Law in Society Series

Law and Society

Other titles in the series

Negotiated Justice
J. BALDWIN AND M. McCONVILLE

The Social Control of Drugs
PHILIP BEAN

Decisions in the Penal Process
A. KEITH BOTTOMLEY

Law and State
KEVIN BOYLE, TOM HADDEN, PADDY HILLYARD

Magistrates' Justice
PAT CARLEN

Censorship and Obscenity
edited by R. DHAVAN and C. DAVIES

Deviant Interpretations
edited by DAVID DOWNES and PAUL ROCK

Inequality and the Law
MARC GALANTER

Pollution, Social Interest and the Law
NEIL GUNNINGHAM

Durkheim and the Law
STEVEN LUKES and ANDREW SCULL

The Politics of Abolition
THOMAS MATHIESEN

Social Needs and Legal Action
P. MORRIS, R. WHITE AND P. LEWIS

The Search for Pure Food
INGEBORG PAULUS

Crime and Conflict
HAROLD E. PEPINSKY

Knowledge and Opinion about Law
PODGORECKI, KAUPEN, VAN HOUTTE, VINKE AND KUTCHINSKY

Deviance, Crime and Socio-Legal Control
ROLAND ROBERTSON AND LAURIE TAYLOR

Sexism and the Law
ALBIE SACHS AND JOAN HOFF WILSON

Law
and Society

EDITED BY

C. M. Campbell
Paul Wiles

LAW IN SOCIETY SERIES

edited by

C. M. Campbell and Paul Wiles

Martin Robertson

First published in 1979 by Martin Robertson & Co. Ltd. 108 Cowley
Road, Oxford OX4 1JF.

ISBN 0 85520 238 6 (paperback)
ISBN 0 85520 239 4 (case edition)

Typeset by Preface Ltd., Salisbury
Printed and bound by Richard Clay (The Chaucer Press) Ltd.,
Bungay, Suffolk

Contents

Introduction

To attempt to conceive of man otherwise than as a social being would be difficult – and probably pointless. It is not just that men live in groups, as many animals do, but that the structure and organization of society delimits and proffers the essential conditions of our existence and identity. Our experience of society is of order, for it is society that provides us with a bounded set of structures and guidelines in what would otherwise be an unmanageable uncertainty of existence. It is order in this mundane sense that enables us to carry on our lives from each day to the next without undue anxiety, and more often than not our dependence upon this order is so complete that, as has been said, it is the 'taken for granted' aspect of our world. It is accepted unthinkingly precisely because it is within its bounds that our everyday reflections upon our society are constructed and formulated. Yet when men consciously attempt more profound reflection on their social existence, the puzzle of how this order is created inevitably must be a central problem.

In everyday conversation, however, references to order usually connote a different sense for the term. Typically such references are to purposive attempts to create a *particular* order for society. In other words the preoccupation is with the kind of institutions and mechanisms of control that are in existence or may be constructed, and that will, together, realize a vision of an ordered society. The consequences, whether intended or unintended, of attempts to manipulate the institutions of society into an order are particular social structures. We can, then, analytically distinguish different senses of the term 'social order', yet in the real world they are closely related. For example, order in the mundane sense is a necessary pre-condition for the remit and implementation of structural plans, whilst the consequences of such plans may affect and change the mundane order of our lives. The resulting ramifications and inter-relationships constitute the social world within which we live, and in this sense the social world is an ordered world. However, the extent to which this order is the result of shared or consensual understandings or, instead, of imposition and manipulation, remains an open question.

It is thus unremarkable that the history of human speculation is full of endeavour to answer questions whose solutions would be of significant help in understanding order. In this book we are concerned with one area of activity that attempts to contribute to that understanding – the sociology of law. The sociology of law attempts to enunciate and explain the part law plays in the ordering of human societies in general, and specific societies in particular. Historically its main focus has been on the role of law and legal institutions in creating and defining the social structures of modern industrialism. However, it should now be obvious that a sociology of law can never limit its inquiry to this question alone; it must inevitably go on to ask about the relationship between law and all aspects of social order, and between law and other institutions which play a part in ordering society.

The problem of order must be of interest to any men inquiring of their conditions. For modern man, however, the problem has a pressing urgency. Many of us live in industrial societies, the very scale and complexity of which make both the achievement and the understanding of order especially difficult. Somehow these societies do seem to achieve social order – for most of us the world is not riddled with existential dread. But when we begin to examine contemporary social structures or attempt to change some part of the order they seek to maintain, we cannot but realize the fragility of our world. We no longer live in a society ordered by traditional beliefs that provide comforting certainty and continuity. Whether we worry about finite natural resources, individual justice, decision-making processes within bureaucracies, or whatever, our contemplation creates doubts and uncertainties. Order is an immanent problem for all of us. Even for men who do not live in industrial societies the desire to *become* industrialized (and in a world where industrialism equals power, it is difficult to gainsay such desire) requires consideration of the social order necessary for that transformation. To study order, and the role of law, in modern societies is, in a way, to take the 'hardest example'. The ramifications of the problem of order are seemingly myriad and are difficult to comprehend. Yet the possibility of rationally controlling our lives' environment dictates that our explanations of order and of law must encompass such contexts.

Within modern industrialized societies law is the most obvious manifestation of the purposive attempt to create order. To some extent this is expressed in the uninformed political slogan of 'law and order'; as if law were the only mechanism that maintains order. Yet the reach of law does seem to be increasing. All of us must have had occasion to note its expanding scope, and the insistent attempts to control more and more activities by legal or quasi-legal control. Increasingly we are required to take account of law in our everyday actions. Indeed it is difficult to identify many aspects of our life that are not subject to some law, to some mechanism of legal control. If we eat food, raise families, get a job or use transport . . . always there is law attempting to pattern our actions. Within modern societies law has become the primary device for attempting to create and control social order. Law, for modern man, has become a metaphor for ordered social life.

The importance of sociology of law in modern societies seems incontestable. Indeed as we shall see, the emergence of industrial societies and the beginnings of sociology – and the sociological study of social order and law – were coextensive. Nevertheless, the development of organized and systematic inquiry in the sociology of law (for example in the universities) was of much more recent origins in many countries. The reasons for this have varied nationally but we may use the particular case of Britain as an illustration. In Britain, such an organized interest is very recent and properly belongs to the last decade. Earlier, English pragmatism and the self-confidence of an industrial society at the height of its power and expansion combined to limit interest in more fundamental problems and instead largely focused such attention as was paid to the social nature of law on questions of practical and immediate efficacy. Contemporary interests may be traced to a declining of that old self-confidence, to the growth of academic legal studies and sociology (and a consequential developing critique of pragmatism and its attendant research methods) and to increasing anxieties among lawyers and those implementing law about the ever-increasing demands being placed on law and the challenges being posed to law. Could law offer suitable or appropriate means for dealing with diverse current problems? The Unilateral Declaration of Independence in Rhodesia, industrial relations over many years, the troubles in Northern Ireland, the need to underwrite racial and sexual equality, all these issues and others raised nagging questions. It came to be realized they would only be answered adequately if more basic questions about the relationship between law and the social order were also examined. There were, of course, many other factors that helped awaken an interest in sociology of law in Britain[1] and in other countries the reasons for renewal of interest in sociology of law have varied the reasons for renewal of interest in sociology of law have varied with the context. But interest has developed or markedly increased in most Western countries over the last two or three decades. If nothing else, such contemporary sociology of law exhibits a shared concern to return to some basic questions about the nature of order – and a critical scepticism of prior, orthodox explanations of the role law does play and can play.

In preparing this book we have tried to select and provide for the reader material that is both a guide and an introduction to some of the more important writings in the sociology of law. The works that are presented comprise attempts to explain and to speculate upon the *actual relationship* between law and the ordering of modern societies. Our hope is that this will help, in some small way, to encourage and inform those who want to develop a sociology of law. As will become clear, the writers we have chosen vary considerably in their approach to this task. Frequently they pose different questions in attempting to explain the general relationship; sometimes they concentrate on the same questions but provide alternative answers; they exhibit considerable diversity in the methods and perspectives they bring to bear in attempting to accomplish the task. Since this is so, the readings in this book are, in a sense, of an eclectic nature. This is not because we believe sociology of law will ultimately develop on the basis of casual eclecticism. Rather it is because we have endeavoured, so that this book may be useful to students of the nature and role of law in society, to represent to the best of our ability the specific approaches and strengths of different writers *on their own terms*. The sociology of law is unfinished, and hardly any of the questions posed within it have yet received anything like definitive answers. In such a state of knowledge, recognition of the diversity of previous work and familiarity with that work are necessary for those who would try to make their own contribution. Conceptual clarification of the questions, attempts to provide new answers, arguments for different priorities, and the development of new theories, all are still open to the student of sociology of law. This book does not, therefore, contain anything that can be regarded as a final statement nor should the collected writings overawe the reader. Instead we hope others might be encouraged by what has been done so far to join in the further inquiries that are necessary.

1. A fuller discussion is contained in C. M. Campbell and P. N. P. Wiles, 'The Study of Law in Society in Britain', *Law and Society Review* (1976) vol. 10, pp. 547–78.

Acknowledgements

We wish to thank the authors and publishers who kindly gave us permission to reproduce portions of copyright material. We also wish to thank Hazel Mount for all the typing and secretarial work involved in producing this book.

CMC
PNPW

I Law and the Social Order

1. Introduction

Modern man lives in industrial societies; his forebears did not. Man in industrial societies is thus, somehow, different from man in pre-industrial societies. Such is the common wisdom that regards industrialization as a crucial turning-point in human history. Certainly those who lived through the process perceived it as such. In Britain, the first country to industrialize, the reaction of thoughtful men was ambiguous. Most of those who reflected upon, and wrote about, contemporary changes acknowledged the potential material advantages of industrial production. Many of us now live in the world of such advantage. However the same men were also worried by the fact that industrialization seemed inevitably to destroy the social order of traditional society. They were concerned about the form of order that was possible in the new world that was emerging. Their interpretations diverged considerably – from those who saw a solution in reaction to those who championed revolution. But from Carlyle to Engels, there was common assent that their world was changing.

In the course of the dramatic changes that took place during industrialization, the way in which men thought about their social world was also to be transformed. A number of factors were relevant. The prevailing theories (whether religious or secular, based on notions of social contract or original states of nature) no longer seemed to provide adequate accounts of societies where tradition and stability were giving way to instrumental reason and endemic change. Equally, in the changing, increasingly complex new societies, the purposive implementation of political visions could no longer rely on tradition and solecism. If the methods of scientific thought had provided knowledge for the new industrial

1

manufactures, might they not also 'deliver' the means for ordering the new societies? Finally, if a new social world was being created, so also was a new social order; this not only presented new problems for reflection, it altered the bounds within which reflection took place. The old theories were simply no longer believable. Men thought anew. They tried to create a science of society. Central to this attempt was the aim of developing scientific theories of the relationship between law, legal control and the social order.

Our excerpts in this section begin with examples of the work of two leading figures of the Scottish Enlightenment — Adam Ferguson and John Millar. In the eighteenth century, men who were aware of the advances in scientific understanding of the natural world contemplated the new social world. Primarily in Scotland (where political economy, the common sense school of philosophy and the use of the 'conjectural method' flourished) and in France (most especially under the influence of Montesquieu's ideas) the importance of examining laws and legal phenomena in their social contexts came to be unambiguously accepted. Scottish moral philosophers, with Hume as catalyst, pondered the nature of knowledge, and became convinced that scientific method, on the basis of observation and experiment, was the means for its production. As far as knowledge of the social world was concerned, they accepted Montesquieu's dictum that 'man is born in society and there he remains'. *A priori* speculation and bifurcated visions of the world were rejected and replaced by humanist and secular perspectives in which society was accepted as fact, and taken as the context within which man's action was to be explained. When the Scottish writers contemplated the *a priori* speculations of earlier writers, they usually did so, as Millar does in the excerpt we reproduce, within the sceptical crucible of correspondence to the observed world. The result was a devastating rejection of old theories, the reformulation of old questions, and the beginnings of a new science of society.

If man was to be understood in his social context, then the nature of men in 'civil society' could only be understood by examining the means by which we had reached the present state. If some of the methods used by the Scottish writers (for example the 'conjectural method') now seem crude, we should allow that they tackled difficult problems with but little reliable data. What they left us as an inheritance was an insistence that historical theories must be empirically grounded. Other aspects of their work also appear to us to be crude (such as a primitive psychologism) or even to be false (such as their attachment to the notion of the 'progress' of civilization). We must remember, however, that they were transitional thinkers, and, had the foundations they provided been built upon in an uninterrupted way, a flourishing, and probably healthier, social scientific tradition would have been maintained in Britain. In the sociological system (and not merely the political economy) of Adam Smith, in the elements of historical materialism in John Millar, in the demographic studies of Adam Ferguson and in the socio-historical appreciation of laws and the legal system in the writings of Lord Kames, are to be found issues and insights that, neglected for decades, deserve acknowledgement as the beginnings of sociological study.

This potential British development did not take place, however. Although the Scottish writers enjoyed much fame in foreign lands, their influence in England was transitory and, in general, of a subdued nature. The political economy of Adam Smith was utilized by the English, but his more radical ideas, and those of others such as Millar, were ignored and buried. The Scottish Enlightenment was a brief interlude whose impact on British thinking was soon consumed under the dull weight of English intellectual dominance. The Revolution in France produced a conservatism in Britain that stultified and then stifled further exploration of the potentially radical issues that the Scottish thinkers had raised. Nineteenth-century England, with its self-confident industrial expansion and imperialist exploitation, found a more congenial approach to the problems of order and law in the utilitarianism of Bentham. The result was a pragmatic approach to such 'problems', which substituted designs of model prisons for models of social order. Even when, later in the nineteenth century, English thinkers took up one theme of the Scots — the idea of progress — they produced a social Darwinism (under the influence of men such as Herbert Spencer) which while providing a theory of history also offered comforting reassurance as to England's place in the scheme of things, and a justification for the (temporary) miseries of the new social world. More broadly, the effects on British thinking entailed a constricted vision of the questions that should be asked about law and the ordering of society, and a practical straight-forward approach to the subject. British sociology was to remain a largely atheoretical enterprise characterized by pragmatically orientated fact gathering, and after Herbert Spencer no British thinker is associated with the development of a major sociological theory.

The two excerpts we reproduce from nineteenth-century English work – those by Maine and Dicey – well illustrate the straightforward strengths, and yet limitations, of developments in England. In case they are forgotten, the strengths need perhaps to be emphasized. After all, English utilitarianism survives long after John Stuart Mill had asknowledged its central weaknesses, precisely because in spite of them it is a tough-minded and practical approach to political thinking. Nineteenth-century English theories about the social nature of law shared this tough-minded practicality, and in addition gave honest recognition to the part that power must play in such theories.

If English writers did not develop the promising beginnings made in the eighteenth century in Scotland and France, they remained equally unaffected by the theorists in continental Europe in the nineteenth and early twentieth centuries who *did* fully explore the contours of sociology of law. Whilst much of Europe rapidly followed the British example and industrialized, the circumstances varied greatly. British industrialization took place in a society where old aristocratic power had already reached a form of political accommodation with the new bourgeosie, and in a unified nation with a strong centralized administration. In Europe on the other hand, the relocation of political power was sometimes achieved by revolution, as in France, by unification by force, as in Germany and Italy, and saw the imposition of heavy-handed bureaucratic administrations, as in Germany. Compared with Britain the transformation to industrialism in Europe often involved overt social upheaval and conflict and made the problems of order more basic and more urgent. The easy-going pragmatism of the English theorists was hardly an adequate answer for the rest of Europe. Faced with social cartharsis, contemporary scholars were forced to inquire more fundamentally into the relationships between law and society. It was in this context that what we now regard as the classical sociological theories were developed.

The classical writings represented here have almost selected themselves. Their scope and influence on later work has been of primordial importance. For this reason we have allowed the classical writers to speak, at length, for themselves.

Marx and Engels, frequently exiled from their native Germany, acquired a broad knowledge of the new societies. For them it was not industrialization that characterized the new societies, but the fact that they rested on the capitalist mode of production, which created class conflicts; and the nature of society was therefore to be explained as a product of this conflict. The modern state and its legal form therefore emerged as a class instrument. Marxist materialism further extended to insisting that ideas of justice, and even consciousness itself, were class products. Their vision was one that could only be exculpated in revolution.

By contrast, Max Weber was concerned with the increasing rationality of modern societies, which he believed underlay industrialism, its economic form in capitalism, its administrative form in bureaucracy, and its legal forms and procedures. In tracing the origins and role of rationalism in modern societies, he never escaped that pessimistic dilemma that so many observers of industrialism shared. He acknowledged the material advantages accruing from the new order, recognized the efficiency of bureaucratic modes of administration, and appreciated the formal justice guaranteed by modern legal systems. Yet he was painfully aware of the potential inhumanity of administration, the substantive injustice of law, and, above all, the spiritual emptiness with which modern societies seemed to face man. He realized the potential for contradictions and confrontations between the new order and democracy.

Emile Durkheim, living in a France that seemed to find the search for political stability after the fall of the Empire particularly difficult, wondered whether the extensive division of labour that characterized the new societies could, in fact, be compatible with an ordered society. Ultimately he demonstrated, to his satisfaction, that it was, but that the possibility was not to be automatically achieved in reality. His later work therefore developed argument and analyses to show why the occupational groups making up the division of labour must develop and sustain moral outlooks if order was to result.

We regard such writers as 'classical' because the world they theorized about is still essentially our world. Their concerns, doubts and passions are relevant to us today.

2. Civil Society

by Adam Ferguson

From An Essay on the History of Civil Society [*1767*] *5th edition, London, P. Cadell (1782) pp. 1–30 and 203–6*

Natural productions are generally formed by degrees. Vegetables are raised on a tender shoot, and animals from an infant state. The latter, being active, extend together their operations and their powers, and have a progress in what they perform, as well as in the faculties they acquire. This progress in the case of man is continued to a greater extent than that of any other animal. Not only the individual advances from infancy to manhood, but the species itself from rudeness to civilization ... Among the writers who have attempted to distinguish, in the human character, its original qualities, and to point out the limits between nature and art, some have represented mankind in their first condition, as possessed of mere animal sensibility, without any exercise of the faculties that render them superior to the brutes, without any political union, without any means of explaining their sentiments, and even without possessing any of the apprehensions and passions which the voice and the gesture are so well fitted to express. Others have made the state of nature to consist in perpetual wars kindled by competition for dominion and interest, where every individual had a separate quarrel with his kind, and where the presence of a fellow creature was the signal of battle. The desire of laying the foundation of a favourable system, or a fond expectation, perhaps, that we may be able to penetrate the secrets of nature, to the very source of existence, have, on this subject, led to many fruitless inquiries, and given rise to many wild suppositions. Among the various qualities which mankind possess, we select one or a few particulars on which to establish a theory, and in framing our account of what man was in some imaginary state of nature, we overlook what he has always appeared within the reach of our own observations, and in the records of history. In every other instance, however, the natural historian thinks himself obliged to collect facts, not to offer conjectures ... He admits, that his knowledge of the material system of the world consists in a collection of facts, or at most, in general tenets derived from particular observations and experiments ... [W]ithout any disparagement to that subtelty which would analyse every sentiment, and trace every mode of being to its source, it may be safely affirmed that the character of man, as he now exists, that the laws of his animal and intellectual system, on which his happiness now depends, deserve our principal study; and that general principles relating to this or any other subject, are useful only insofar as they are founded on just observation, and lead to the knowledge of important consequences, or insofar as they enable us to act with success when we would apply either the intellectual or the physical powers of nature, to the purposes of human life.

If both the earliest and the latest accounts collected from every quarter of the earth, represent mankind as assembled in troops and companies; and the individual always joined by affection to party, while he is possibly opposed to another; employed in the exercise of recollection and foresight; inclined to communicate his own sentiments, and to be acquainted with those of others; these facts must be admitted as the foundation of all the reasoning relative to man ... Mankind are to be taken in groups, as they have always subsisted. The history of the individual is but a detail of the sentiments and the thoughts he has entertained in the view of his species; and every experiment relative to this subject should be made with entire societies, not with single men.

The individual, in every age, has the same race to run from infancy to manhood, and every infant, or ignorant person now, is a model of what man was in his original state. He enters on his career with advantages peculiar to his age; but his natural talent is probably the same. The use and application of this talent is changing, and men continue their works in progression through many ages together: they build on foundations laid by their ancestors; and in a succession of years, tend to a perfection in the application of their faculties, to which the aid of long experience is required, and which many generations must have combined in their endeavours. ... If we would know [man], we must attend to himself, to the course of his life, and the tenor of his conduct. With him the society appears to be as old as the individual, and the use of the tongue as universal as that of the hand or the foot. If there was a time in which he had his acquaintance with his own species to make, and his faculties to acquire, it is a time of which we have no record, and in relation to which our opinions can serve no purpose, and are supported by no evidence.

Man finds his lodgement alike in the cave, the cottage, and the palace; and his subsistence equally in the woods, in the dairy, or the farm. He assumes the distinction of titles, equipage, and dress; he devises regular systems of government, and a complicated body of laws; or naked in the woods has no badge of superiority but the strength of his limbs and the sagacity of his mind; no rule of conduct but choice; no tie with his fellow creatures but affection, the love of company and the desire of safety. Capable of a great variety of arts, but dependent upon none in particular for the preservation of his being; to whatever length he has carried his artifice, there he seems to enjoy the conveniences that suit his nature, and to have found the condition for which he is destined. The tree which an American, on the banks of the Oronoko, has chosen to climb for the retreat, and the lodgement of his family, is to him a convenient dwelling. The sofa, the vaulted dome and the colonnade, do not more effectually content their native inhabitant.

If we are asked therefore, where the state of nature is to be found? We may answer, It is here; and it matters not whether we are understood to speak on the Island of Great Britain, at the Cape of Good Hope, or the Straits of Magellan. While this active being is in the train of employing his talents, and of operating on the subjects around him, all situations are equally natural. ... If the palace be unnatural, the cottage is so no less; and the highest refinements in political and moral apprehension, are not more artificial in their kind, than the first operations of sentiment and reason. If we admit that man is sensible of improvement and has in himself a principle of progression, and a desire of perfection, it appears improper to say, that he has quitted the state of his nature, when he has begun to proceed; or that he finds a station for which he was not intended, while, like other animals, he only follows the disposition, and employs the power that nature has given. ...

'Man is born in society', says Montesquieu, 'and there he remains.' The charms that detain him are known to be manifold. Together with the parental affection, which, instead of deserting the adult, as among the brutes, embraces more close, as it becomes mixed with esteem, and the memory of its early effects; we may reckon a propensity common to man and other animals, to mix with the herd, and, without reflection, to follow the crowd of his species. What this propensity was in the first moment of its operation, we know not; but with men accustomed to company, its enjoyments and disappointments are reckoned among the principal pleasures or pains of human life. Sadness and melancholy are connected with solitude; gladness and pleasure with the concourse of men. The track of a Lapplander on the snowy shore, gives joy to the lonely mariner; and the mute signs of cordiality and kindness which are made to him, awaken the memory of pleasures which are felt in society. . . . But neither a propensity to mix with the herd, nor the sense of advantages enjoyed in that condition, comprehend all the principles by which men are united together. Those bands are even of a feeble texture, compared to the resolute ardour with which man adheres to his friends, or to his tribe, after they have for some time run the career of fortune together. Mutual discoveries of generosity, joint trials of fortune, redouble the ardours of friendship, and kindle a flame in the human breast, which the considerations of personal interest of safety cannot suppress. The most lively transports of joy are seen, and the loudest shrieks of despair are heard, when the objects of a tender affection are beheld in a state of triumph or of suffering.

Mere acquaintance and habitude nourish affection, and the experience of society brings every passion of the human mind upon its side. Its triumphs and prosperities, its calamities and its stresses, bring a variety and a force of emotion, which can only have place in the company of our fellow creatures. It is here that a man is made to forget his weakness, his cares of safety, and his subsistence; and to act from those passions which make him discover his force . . . That condition is surely favourable to the nature of any being, in which his force is increased; and if courage be the gift of society to man, we have reason to consider his union with his species as the noblest part of his fortune. From this source are derived, not only the force, but the very existence of his happiest emotions; not only the better part, but almost the whole of his rational character. Send him to the desert alone, he is a plant drawn from its roots, the form indeed may remain, but every faculty droops and withers; the human personage and the human character cease to exist.

We have . . . observed mankind, either united together on terms of equality, or disposed to admit of a subordination founded merely on the voluntary respect and attachment which they paid to their leaders; but, in both cases, without any concerted plan of government, or system of laws. The savage, whose fortune is comprised in his cabin, his fur, and his arms, is satisfied with that provision, and with that degree of security, he himself can procure. He perceives, in treating with his equal, no subject of discussion that should be referred to the decision of a judge; nor does he find in any hand the badges of magistracy, or the ensigns of a perpetual command. The barbarian, though induced by his admiration of personal qualities, the lustre of a heroic race, or a superiority of fortune, to follow the banners of a leader, and to act a subordinate part in his tribe, knows not, that what he performs from choice, is to be made a subject of obligation. He acts from affections unacquainted with forms; and when provoked, or when engaged in disputes, he recurs to the sword, as the ultimate means of decision, in all questions of right. Human affairs in the meantime, continue their progress. What was in one generation a propensity to herd with the species, becomes in the ages which follow a principle of natural union. What was originally an alliance for common defense becomes a concerted plan of political force; the case of subsistence becomes an anxiety for accumulating wealth, and the foundation of commercial arts.

Mankind, in following the present sense of their minds, in striving to remove inconveniences, or to gain apparent and continuous advantages, arrive at ends which even their imagination could not anticipate; and pass on, like other animals, in the tract of their nature, without perceiving its end. He who first said, 'I will appropriate this field; I will leave it to my heirs'; did not perceive, that he was laying the foundation of civil laws and of political establishments. He who first arranged himself under a leader, did not perceive, that he was setting the example of a permanent subordinate nation, under the pretence of which the rapacious were to seize his possessions, and the arrogant to lay claim to his services.

Men, in general, are sufficient disposed to occupy themselves in forming projects and schemes; but he who would scheme and project for others, will find an opponent in every person who is disposed to scheme for himself. Like the winds that come we know not whence, and blow whithersoever they lift, the forms of society are derived from an obscure and distant origin; they arise, long before the date of philosophy, from the instincts, not from the speculations of men. The crowd of mankind, are directed in their establishments and measures, by the circumstances in which they are placed; and seldom are turned from their way, to follow the plan of any single projector.

Every step and every movement of the multitude, even in what are termed enlightened ages, are made with equal blindness to the future; and nations stumble upon establishments, which are indeed the result of human action, but not the execution of any human design. If Cromwell said, that a man never mounts higher, than when he knows not whither he is going; it may with more reason be affirmed of communities, that they admit of the greatest revolutions where no change is intended, and that the most refined politicians do not always know whether they are leading the state by their projects. If we listen to the testimony of modern history, and to that of the most authentic parts of the ancient; if we attend to the practice of nations in every quarter of the world, and in every condition, whether that of the barbarian or the polished, we will find very little reason to retract this assertion. No constitution is formed by concert, no government is copied from a plan, the members of a small state contend for equality; the members of a greater, find themselves classed in a certain manner that lays a foundation for monarchy. They proceed from one form of government to another, by easy transitions, and frequently under old names adopt a new constitution. The seeds of every form are lodged in human nature; they spring up and ripen with the season. The prevalence of a particular species is often derived from an imperceptible ingredient mingled in the soil. We are therefore to receive, with caution, the traditionary histories of ancient legislators, and founders of states. Their names have long been celebrated; their supposed plans have been admired; and what were probably the consequences of an early situation, is, in every instance, considered as an effect of design.

3. Authority, Social Inequality and the Law

by John Millar

From An Historical View of English Government [*1787*] *4 vols, London, J. Mawman (1803) vol. 4, pp. 286–96 and 143–61*

All government appears to be ultimately derived from two great principles. The first which I shall call *authority*, is the immediate effect of the peculiar qualities or circumstances, by which any one member of society may be exalted above another. The second is a consideration of the advantages to be derived from any political establishment.

1. Superior bodily qualities, agility, strength; dexterity of hand, especially in using the weapons employed in fighting; as well as uncommon mental endowments; wisdom, knowledge, fidelity, generosity, courage, are the natural sources of admiration and respect, and consequently of deference and submission. A schoolboy superior to his companions in courage and feats of activity, becomes often a leader of the school, and acquires a very despotic authority. ... The patriarchical government in a primitive age of the world, and the authority possessed by the leaders of barbarous tribes in those periods which preceded the accumulation of property, are known to have arisen from similar circumstances. The heroes and demi-gods of antiquity, were indebted solely to their valour, and their wonderful exploits, for that enthusiastic admiration which they excited, and for that sovereign power to which they were frequently exalted. The acquisition of property, whether derived from occupancy and labour in conformity to the rules of justice, or from robbery and oppression, in defiance of every law, human and divine, became another and a more extensive source of authority. Wealth, however improperly in the eyes of a strict moralist, seldom fails to procure a degree of admiration and respect. The poor are attracted and dazzled by the apparent happiness and splendour of the rich; and they regard a man of large fortune with a sort of wonder, and partial pre-possession which disposes them to magnify and over-rate all his advantages. If they are so far beneath them as not to be soured in the malignancy of envy, they behold with pleasure and satisfaction the sumptousness of his table, the magnificance of his equipage, the facility and quickness with which he is whirled from place to place, the number of his attendants, the readiness with which they observe all his movements, and run to promote his wishes. Delighted with the situation which appears to them so agreeable, and catching from one another the contagion of sympathetic feelings, they are often prompted by an enthusiastic fervour, to exalt his dignity and promote his enjoyments, and to favour his pursuits. Without distinguishing the objects which figure in their imagination, they transfer to his person that superiority which belongs properly to his condition, and are struck with those accomplishments, and modes of behaviour, which his education has taught him to acquire, and which his rank and circumstances have rendered habitual to him. They are of course embarrassed in his

presence by impressions of awe and reverence, and losing sometimes the exercise of their natural powers are sunk in abasement and stupidity.

The authority, however, of the rich over the poor is, doubtless, chiefly supported by selfish considerations. As in spending a great fortune, the owner gives employment and consequential subsistence to many individuals, all those who, in this manner, obtain or expect any advantage have more or less an interest in paying respect and submission. The influence which may be traced from this origin, operates in such various directions, is distributed in such different proportions, and so diffused through every corner of society, that it appears in its degree and extent to be incalculable. Uncommon personal talents occur but seldom; and the sphere of their activity, so to speak, is very often limited. But the inequalities in the division of wealth are varied without end; and though their effect is greater in some situations of mankind than in others, they never cease, in any, to introduce a correspondent gradation and subordination of ranks.

These original circumstances, from which authority is derived, are gradually confirmed and strengthened by their having long continued to flow in the same channel. The force of habit, the great controller and governor of our actions, is in nothing more remarkable than in promoting the respect and submission claimed by our superiors. By living in a state of inferiority and dependence, the mind is enured to subjection; and the ascendant which has been once gained is gradually rendered more complete and powerful. [T]he force of habit is much more effectual in confirming the authority derived from wealth, than that which is found in personal qualities . . . [W]ealth . . . in the ordinary course of things, is transmitted, by lineal succession, from father to son and remain[s] for many generations in the same family. The possessor of that estate, therefore, who bears the name, and who exercises the powers which belong to his ancestors, obtains not only the original means of creating dependence which they enjoyed, but seems to inherit, in some degree, that consideration and respect, that influence or attachment, which, by their high station, and by the distribution of their favours during a long period they were able to accumulate. This is the origin of what is called *birth*, as the foundation of authority which creates a popular prepossession for the representative of an ancient family, giving him the preference to an upstart, though the latter should possess the greater abilities and virtues.

From the operation of these different circumstances; from the accidental superiority of personal qualities, and from the unequal distribution of wealth, aided and confirmed by the force of habit, systems of government have grown up, and been variously modified, without exciting any inquiry into their consequences, and without leading the people to examine the grounds of their submission to the constituted authorities.

2. But when in the course of political transactions, particular persons grossly abuse their powers, or when competitions arise among individuals possessing influence and authority, and of consequence parties are formed, who espouse the interests of the respective leaders, the public attention is aroused to scrutinise the pretentions of the several candidates, to compare the different modes of government which they may propose to introduce, and to examine their title to demand obedience from the rest of the community. In such inquiries, it is hardly possible to avoid suggesting another principle, more satisfactory than that of mere authority; the general *utility* of government; or rather its absolute necessity, for preventing the disorders incident to human society. . . .

There are natural rights, which belong to mankind antecedent to the formation of civil society. We may easily conceive, that, in the state of nature, we should be entitled to maintain our personal safety, to exercise our natural liberty, so far as it does not encroach on the rights of others; and even to maintain a property in those things which we have come to possess, by original occupancy, or by labour in producing them. These rights are not lost, though they may be differently modified when we enter into society. A part of them, doubtless, must be resigned for the sake of those advantages to be derived from the social state. We must resign, for example, the privilege of avenging injuries, for the advantage of being protected by courts of justice. We must give up a part of our property, so that the public may be enabled to afford that protection. We must yield obedience to the legislative power, that we may enjoy that good order and tranquility to be expected from its cool and dispassionate regulations. But the rights which we resign, ought, in all these cases, to be compensated by the advantages obtained; and the restraints, or burdens imposed, ought neither to be greater, nor more numerous, than are necessary for the general prosperity and happiness. Were we to examine, according to this criterion, the various political systems which take place in the world, how many might be weighed in the balance and found wanting? Some are defective by too great strictness or regulation, confining and hampering natural liberty by minute and trivial restraints; more have deviated widely from the purpose by too great laxity, admitting an excessive licence to the various modifications of knavery and violence; but the greatest number have almost totally failed in producing happiness or security, from the tyranny of individuals, or of particular orders and ranks, who, by the accidental concurrence of circumstances, acquiring exhorbitant power, have reduced their fellow citizens into a state of servile subjection. It is a mortifying reflection, to observe, that, while many other branches of knowledge have attained a high degree of maturity, the masterpiece of science, the guardian of rights, and of everything valuable, should, in many enlightened parts of the world, still remain in a state of gross imperfection. Even in countries where the people have made vigorous efforts to ameliorate their government, how often have the collusion of parties, the opposite attraction of public and private interests, the fermentation of numberless discordant elements, introducing nothing at last but a residue of despotism.

There can be no doubt that [the] division in the labours, both of art and of science, is calculated for promoting their improvement. From the limited powers both of the mind and of the body, the exertions of an individual are likely to be more vigorous and successful when confined to a particular channel, than when diffused over boundless expanse. The athlete who limited his application to one of the gymnastic exercises was commonly enabled to practice it with more dexterity than he who studied to become proficient in them all.

But though the separation of different trades and professions, together with a consequent division of labour, and application in the exercise of them, has a tendency to improve in the art of science, it has frequently an opposite effect upon the personal qualities of those individuals who are engaged in such employments. In the sciences, indeed, and even in the liberal arts, the application of those who follow particular professions can seldom be so much limited as to prove destructive to general knowledge ... But the mechanical arts admit such minute divisions of labour, that the workmen belonging to a manufacture are each of them employed, for the most part, in a single manual operation, and have no concern in the results of their several productions. It is hardly possible that these mechanics should acquire extensive information or intelligence. In proportion as the operation which they perform is narrow, it will supply them with few ideas; and according as the necessity for obtaining a livelihood obliges them to double their industry, they have the less opportunity of leisure to procure the means of observation, or to find topics for reflection from other quarters. As their employment requires constant attention to an object which can afford no variety of occupation to their minds, they are apt to acquire a habitual vacancy of thought, unenlivened by any prospects, but such as are derived from the future wages of their labour, or from the grateful returns of bodily repose and sleep. They become, like machines, actuated by a regular weight, and performing certain movements with great celerity and exactness, in a small compass, and unfitted for any other use. In the intervals of their work, they can draw but little improvement from the society of companions, bred to similar employments, with whom, if they have much intercourse, they are most likely to seek amusement in drinking and dissipation ...

Even in the same country there is a sensible difference between different professions; and, according as every separate employment gives rise to a greater subdivision of workmen and artificers, it has a greater tendency to withdraw from them the means of intellectual improvement. The business of agriculture, for example, is less capable of a minute subdivision of labour than the greater part of mechanical employments. The same workman has often occasion to plough, to sow, to reap, to cultivate the ground for different purposes, and to prepare its various productions for the market. He is obliged alternatively to handle very opposite tools and instruments; to repair, and even sometimes, to make them for his own use; and always to accommodate the different parts of his labour to the change of the scenes and to the variations of the weather. He is employed in the management and rearing of cattle, becomes frequently a grazier and a corn merchant, and is unavoidably initiated in the mysteries of the horse jockey. What an extent of knowledge, therefore, must he possess! What a diversity of talent must he exercise, in comparison with a mechanic, who employs his whole labour in sharpening the point, or in putting on a head of a pin; how different the education of these two persons. The pin maker, who commonly lives in a town, will have more of the fashionable improvements of society than the peasant; he will undoubtedly be better dressed; he will, in all probability, have more book learning, as well as less coarseness in the tone of his voice, and less uncouthness in his appearance and deportment ... But in a bargain he would, assuredly, be no match for his rivals. He would be greatly inferior in real intelligence and acuteness; much less qualified to converse with his superiors, to take advantage of their foibles, to give a plausible account of his measures, or to adapt his behaviour to any peculiar and unexpected emergency.

The circumstances now mentioned offers a view not very pleasant in the history of human society. It were to be wished that wealth and knowledge should go hand in hand, and that the acquisition of the former should lead to the possession of the latter. Considering the state of nations at large, it will, perhaps, be found that opulence and intellectual improvements are pretty well balanced, and that the same progress in commerce and manufactures which occasions an increase of the one, creates a proportional accession of the other. But, among individuals, this distribution of things is far from being so uniformly established; and, in the lower order of the people, it appears to be completely reversed. The class of mechanics and labourers, by far the most numerous in commercial nations, are apt, according as they attain more affluence and independent circumstances, to be more withdrawn and debarred from extensive information; and are likely, in proportion as the rest of the community advance in knowledge and literature, to be involved in a thicker cloud of ignorance and prejudice. Is there not reason to apprehend, that the common people, instead of sharing the advantages of national prosperity, are thus in danger of losing their importance, or becoming the dupes of their superiors, and of being degraded from the rank which they held in the scale of society? ...

The doctrine maintained by some politicians, that the ignorance of the labouring people is of advantage, by securing their patience and submission under the yoke which their unequal fortune has imposed upon them, is not less absurd than it is revolting to all the feelings of humanity. The security derived from so mean a source is temporary and fallacious. It is liable to be undermined by the intrigues of any plausible projector, or suddenly overthrown by the casual breath of popular opinion.

As the circumstances of commercial society are unfavourable to the mental improvements of the populus, it ought to be the great aim

of the public to counteract, in this respect, the natural tendency of
mechanical employments, and by the institutions of those in
seminaries of education, to communicate, as far as possible, to the
most useful, but humble class of citizens, that knowledge which their
way of life has, in some degree, prevented them from acquiring. It is
needless to observe how imperfect such institutions have hitherto
been. The principal schools and colleges of Europe have been
intended for the benefit merely of the higher orders; and even for this
purpose, the greater part of them are not very judiciously modelled.
But men of rank and fortune, and in general those who are exempted
from bodily labour, have little occasion in this respect, for the aid of
the public, and perhaps would be better supplied, if left, in a great
measure, to their own exertions. The execution, however, of a liberal
plan for the instruction of the lower orders, would be a valuable
addition to those efforts for the maintenance of the poor, for the
relief of the diseased and infirm, and for the correction of the
malefactor, which have proceeded from the humanity and public
spirit of the present age.

4. Law in Progressive Societies

by Henry Sumner Maine

From Ancient Law [*1861*] *London, John Murray (1912) chapters 2, pp. 26–29
and 5, pp. 123–174.*

When primitive law has once been embodied in a Code, there is an
end to what may be called its spontaneous development. Hence-
forward the changes effected in it, if effected at all, are effected
deliberately and from without . . . A new era begins with the Codes.
Wherever, after this epoch, we trace the course of legal modification,
we are able to attribute it to the conscious desire of improvement, or
at all events of compassing objects other than those which were
aimed at in the primitive times.

It may seem at first sight that no general propositions worth trust-
ing can be elicited from the history of legal systems subsequent to the
codes. The field is too vast. We cannot be sure that we have included

a sufficient number of phenomena in our observations, or that we accurately understand those which we have observed. But the undertaking will be seen to be more feasible, if we consider that after the epoch of codes the distinction between stationary and progressive societies begins to make itself felt. It is only with the progressive societies that we are concerned, and nothing is more remarkable than their extreme fewness. In spite of overwhelming evidence, it is most difficult for a citizen of Western Europe to bring thoroughly home to himself the truth that the civilisation which surrounds him is a rare exception in the history of the world. The tone of thought common among us, all our hopes, fears, and speculations, would be materially affected, if we had vividly before us the relation of the progressive races to the totality of human life. It is indisputable that much the greatest part of mankind has never shown a particle of desire that its civil institutions should be improved since the moment when external completeness was first given to them by their embodiment in some permanent record. One set of usages has occasionally been violently overthrown and superseded by another; here and there a primitive code, pretending to a supernatural origin, has been greatly extended, and distorted into the most surprising forms, by the perversity of sacerdotal commentators; but, except in a small section of the world, there has been nothing like the gradual amelioration of a legal system. There has been material civilisation, but, instead of the civilisation expanding the law, the law has limited the civilisation... The difference between the stationary and progressive societies is one of the great secrets which inquiry has yet to penetrate ... It may be remarked that no one is likely to succeed in the investigation who does not clearly realise that the stationary condition of the human race is the rule, the progressive the exception.

I confine myself in what follows to the progressive societies. With respect to them it may be laid down that social necessities and social opinion are always more or less in advance of Law. We may come indefinitely near to the closing of the gap between them, but it has a perpetual tendency to reopen. Law is stable; the societies we are speaking of are progressive. The greater or less happiness of a people depends on the degree of promptitude with which the gulf is narrowed.

A general proposition of some value may be advanced with respect to the agencies by which Law is brought into harmony with society. These instrumentalities seem to me to be three in number, Legal Fictions, Equity, and Legislation.. Their historical order is that in which I have placed them. Sometimes two of them will be seen operating together, and there are legal systems which have escaped the influence of one or other of them. But I know of no instance in which the order of their appearance has been changed or inverted.

The necessity of submitting the subject of jurisprudence to scientific treatment has never been entirely lost sight of in modern times, and the essays which the consciousness of this necessity has produced have proceeded from minds of very various calibre, but there is not much presumption, I think, in asserting that what has hitherto stood in the place of science has for the most part been a set of guesses (similar to those of the Roman lawyers). A series of explicit statements, recognising and adopting these conjectural theories of a natural state, and of a system of principles congenial to it, has been continued with but brief interruption from the days of their inventors to our own.

There is such wide-spread dissatisfaction with existing theories of jurisprudence, and so general a conviction that they do not really solve the questions they pretend to dispose of, as to justify the suspicion that some line of inquiry, necessary to a perfect result, has been incompletely followed or altogether omitted by their authors. And indeed there is one remarkable omission with which all these speculations are chargeable, except perhaps those of Montesquieu. They take no account of what law has actually been at epochs remote from the particular period at which they made their appearance. Their originators carefully observed the institutions of their own age and civilisation, and those of other ages and civilisations with which they had some degree of intellectual sympathy, but, when they turned their attention to archaic states of society which exhibited much superficial difference from their own, they uniformly ceased to observe and began guessing. The mistake which they committed is therefore analogous to the error of one who, in investigating the laws of the material universe, should commence by contemplating the existing physical world as a whole, instead of beginning with the particles which are its simplest ingredients. One does not certainly see why such a scientific solecism should be more defensible in jurisprudence than in any other region of thought. It would seem antecedently that we ought to commence with the simplest social forms in a state as near as possible to their rudimentary condition. In other words, if we followed the course usual in such inquiries, we should penetrate as far up as we could in the history of primitive societies. The phenomena which early societies present us with are not easy at first to understand, but the difficulty of grappling with them bears no proportion to the perplexities which beset us in considering the baffling entanglement of modern social organisation. It is a difficulty arising from their strangeness and uncouthness, not from their number and complexity. One does not readily get over the surprise which they occasion when looked at from a modern point of view; but when that is surmounted they are few enough and simple enough. But, even if they gave more trouble than they do, no pains would be wasted in ascertaining the germs out of which has assuredly been unfolded every form of moral restraint which controls our actions and shapes our conduct at the present moment . . .

We have now examined all parts of the ancient Law of Persons which fall within the scope of this treatise, and the result of the inquiry is I trust, to give additional definiteness and precision to our view of the infancy of jurisprudence. The Civil laws of States first make their appearance as the Themistes of a patriarchal sovereign, and we can now see that these Themistes are probably only a developed form of the irresponsible commands which, in a still earlier condition of the race, the head of each isolated household may have addressed to his wives, his children, and his slaves. But, even after the State has been organised, the laws have still an extremely limited application. Whether they retain their primitive character as Themistes, or whether they advance to the condition of Customs or Codified Texts, they are binding not on individuals, but on Families. Ancient jurisprudence, if a perhaps deceptive comparison may be employed, may be likened to International Law, filling nothing, as it were, excepting the interstices between the great groups which are the atoms of society. In a community so situated, the legislation of assemblies and the jurisdiction of Courts reach only to the heads of families, and to every other individual the rule of conduct is the law of his home, of which his Parent is the legislator. But the sphere of civil law, small at first, tends to enlarge itself. The agents of legal change, Fictions, Equity, and Legislation, are brought in turn to bear on the primeval institutions, and at every point of the progress, a greater number of personal rights and a larger amount of property are removed from the domestic forum to the cognisance of the public tribunals. The ordinances of the government obtain gradually the same efficacy in private concerns as in matters of state, and are no longer liable to be overridden by the behests of a despot enthroned by each hearthstone. We have in the annals of Roman law a nearly complete history of the crumbling away of an archaic system, and of the formation of new institutions from the recombined materials, institutions some of which descended unimpaired to the modern world, while others, destroyed or corrupted by contact with barbarism in the dark ages, had again to be recovered by mankind. When we leave this jurisprudence at the epoch of its final reconstruction by Justinian, few traces of archaism can be discovered in any part of it except in the single article of the extensive powers still reserved to the living Parent. Everywhere else principles of convenience, or of symmetry, or of simplification–new principles at any rate–have usurped the authority of the jejune considerations which satisfied the conscience of ancient times. Everywhere a new morality has displaced the canons of conduct and the reasons of acquiescence which were in unison with the ancient usages, because in fact they were born of them.

The movement of the progressive societies has been uniform in one respect. Through all its course it has been distinguished by the gradual dissolution of family dependency and the growth of individual obligation in its place. The Individual is steadily substituted for the Family, as the unit of which civil laws take account. The advance has been accomplished at varying rates of celerity, and there are societies not absolutely stationary in which the collapse of the ancient organisation can only be perceived by careful study of the phenomena they present. But, whatever its pace, the change has not been subject to reaction or recoil, and apparent retardations will be found to have been occasioned through the absorption of archaic ideas and customs from some entirely foreign source. Nor is it difficult to see what is the tie between man and man which replaces by degrees those forms of reciprocity in rights and duties which have their origin in the Family. It is Contract. Starting, as from one terminus of history, from a condition of society in which all the relations of Persons are summed up in the relations of Family, we seem to have steadily moved towards a phase of social order in which all these relations arise from the free agreement of Individuals. In Western Europe the progress achieved in this direction has been considerable. Thus the status of the Slave has disappeared–it has been superseded by the contractual relation of the servant to his master. The status of the Female under Tutelage, if the tutelage be understood of persons other than her husband, has also ceased to exist; from her coming of age to her marriage all the relations she may form are relations of contract. So too the status of the Son under Power has no true place in the law of modern European societies. If any civil obligation binds together the Parent and the child of full age, it is one to which only contract gives its legal validity. The apparent exceptions are exceptions of that stamp which illustrates the rule. The child before years of discretion, the orphan under guardianship, the adjudged lunatic, have all their capacities and incapacities regulated by the Law of Persons. But why? The reason is differently expressed in the conventional language of different systems, but in substance it is stated to the same effect by all. The great majority of Jurists are constant to the principle that the classes of persons just mentioned are subject to extrinsic control on the single ground that they do not possess the faculty of forming a judgment on their own interests; in other words, that they are wanting in the first essential of an engagement by Contract.

The word Status may be usefully employed to construct a formula expressing the law of progress thus indicated, which, whatever be its value, seems to me to be sufficiently ascertained. All the forms of Status taken notice of in the Law of Persons were derived from, and to some extent are still coloured by, the powers and privileges anciently residing in the Family. If then we employ Status, agreeably with the usage of the best writers, to signify these personal conditions only, and avoid applying the term to such conditions as are the immediate or remote result of agreement, we may say that the movement of the progressive societies has hitherto been a movement *from Status to Contract*.

5. Public Opinion and Law
by A. V. Dicey

From Law and Public Opinion in England [*1905*] *London, Macmillan (1963) chapter 1, pp. 1–16.*

My aim in these lectures is to exhibit the close dependence of legislation, and even of the absence of legislation, in England during the nineteenth century upon the varying currents of public opinion.

The fact of this dependence will be assumed by most students with even too great readiness. We are all of us so accustomed to endow public opinion with a mysterious or almost supernatural power, that we neglect to examine what it is that we mean by public opinion, to measure the true limits of its authority, and to ascertain the mode of its operation. Surprise may indeed be felt, not at the statement that the law depends upon opinion, but at this assertion being limited to England, and to England during the last century. The limitation, however, is intentional, and admits of full justification.

True indeed it is that the existence and the alteration of human institutions must, in a sense, always and everywhere depend upon the beliefs or feelings, or, in other words, upon the opinion of the society in which such institutions flourish.

'As force', writes Hume, 'is always on the side of the governed, the governors have nothing to support them but opinion. It is, therefore, on opinion only that government is founded; and this maxim extends to the most despotic and most military governments, as well as to the most free and most popular.'[1]

But, though obedience to law must of necessity be enforced by opinion of some sort, and Hume's paradox thus turns out to be a truism, this statement does not involve the admission that the law of every country is itself the result of what we mean by 'public opinion'. This term, when used in reference to legislation, is merely a short way of describing the belief or conviction prevalent in a given society that particular laws are beneficial, and therefore ought to be maintained, or that they are harmful, and therefore ought to be modified or repealed. And the assertion that public opinion governs legislation in a particular country, means that laws are there maintained or repealed in accordance with the opinion or wishes of its inhabitants. Now this assertion, though it is, if properly understood, true with regard to England at the present day, is clearly not true of all countries, at all times, and indeed has not always been true even of England.

For, in the first place, there exist many communities in which public opinion – if by that term be meant speculative views held by the mass of the people as to the alteration or improvement of their institutions – can hardly be said to have any existence. The members of such societies are influenced by habits rather than by thoughts. Their mode of life is determined by customary rules, which may indeed have originated in the necessities of a given social condition, or even in speculative doctrines entertained by ancient law-givers,

but which, whatever be their origin, assuredly owe their continuance
to use and wont. It is, in truth, only under the peculiar conditions of
an advanced civilisation that opinion dictates legislative change.

It is possible, in the second place, to point to realms where laws
and institutions have been altered or revolutionised in deference to
opinion, but where the beliefs which have guided legislative reform
have not been what we mean in England by 'public' opinion. They
have been, not ideas entertained by the inhabitants of a country, or
by the greater part thereof, but convictions held by a small number
of men, or even by a single individual who happened to be placed in a
position of commanding authority. We must, indeed, remember that
no ruler, however powerful, can stand completely alone, and that the
despots who have caused or guided revolutions have been influenced
by the opinion, if not of their own country, yet of their generation.

In the third place, the law of a country may fail, for a time, to
represent public opinion owing to the lack of any legislative organ
which adequately responds to the sentiment of the age. A portion, at
least, of that accumulation of abuses, which was the cause or the
occasion of the French Revolution, may fairly be ascribed to the
want of any legislative body possessing both the power and the will
to carry out reforms which had long been demanded by the intelligence of the French nation. Nor can it be denied that even in England
defective legislative machinery has at times lessened the immediate
influence of opinion. The chief cause, no doubt, of the arrest of
almost every kind of reform during the latest years of the eighteenth
and the earlier part of the nineteenth century, was a state of feeling so
hostile to revolution that it forbade the most salutary innovations.
But 'legislative stagnation', as it has been termed, lasted in England
for at least ten or twenty years beyond the date when it ought
naturally to have come to an end; and it can hardly be disputed that
this delay in the improvement of English institutions was due in part
to the defects of the unreformed Parliament – that is, to the non-
existence of a satisfactory legislative organ.

The close and immediate connection then, which in modern
England exists between public opinion and legislation is a very
peculiar and noteworthy fact, to which we cannot easily find a
parallel. Nowhere have changes in popular convictions or wishes
found anything like such rapid and immediate expression in alterations of the law as they have in Great Britain during the nineteenth
century, and more especially during the last half thereof. France is
the land of revolution, England is renowned for conservatism, but a

glance at the legal history of each country suggests the existence of some error in the popular contrast between French mutability and English unchangeableness. From whatever point of view, in short, the matter be regarded, it becomes apparent that during the last seventy-five years or more public opinion has exercised in England a direct and immediate control over legislation which it does not even now exert in most other civilised countries.

In England, the beliefs or sentiments which, during the nineteenth century, have governed the development of the law have in strictness been public opinion, for they have been the wishes and ideas as to legislation held by the people of England, or, to speak with more precision, by the majority of those citizens who have at a given moment taken an effective part in public life.

The principle that the development of law depends upon opinion is, however, open to one objection. Men legislate, it may be urged, not in accordance with their opinion as to what is a good law, but in accordance with their interest, and this, it may be added, is emphatically true of classes as contrasted with individuals, and therefore of a country like England, where classes exert a far more potent control over the making of laws than can any single person.

Now it must at once be granted that in matters of legislation men are guided in the main by their real or apparent interest. So true is this, that from the inspection of the laws of a country it is often possible to conjecture, and this without much hesitation, what is the class which holds, or has held, predominant power at a given time. No man could cast a glance at the laws and institutions of the middle ages without seeing that power then went with ownership of land. The criminal law of the eighteenth century, and also many of its trade laws, bear witness to the growing influence of merchants. The free-trade legislation of 1846 and the succeeding years tells us that political authority had come into the hands of manufacturers and traders. Nor would any man, even though he knew not the history of our Parliamentary Reform Acts, hesitate, from the gist of modern statutes, to infer that during the nineteenth century, first the middle classes, then the artisans of our towns, and lastly the country labourers, had obtained an increase of political power. The connection, however, between legislation and the supposed interests of the legislators is so obvious that the topic hardly requires illustration.

The answer to the objection under consideration is, however, easy to find.

'Though man', to use the words of Hume, 'be much governed by interest, yet even interest itself, and all human affairs, are entirely governed by *opinion*.'[2] Even, therefore, were we to assume that the persons who have power to make law are solely and wholly influenced by the desire to promote their own personal and selfish interests, yet their view of their interest and therefore their legislation must be determined by their opinion; and hence, where the public has influence, the development of the law must of necessity be governed by public opinion.

But though this answer is sufficient, there exists so much misunderstanding as to the connection between men's interests and their beliefs that it is well to pursue the matter a step further. The citizens of a civilised country, such as England, are for the most part not recklessly selfish in the ordinary sense of the word; they wish, no doubt, to promote their own interests – that is, to increase their own pleasures and to diminish their own discomforts, but they certainly do not intend to sacrifice, to their own private advantage or emolument, either the happiness of their neighbours or the welfare of the State. Individuals, indeed, and still more frequently classes, do constantly support laws or institutions which they deem beneficial to themselves, but which certainly are in fact injurious to the rest of the world. But the explanation of this conduct will be found, in nine cases out of ten, to be that men come easily to believe that arrangements agreeable to themselves are beneficial to others. A man's interest gives a bias to his judgment far oftener than it corrupts his heart. It is well to insist upon the true relation between self-interest and belief, because ardent reformers, and notably Bentham and his disciples, have at times misunderstood it, and have used language which implied that every opponent of progress was, if not a fool, then a rogue, who deliberately preferred his own private advantage to the general benefit of mankind, whereas in reality he will be found in most cases to have been an honest man of average ability, who has opposed a beneficial change not through exceptional selfishness, but through some intellectual delusion unconsciously created by the bias of a sinister interest. Take the extreme case of American slave-owners. It will not be denied that, at the outbreak of the War of Secession, there were to be found in the South many fervent enthusiasts for slavery (or rather for the social system of which it was a necessary part), just as there were to be found in the North a far greater number of ardent enthusiasts for abolition. Some Southerners at least did undoubtedly hold the bona fide belief that slavery was the source of benefit, not only to the planters, but to the slaves, and indirectly to the whole civilised world. Such Southern fanatics were wrong and the Abolitionists were right. The faith in slavery was a delusion; but a delusion, however largely the result of self-interest, is still an intellectual error, and a different thing from callous selfishness. It is at any rate an opinion. In the case, therefore, of Southerners who resisted the passing of any law for the abolition of slavery, as in all similar instances, we are justified in saying that it is at bottom opinion which controls legislation.

1. David Hume, *Essays*, vol. I, Essay IV, p. 110.
2. David Hume, *Essays*, vol. I, Essay VII, p. 125.

6. The State and Law
by Karl Marx and Frederick Engels

From (i) Karl Marx, 'Contribution to the Critique of Hegel's Philosophy of Law' [written 1843, and its Introduction some time later] in Collected Works, vol. 3, London, Lawrence and Wishart (1975) pp. 175–87 and 29–81 (sub-headings inserted by editors); (ii) Karl Marx and Frederick Engels, The German Ideology [written 1846] London, Lawrence and Wishart (1965) pp. 78–80 and 365–8; (iii) letter from Engels to C. Schmidt [London, 27 October 1890, edited] in Selected Correspondence, Moscow, Foreign Languages Publishing House (n.d.) pp. 503–5; (iv) Frederick Engels, The Origin of the Family, Private Property and the State [written 1884] London Lawrence and Wishart (1973) pp. 229–32; (v) Frederick Engels, Anti-Dühring [written 1877–8] London, Lawrence and Wishart (1969) pp. 36–7 and 101–15; (vi) Karl Marx and Frederick Engels, Manifesto of the Communist Party [written 1847] Moscow, Progress Publishers (1967) pp. 52–68.

(i) Critique of Hegel's Philosophy of Law

Critique of the German State and Hegelian Philosophy of Law: Theory and Practice
For Germany the *criticism of religion* is in the main complete, and criticism of religion is the premise of all criticism.

The *profane* existence of error is discredited after its *heavenly oratio pro aris et focis* have been disproved. Man, who looked for a superhuman being in the fantastic reality of heaven and found nothing there but the *reflection* of himself, will not longer be disposed to find but the *semblance* of himself, only an inhuman being, where he seeks and must seek his true reality.

The basis of irreligious criticism is: *Man makes religion*, religion does not make man. Religion is the self-consciousness and self-esteem of man who has either not yet found himself or has already lost himself again. But *man* is no abstract being encamped outside the world. Man is *the world of man*, the state, society. This state, this society, produce religion, an *inverted world-consciousness*, because they are an *inverted world*. Religion is the general theory of that world, its encyclopaedic compendium, its logic in a popular form, its spiritualistic *point d'honneur*, its enthusiasm, its moral sanction, its solemn complement, its universal source of consolation and justi-fication. It is the *fantastic realisation* of the human essence because the *human essence* has no true reality. The struggle against religion is therefore indirectly a fight against *the world* of which religion is the spiritual *aroma*.

Religious distress is at the same time the *expression* of real distress and also the *protest* against real distress. Religion is the sigh of the oppressed creature, the heart of a heartless world, just as it is the spirit of spiritless conditions. It is the *opium* of the people.

To abolish religion as the *illusory* happiness of the people is to demand their *real* happiness. The demand to give up illusions about the existing state of affairs is the *demand to give up a state of affairs which needs illusions*. The criticism of religion is therefore *in embryo the criticism of the vale of tears*, the *halo* of which is religion.

The *task of history*, therefore, once the *world beyond* the truth has disappeared, is to establish the *truth of this world*. The immediate *task of philosophy*, which is at the service of history, once the *holy form* of human self-estrangement has been unmasked, is to unmask self-estrangement in its *unholy forms*. Thus the criticism of heaven turns into the criticism of the earth, the *criticism of religion* into the *criticism of law* and the *criticism of theology* into the *criticism of politics*.

The following exposition – a contribution to that task – deals immediately not with the original, but with a copy, the German *philosophy* of state and of law, for no other reason than that it deals with *Germany*.

If one wanted to proceed from the *status quo* itself in Germany, even in the only appropriate way, i.e., negatively, the result would still be an *anachronism*. Even the negation of our political present is a reality already covered with dust in the historical lumber-room of modern nations. If I negate powdered pigtails, I am still left with unpowdered pigtails.

As the ancient peoples went through their pre-history in imagination, in *mythology*, so we Germans have gone through our post-history in thought, in *philosophy*. We are *philosophical* contemporaries of the present without being its *historical* contemporaries. German philosophy is the *ideal prolongation* of German history. If therefore, instead of the *oeuvres incomplètes* of our real history, we criticise the *oeuvres posthumes* of our ideal history, *philosophy*, our criticism is among the questions of which the present says: *That is the question*. What in advanced nations is a *practical* break with modern political conditions, is in Germany, where even those conditions do not yet exist, at first a *critical* break with the philosophical reflection of those conditions.

German philosophy of law and state is the only *German history* which is *al pari* with the *official* modern reality. The German nation must therefore take into account not only its present conditions but also its dream-history, and subject to criticism not only these existing conditions but at the same time their abstract continuation. Its future cannot be *limited* either to the immediate negation of its real conditions of state and law or to the immediate implementation of its ideal state and legal conditions, for it has the immediate negation of its real conditions in its ideal conditions, and it has almost *outlived* the immediate implementation of its ideal conditions in the contemplation of neighbouring nations.

The criticism of the *German philosophy of state and law*, which attained its most consistent, richest and final formulation through *Hegel*, is both a critical analysis of the modern state and of the reality connected with it, and the resolute negation of the whole *German political and legal consciousness* as *practised* hitherto, the most distinguished, most universal expression of which, raised to the level of a *science*, is the *speculative philosophy of law* itself. If the speculative philosophy of law, that abstract extravagant *thinking* on the modern state, the reality of which remains a thing of the beyond, if only beyond the Rhine, was possible only in Germany, inversely the *German* thought-image of the modern state which disregards *real man* was possible only because and insofar as the modern state itself disregards *real man* or satisfies the *whole* of man only in imagination. In politics the Germans *thought* what other nations *did*. Germany was their *theoretical consciousness*. The abstraction and conceit of its thought always kept in step with the one-sidedness and stumpiness of its reality. If therefore the *status quo of German statehood* expresses the *perfection of the ancien regime*, the perfection of the thorn in the flesh of the modern state, the *status quo of German political theory* expresses the *imperfection of the modern state*, the defectiveness of its flesh itself.

Even as the resolute opponent of the previous form of *German* political consciousness the criticism of speculative philosophy of law turns, not towards itself, but towards *problems* which can only be solved by one means – *practice*.

It is not the *radical* revolution, not the *general human* emancipation which is a utopian dream for Germany, but rather the partial, the *merely* political revolution, the revolution which leaves the pillars of the house standing. On what is a partial, a merely political revolution based? On the fact that *part of civil society* emancipates itself and attains *general* domination; on the fact that a definite class, proceeding from its *particular situation*, undertakes the general emancipation of society. This class emancipates the whole of society but only provided the whole of society is in the same situation as this class, e.g., possesses money and education or can acquire them at will.

No class of civil society can play this role without arousing a moment of enthusiasm in itself and in the masses, a moment in which it fraternises and merges with society in general, becomes confused with it and is perceived and acknowledged as its *general representative*; a moment in which its demands and rights are truly the rights and demands of society itself; a moment in which it is truly the social head and the social heart. Only in the name of the general rights of society can a particular class lay claim to general domination. For the storming of this emancipatory position, and hence for the political exploitation of all spheres of society in the interests of its own sphere, revolutionary energy and intellectual self-confidence alone are not sufficient. For the *revolution of a nation* and the *emancipation of a particular class* of civil society to coincide, for *one* estate to be acknowledged as the estate of the whole society, all the defects of society must conversely be concentrated in another class, a particular estate must be the general stumbling-block, the incorporation of the general limitation, a particular social sphere must be looked upon as the *notorious crime* of the whole of society, so that liberation from that sphere appears as general self-liberation. For *one* estate to be *par excellence* the estate of liberation, another estate must conversely be the obvious estate of oppression. The negative general significance of the French nobility and the French clergy determined the positive general significance of the immediately adjacent and opposed class of the *bourgeoisie*.

But no particular class in Germany has the consistency, the severity, the courage or the ruthlessness that could mark it out as the negative representative of society. No more has any estate the breadth of soul that identifies itself, even for a moment, with the soul of the nation, the genius that inspires material might to political violence, or that revolutionary audacity which flings at the adversary the defiant words: *I am nothing and I should be everything*.

In Germany, on the contrary, where practical life is as spiritless as spiritual life is unpractical, no class in civil society has any need or capacity for general emancipation until it is forced by its *immediate* condition, by *material* necessity, by its *very chains*.

Where, then, is the *positive* possibility of a German emancipation? *Answer*: In the formation of a class with *radical chains*, a class of civil society which is not a class of civil society, an estate which is the dissolution of all estates, a sphere which has a universal character by its universal suffering and claims no *particular right* because no *particular wrong* but *wrong generally* is perpetrated against it; which can no longer invoke a *historical* but only a *human* title: which does not stand in any one-sided antithesis to the consequences but in an all-round antithesis to the premises of the German state: a sphere, finally, which cannot emancipate itself without emancipating itself from all other spheres of society and thereby emancipating all other spheres of society, which, in a word, is the *complete loss* of man and hence can win itself only through the *complete rewinning of man*. This dissolution of society as a particular estate is the *proletariat*.

The proletariat is coming into being in Germany only as a result of the rising *industrial* development. For it is not the *naturally arising* poor but the *artificially impoverished*, not the human masses mechanically oppressed by the gravity of society but the masses resulting from the *drastic dissolution* of society, mainly of the middle estate, that form the proletariat, although it is obvious that gradually the naturally arising poor and the Christian–Germanic serfs also join its ranks.

By proclaiming the *dissolution of the hitherto existing world order* the proletariat merely states the *secret of its own existence*, for it *is in fact* the dissolution of that world order. By demanding the *negation of private property*, the proletariat merely raises to the rank of a *principle of society* what society has made the principle of the *proletariat*. What, without its own co-operation, is already incorporated in *it* as the negative result of society. In regard to the world which is coming into being the proletarian then finds himself possessing the same right as the *German king* in regard to the world which has come into being when he calls the people *his* people as he calls the horse *his* horse. By declaring the people his private property the king simply states that the property owner is king.

As philosophy finds its *material* weapons in the proletariat, so the proletariat find its *spiritual* weapons in philosophy. And once the lightning of thought has squarely struck this ingenuous soil of the people the emancipation of the *Germans* into *human beings* will take place. ...

Man and the State under True Democracy (Communism), and under other State Forms

Hegel starts from the state and makes man the subjectified state; (true) democracy starts from man and makes the state objectified man. Just as it is not religion which creates man but man who creates religion, so it is not the constitution which creates the people but the people which creates the constitution ... To democracy all other forms of state stand as its Old Testament. Man does not exist for the law but the law for man – it is a *human manifestation*; whereas in the other forms of state man is a legal manifestation. That is the fundamental distinction of democracy.

All other *state forms* are definite, distinct, *particular forms of state*. In democracy the *formal* principle is at the same time the *material* principle. Only democracy, therefore, is the true unity of the general and the particular ... The French have recently interpreted this as meaning that in true democracy the *political state is annihilated*. This is correct insofar as the political state *qua* political state, as constitution, no longer passes for the whole.

In all states other than democratic ones the *state*, the *law*, the *constitution* is what rules, without really ruling – i.e., without materially permeating the content of the remaining, non-political spheres. In (true) democracy the constitution, the law, the state itself, insofar as it is a political constitution, is only the self-determination of the people, and a particular content of the people.

Incidentally, it goes without saying that all forms of state have democracy *for* their truth and that they are therefore untrue insofar as they are not democracy.

The abstraction of the *state as such* belongs only to modern times, because the abstraction of private life belongs only to modern times. The abstraction of the *political state* is a modern product.

The Separation of the Modern State from Civil Society

For Hegel on the one side are placed, always as identical, state and government; on the other, the nation, resolved into particular spheres and individuals. The estates stand between the two as a *mediating* organ.

The identity Hegel is asserting was at its most complete, as he himself admits, in the *Middle Ages*. Here the *estates of civil society* as such and the *estates in the political sense* were identical. One can express the spirit of the Middle Ages in this way: the estates of civil society and the estates in the political sense were identical, because civil society was political society.

Hegel, however, takes as his starting point the *separation* of '*civil society*' and the '*political state*' as two fixed opposites, two really different spheres. This separation does indeed *really* exist in the *modern* state . . . Only the *separation* of the civil and political estates expresses the *true* relationship of *modern* civil and political society.

The Modern State and Alienated Man

In describing civil society as civil estate, Hegel has declared the distinctions of estate in civil society to be *non*-political distinctions, and civil and political life to be heterogeneous, even *opposites*.

The *general law* here appears in the individual. Civil society and state are separated. Hence the citizen of the state is also separated from the citizen as the member of civil society. He must therefore effect a *fundamental division* within himself. As an *actual citizen* he finds himself in a twofold organisation: the *bureaucratic* organisation, which is an external, formal feature of the distant state, the executive, which does not touch him or his independent reality, and the *social* organisation, the organisation of civil society. But in the latter he stands as a *private person* outside the state; this social organisation does not touch the political state as such. The former is a state organisation for which he always provides the *material*. The second is a *civil organisation* the material of which is not the state. In the former the state stands as formal antithesis to him, in the second he stands as material antithesis to the state. Hence, in order to behave as an *actual citizen of the state*, and to attain political significance and effectiveness, he must step out of his civil reality, disregard it, and withdraw from this whole organisation into his individuality; for the sole existence which he finds for his citizenship of the state is his sheer, blank, *individuality*, since the existence of the state as executive is complete without him, and his existence in civil society is complete without the state. He can be a *citizen of the state* only in contradiction to these *sole available communities*, only as an *individual*. His existence as a citizen of the state is an existence outside his *communal* existences and is therefore purely *individual*. ... The separation of civil society and political state necessarily appears as a separation of *political* citizen, the citizen of the state, from civil society, from his own, actual, empirical reality.

[In] the modern era, *civilisation* separates the *objective* essence of the human being from him as merely something *external*, material. It does not accept the content of the human being as his true reality.

(ii) The Relation of State and Law to Property

The first form of property, in the ancient world as in the Middle Ages, is tribal property, determined with the Romans chiefly by war, with the Germans by the rearing of cattle. In the case of the ancient peoples, since several tribes live together in one town, the tribal property appears as State property, and the right of the individual to it as mere 'possession' which, however, like tribal property as a whole, is confined to landed property only. Real private property began with the ancients, as with modern nations, with movable property. – (Slavery and community) (dominium ex jure Quiritum) [Ownership in accordance with the law applying to full Roman citizens – eds.] In the case of the nations which grew out of the Middle Ages, tribal property evolved through various stages – feudal landed property, corporative moveable property, capital invested in manufacture – to modern capital, determined by big industry and universal competition, i.e. pure private property, which has cast off all semblance of a communal institution and has shut out the State from any influence on the development of property. To this modern private property corresponds the modern State, which, purchased gradually by the owners of property by means of taxation, has fallen entirely into their hands through the national debt, and its existence has become wholly dependent on the commercial credit which the owners of property, the bourgeois, extent to it, as reflected in the rise and fall of State funds on the stock exchange. By the mere fact that it is a *class* and no longer an *estate*, the bourgeoisie is forced to organise itself no longer locally, but nationally, and to give a general form to its mean average interest. Through the emancipation of private property from the community, the State has become a separate entity, beside and outside civil society; but it is nothing more than the form of organisation which the bourgeois necessarily adopt both for internal and external purposes, for the mutual guarantee of their property and interests. The independence of the State is only found nowadays in those countries where the estates have not yet completely developed into classes, where the estates, done away with in more advanced countries, still have a part to play, and where there exists a mixture; countries, that is to say, in which no one section of the population can achieve dominance over the others. This is the case particularly in Germany. The most perfect example of the modern State is North America. The modern French, English and American writers all express the opinion that the State exists only for the sake of private property, so that this fact has penetrated into the consciousness of the normal man.

Since the State is the form in which the individuals of a ruling class assert their common interests, and in which the whole civil society of an epoch is epitomised, it follows that the State mediates in the formation of all common institutions and that the institutions receive a political form. Hence the illusion that law is based on the will, and indeed on the will divorced from its real basis – on *free* will. Similarly, justice is in its turn reduced to the actual laws.

Civil law develops simultaneously with private property out of the disintegration of the natural community. With the Romans the development of private property and civil law had no further industrial and commercial consequences, because their whole mode of production did not alter. With modern peoples, where the feudal community was disintegrated by industry and trade, there began with the rise of private property and civil law a new phase, which was capable of further development. The very first town which carried on an extensive maritime trade in the Middle Ages, Amalfi, also developed maritime law. As soon as industry and trade developed private property further, first in Italy and later in other countries, the highly developed Roman civil law was immediately adopted again and raised to authority. When later the bourgeoisie had acquired so much power that the princes took up its interests in order to overthrow the feudal nobility by means of the bourgeoisie, there began in all countries – in France in the sixteenth century – the real development of law, which in all countries except England proceeded on the basis of the Roman Codex. In England, too, Roman legal principles had to be introduced to further the development of civil law (especially in the case of movable property). (It must not be forgotten that law has just as little an independent history as religion.)

In actual history, those theoreticians who regarded *power* as the basis of right, were in direct contradiction to those who looked on *will* as the basis of right. If power is taken as the basis of right, as Hobbes, etc., do, then right, law, etc. are merely the symptom, the expression of *other* relations upon which State power rests. The material life of individuals, which by no means depends merely on their 'will', their mode of production and form of intercourse, which mutually determine each other – this is the real basis of the State and remains so at all the stages at which division of labour and private property are still necessary, quite independently of the *will* of individuals. These actual relations are in no way created by the State power; on the contrary they are the power creating it. The individuals who rule in these conditions, besides having to constitute their power in the form of the *State*, have to give their will, which is determined by these definite conditions, a universal expression as the will of the State, as law – an expression whose content is always determined by the relations of this class, as the civil and criminal law demonstrates in the clearest possible way. Just as the weight of their bodies does not depend on their idealistic will or on their arbitrary decision, so also the fact that they enforce their own will in the form of law, and at the same time make it independent of the personal arbitrariness of each individual among them, does not depend on their idealistic will. Their personal rule must at the same time be constituted as average rule. Their personal power is based on conditions of life which as they develop are common to many individuals, and the continuance of which they, as ruling individuals, have to maintain against others and, at the same time, maintain that they hold good for all. The expression of this will, which is determined by their common interest, is law. It is precisely because individuals who are independent of one another assert themselves and their own will, which on this basis is inevitably egoistical in their mutual relations, that self-denial is made necessary in law and right, self-denial in the exceptional case, and self-assertion of their interests in the average case (which, therefore, not *they*, but only the 'egoist in agreement with himself' regards as self-denial). The same applies to the classes which are ruled, whose will plays just as small a part in determining the existence of law and the State. For example, so long as the productive forces are still insufficiently developed to make competition superfluous, and therefore would give rise to competition over and over again, for so long the classes which are ruled would be wanting the impossible if they had the 'will' to abolish competition and with it the State and the law. Incidentally, too, it is only in the imagination of the ideologist that this 'will' arises before conditions have developed far enough to make its production possible. After conditions have developed sufficiently to produce it, the ideologist is able to imagine this will as being purely arbitrary and therefore as conceivable at all times and under all circumstances.

Like right, so crime, i.e., the struggle of the isolated individual against the prevailing conditions, is not the result of pure arbitrariness. On the contrary, it depends on the same conditions as that rule. The same visionaries who see in right and law the domination of some independently existing, general will can see in crime the mere violation of right and law. Hence the State does not exist owing to the ruling will, but the State which arises from the material mode of life of individuals has also the form of a ruling will. If the latter loses its domination, it means that not only has the will changed but also the material existence and life of the individuals, and only for that reason has their will changed. It is possible for rights and laws to be 'inherited'. But in that case they are no longer ruling, but nominal, of which striking examples are furnished by the history of ancient Roman law and English law. We saw earlier how a theory and history of pure thought could arise among philosophers owing to the divorce between ideas and the individuals and their empirical relations which serve as the basis of these ideas. In the same way, here too one can divorce right from its real basis, whereby one obtains a 'ruling will' which in different epochs becomes modified in various ways and has its own, independent history in its creations, the laws. On this account, political and civil history becomes ideologically merged in the history of the rule of successive laws. This is the specific illusion of lawyers and politicians that Jacques le bonhomme adopts *sans façon*.

(iii) Law and Economic Development

The reaction of the state power upon economic development can be of three kinds: it can run in the same direction, and then development is more rapid; it can oppose the line of development, in which case nowadays it will go to pieces in the long run in every great people; or it can prevent the economic development from proceeding along certain lines, and prescribe other lines. This case ultimately reduced itself to one of the two previous ones. But it is obvious that in cases two and three the political power can do great damage to the economic development and cause a great squandering of energy and material.

Then there is also the case of the consequent and brutal destruction of economic resources, by which, in certain circumstances, a whole local or national economic development could formerly be ruined. Nowadays such a case usually has the opposite effect, at least with great peoples: in the long run the vanquished often gains more economically, politically and morally than the victor.

Similarly with law. As soon as the new division of labour which creates professional lawyers becomes necessary, another new and independent sphere is opened up which, for all its general dependence on production and trade, has also a special capacity for reacting upon these spheres. In a modern state, law must not only correspond to the general economic condition and be its expression, but must also be an *internally coherent* expression which does not, owing to inner contradictions, reduce itself to nought. And in order to achieve this, the faithful reflection of economic conditions suffers increasingly. All the more so the more rarely it happens that a code of law is the blunt, unmitigated, unadulterated expression of the domination of a class – this in itself would offend the 'conception of right'. Even in the *Code Napoleon* the pure, consistent conception of right held by the revolutionary bourgeoisie of 1792–96 is already adulterated in many ways, and, in so far as it is embodied there, has daily to undergo all sorts of attenuations owing to the rising power of the proletariat. This does not prevent the *Code Napoleon* from being the statute book which serves as the basis of every new code of law in every part of the world. Thus to a great extent the course of the 'development of right' consists only, first, in the attempt to do away with the contradictions arising from the direct translation of economic relations into legal principles, and to establish a harmonious system of law, and then in the repeated breaches made in this system by the influence and compulsion of further economic development, which involves it in further contradictions. (I am speaking here for the moment only of civil law.)

The reflection of economic relations as legal principles is necessarily also a topsy-turvy one: it goes on without the person who is acting being conscious of it; the jurist imagines he is operating with *a priori* propositions, whereas they are really only economic reflexes; so everything is upside down. And it seems to me obvious that this inversion, which, so long as it remains unrecognised, forms what we call *ideological outlook*, reacts in its turn upon what we call *ideological outlook*, reacts in its turn upon the economic basis and may, within certain limits, modify it. The basis of the right of inheritance – assuming that the stages reached in the development of the family are the same – is an economic one. Nevertheless, it would be difficult to prove, for instance, that the absolute liberty of the testator in England and the severe restrictions in every detail imposed upon him in France are due to economic causes alone. Both react back, however, on the economic sphere to a very considerable extent, because they influence the distribution of property.

(iv) The Historical Nature of the Capitalist State

The state is by no means a power imposed on society from without; just as little is it 'the reality of the moral idea', 'the image and the reality of reason', as Hegel maintains. Rather, it is a product of society at a particular stage of development; it is the admission that this society has involved itself in insoluble self-contradiction and is cleft into irreconcilable antagonisms which it is powerless to exorcise. But in order that these antagonisms, classes with conflicting economic interests, shall not consume themselves and society in fruitless struggle, a power, apparently standing above society, has become necessary to moderate the conflict and keep it within the bounds of 'order'; and this power, arisen out of society but placing itself above it and increasingly alienating itself from it, is the state.

In contrast to the old gentile organisation, the state is distinguished firstly by the grouping of its members *on a territorial basis*. The second distinguishing characteristic is the institution of a *public force* which is no longer immediately identical with the people's own organization of themselves as an armed power. This special public force is needed because a self-acting armed organisation of the people has become impossible since their cleavage into classes . . . This public force exists in every state; it consists not merely of armed men but also of material appendages, prisons and coercive institutions of all kinds, of which gentile society knew nothing. It may be very insignificant, practically negligible, in societies with still undeveloped class antagonisms and living in remote areas, as at times and in places in the United States of America. But it becomes stronger in proportion as the class antagonisms within the state become sharper and as adjoining states grow larger and more populous. It is enough to look at Europe today, where class struggle and rivalry in conquest have brought the public power to a pitch that it threatens to devour the whole of society and even the state itself.

In order to maintain this public power, contributions from the citizens are necessary – *taxes*. There were completely unknown to gentile society. We know more than enough about them today. With advancing civilisation, even taxes are not sufficient; the state draws drafts on the future, contracts loans – *state debts*. Our old Europe can tell a tale about these, too.

In possession of the public power and the right of taxation, the officials now present themselves as organs of society standing *above* society. The free, willing respect accorded to the organs of the gentile constitution is not enough for them, even if they could have it. Representatives of a power which estranges them from society, they have to be given prestige by means of special decrees which invest them with a peculiar sanctity and inviolability. The lowest police officer of the civilised state has more 'authority' than all the organs of gentile society put together; but the mightiest prince and the greatest statesman or general of civilization might envy the humblest of the gentile chiefs, the unforced and unquestioned respect accorded to him. For the one stands in the midst of society; the other is forced to pose as something outside and above it.

As the state arose from the need to keep class antagonisms in check, but also arose in the thick of the fight between the classes, it is normally the state of the most powerful, economically dominant class, which by its means becomes also the politically dominant class and so acquires new means of holding down and exploiting the oppressed class. The ancient state was, above all, the state of the slave owners for holding down the slaves, just as the feudal state was the organ of the nobility for holding down the peasant serfs and bondsmen, and the modern representative state is an instrument for exploiting wage labour by capital. Exceptional periods, however, occur when the warring classes are so nearly equal in forces that the state power, as apparent mediator, acquires for the moment a certain independence in relation to both. This applies to the absolute monarchy of the 11th and 18th centuries, which balanced the nobility and the bourgeoisie against one another, and to the Bonapartism of the First and particularly of the Second French Empire, which played off the proletariat against the bourgeoisie and the bourgeoisie against the proletariat. The latest achievement in this line, in which ruler and ruled look equally comic, is the new German Empire of the Bismarckian nation; here the capitalists and the workers are balanced against one another and both of them fleeced for the benefit of the decayed Prussian cabbage Junkers.

Further, in most historical states the rights conceded to citizens are graded on a property basis whereby it is directly admitted that the state is an organisation for the protection of the possessing class against the non-possessing class. This is already the case in the Athenian and Roman property classes; similarly in the medieval feudal state in which the extent of political power was determined by the extent of land-ownership; similarly, also, in the electoral qualifications in modern parliamentary states. This political recognition of property differences is, however, by no means essential. On the contrary, it marks a low stage in the development of the state. The highest form of the state, the democratic republic, which in our modern social condition becomes more and more an unavoidable necessity and is the form of state in which alone the last decisive battle between proletariat and bourgeoisie can be fought out – the democratic republic no longer officially recognises differences of property. Wealth here employs its power indirectly, but all the more surely. It does this in two ways: by plain corruption of officials, of which America is the classic example; and by an alliance between the government and the stock exchange, which is effected all the more easily the higher the state debt mounts and the more the joint-stock companies concentrate in their hands not only transport but also production itself, and themselves have their own centre in the stock exchange. In addition to America, the latest French republic illustrates this strikingly, and honest little Switzerland has also given a creditable performance in this field. But that a democratic republic is not essential to this brotherly bond between government and stock exchange is proved not only by England but also by the new German Empire, where it is difficult to say who scored most by the introduction of universal suffrage, Bismarck or the Bleichröder bank. And lastly the possessing class rules directly by means of universal suffrage. As long as the oppressed class – in our case, therefore, the proletariat – is not yet ripe for its self-liberation, so long will it in its majority recognise the existing order of society as the only possible one and remain politically the tail of the capitalist class, its extreme left wing. But in the measure in which it matures towards its self-emancipation, in the same measure it constitutes itself as its own party and votes for its own representatives, not those of the capitalists. Universal suffrage is thus the gauge of the maturity of the working class. It cannot and never will be anything more in the modern state; but that is enough. On the day when the thermometer of universal suffrage shows boiling point among the workers, they as well as the capitalists will know where they stand.

The state, therefore, has not existed from all eternity. There have been societies which have managed without it, which had no notion of the state or state power. At a definite stage of economic development, which necessarily involved the cleavage of society into classes, the state became a necessity because of this cleavage. We are now rapidly approaching a stage in the development of production at which the existence of these classes has not only ceased to be a necessity but becomes a positive hindrance to production. They will fall as inevitably as they once arose. The state inevitably falls with them. The society which organises production anew on the basis of free and equal association of the producers will put the whole state machinery where it will then belong–into the museum of antiquities, next to the spinning wheel and the bronze axe.

(v) Law, Morality and Justice

The revolution in the conception of nature could only be made in proportion to the corresponding positive materials furnished by research; already much earlier certain historical facts had occurred which led to a decisive change in the conception of history. In 1831, the first working-class rising took place in Lyons; between 1838 and 1842, the first national working-class movement, that of the English Chartists, reached its height. The class struggle between proletariat and bourgeoisie came to the front in the history of the most advanced countries in Europe, in proportion to the development, upon the one hand, of modern industry, upon the other, of the newly-acquired political supremacy of the bourgeoisie. Facts more and more strenuously gave the lie to the teachings of bourgeois economy as to the identity of the interests of capital and labour, as to the universal harmony and universal prosperity that would be the consequence of unbridled competition. All these things could no longer be ignored, any more than the French and English socialism, which was their theoretical, though very imperfect, expression. But the old idealist conception of history, which was not yet dislodged, knew nothing of class struggles based upon economic interests, knew nothing of economic interests; production and all economic relations appeared in it only as incidental, subordinate elements in the 'history of civilisation'.

The new facts made imperative a new examination of all past history. Then it was seen that *all* past history (with the exception of its primitive stages) was the history of class struggles; that these warring classes of society are always the products of the modes of production and of exchange–in a word, of the *economic* conditions of their time; that the economic structure of society always furnishes the real basis, starting from which we can alone work out the ultimate explanation of the whole superstructure of juridical and political institutions as well as of the religious, philosophical, and other ideas of a given historical period. [Hegel] had freed history from metaphysics–he made it dialectic; but his conception of history was essentially idealistic. But now idealism was driven from its last refuge, the philosophy of history; now a materialistic treatment of history was propounded, and a method found of explaining man's 'knowing' by his 'being', instead of, as heretofore, his 'being' by his 'knowing' . . .

It is just the same with eternal truths. Are there then any truths which are so securely based that any doubt of them seems to us to be tantamount to insanity? That twice two makes four, etc. Certainly there are. We can divide the whole realm of knowledge in the traditional way into three great departments. The first includes all sciences that deal with inanimate nature and are to a greater or lesser degree susceptible of mathematical treatments ... If it gives anyone any pleasure to use mighty words for very simple things, it can be asserted that *certain* results obtained by these sciences are eternal truths ...

The second department of science is the one which covers the investigation of living organisms. In this field there is such a multiplicity of interrelationships and causalities that the need for a systematic presentation of interconnections makes it necessary again and again to surround the final and ultimate truths with a luxuriant growth of hypotheses ...

But eternal truths are in an even worse plight in the third, the historical group of sciences. The subjects investigated by these, in their historical sequence and in their present resultant state, are the conditions of human life, social relationships, forms of law and government, with their ideological superstructure in the shape of philosophy, religion, art, etc. ... In social history, [however] the repetition of conditions is the exception and not the rule ... Therefore, knowledge is here essentially relative, inasmuch as it is limited to the investigation of interconnections and consequences of certain social and state forms which exist only in a particular epoch and among particular peoples and are by their very nature transitory.

Now it is a remarkable thing that it is precisely in this sphere that we most frequently encounter truths which claim to be eternal, final and ultimate and all the rest of it. That twice two makes four, that birds have beaks, and similar statements, are proclaimed as eternal truths only by those who aim at deducing, from the existence of eternal truths in general, the conclusion that there are also eternal truths in the sphere of human history–eternal morality, eternal justice, and so on–which claim a validity and scope similar to those of the theorems and applications of mathematics.

If, then, we have not made much progress with truth and error, we can make even less with good and evil. This opposition manifests itself exclusively in the domain of morals, that is, a domain belonging to the history of mankind, and it is precisely in this field that final and ultimate truths are most sparsely sown. The conceptions of good and evil have varied so much from nation to nation and from age to age that they have often been in direct contradiction to each other.

But how do things stand today? What morality is preached to us today? There is first Christian-feudal morality, inherited from earlier religious times; and this is divided, essentially, into a Catholic and a Protestant morality, each of which has no lack of subdivisions. Alongside these we find the modern-bourgeois morality and beside it also the proletarian morality of the future, so that in the most advanced European countries alone the past, present and future provide three great groups of moral theories which are in force simultaneously and alongside each other. Which then, is the true one? Not one of them, in the sense of absolute finality; but certainly that morality contains the maximum elements promising permanence which, in the present, represents the overthrow of the present, represents the future, and that is proletarian morality.

But when we see that the three classes of modern society, the feudal aristocracy, the bourgeoisie and the proletariat, each have a morality of their own, we can only draw the one conclusion: that men, consciously or unconsciously, derive their ethical ideas in the last resort from the practical relations on which their class position is based–from the economic relations in which they carry on production and exchange.

But nevertheless there is quite a lot which the three moral theories mentioned above have in common–is this not at least a portion of a morality which is fixed once and for all? These moral theories represent three different stages of the same historical development, have therefore a common historical background, and for that reason alone they necessarily have much in common. Even more. At similar or approximately similar stages of economic development moral theories must of necessity be more or less in agreement. From the moment when private ownership of movable property developed, all societies in which this private ownership existed had to have this moral injunction in common: Thous shalt not steal. Does this injunction thereby become an eternal moral injunction? By no means. In a society in which all motives for stealing have been done away with, in which therefore at the very most only lunatics would ever steal, how the preacher of morals would be laughed at who tried solemnly to proclaim the eternal truth: Thou shalt not steal!

We therefore reject every attempt to impose on us any moral dogma whatsoever as an eternal, ultimate and for ever immutable ethical law on the pretext that the moral world, too, has its permanent principles which stand above history and the differences between nations. We maintain on the contrary that all moral theories have been hitherto the product, in the last analysis, of the economic conditions of society obtaining at the time. And as society has hitherto moved in class antagonisms, morality has always been class morality; it has either justified the domination and the interests of the ruling class, or, ever since the oppressed class became powerful enough, it has represented its indignation against this domination and the future interests of the oppressed. That in this process there has on the whole been progress in morality, as in all other branches of human knowledge, no one will doubt. But we have not yet passed beyond class morality. A really human morality which stands above class antagonisms and above any recollection of them becomes possible only at a stage of society which has not only overcome class antagonisms but has even forgotten them in practical life.

(vi) Manifesto of the Communist Party

The immediate aim of the Communists is the same as that of all the other proletarian parties: formation of the proletariat into a class, over-throw of the bourgeois supremacy, conquest of political power by the proletariat.

The theoretical conclusions of the Communits are in no way based on ideas or principles that have been invested, or discovered, by this or that would-be universal reformer.

They merely express, in general terms, actual relations springing from an existing class struggle, from a historical movement going on under our very eyes. The abolition of existing property relations is not at all a distinctive feature of Communism.

All property relations in the past have continually been subject to historical change consequent upon the change in historical conditions.

The French Revolution, for example, abolished feudal property in favour of bourgeois property.

The distinguishing feature of Communism is not the abolition of property generally, but the abolition of bourgeois property. But modern bourgeois private property is the final and most complete expression of the system of producing and appropriating products, that is based on class antagonisms, on the exploitation of the many by the few.

In this sense, the theory of the Communists may be summed up in the single sentence: Abolition of private property.

We Communists have been reproached with the desire of abolishing the right of personally acquiring property as the fruit of a man's own labour, which property is alleged to be the ground work of all personal freedom, activity and independence.

Hard-won, self-acquired, self-earned property! Do you mean the property of the petty artisan and of the small peasant, a form of property that preceded the bourgeois form? There is no need to abolish that; the development of industry has to a great extent already destroyed it, and is still destroying it daily.

Or do you mean modern bourgeois private property?

But does wage labour create any property for the labourer? Not a bit. It creates capital, i.e., that kind of property which exploits wage labour, and which cannot increase except upon condition of begetting a new supply of wage labour for fresh exploitation. Property, in its present form, is based on the antagonism of capital and wage labour. Let us examine both sides of this antagonism.

To be a capitalist, is to have not only a purely personal, but a social *status* in production. Capital is a collective product, and only by the united action of many members, nay, in the last resort, only by the united action of all members of society, can it be set in motion.

Capital is, therefore, not a personal, it is a social power.

When, therefore, capital is converted into common property, into the property of all members of society, personal property is not thereby transformed into social property. It is only the social character of the property that is changed. It loses its class character.

Let us now take wage labour.

The average price of wage labour is the minimum wage, i.e., that quantum of the means of subsistence, which is absolutely requisite to keep the labourer in bare existence as a labourer. What, therefore, the wage labourer appropriates by means of his labour, merely suffices to prolong and reproduce a bare existence. We by no means intend to abolish this personal appropriation of the products of labour, an appropriation that is made for the maintenance and repro-duction of human life, and that leaves no surplus wherewith to command the labour of others. All that we want to do away with is the miserable character of this appropriation, under which the labourer lives merely to increase capital, and is allowed to live only in so far as the interest of the ruling class requires it.

In bourgeois society, living labour is but a means to increase accumulated labour. In Communist society, accumulated labour is but a means to widen, to enrich, to promote the existence of the labourer.

In bourgeois society, therefore, the past dominates the present; in Communist society, the present dominates the past. In bourgeois society capital is independent and has individuality, while the living person is dependent and has no individuality.

And the abolition of this state of things is called by the bourgeois, abolition of individuality and freedom! And rightly so. The abolition of bourgeois individuality, bourgeois independence, and bourgeois freedom is undoubtedly aimed at.

By freedom is meant, under the present bourgeois conditions of product, free trade, free selling and buying.

But if selling and buying disappears, free selling and buying disappears also. This talk about free selling and buying, and all the other 'brave words' of our bourgeoisie about freedom in general, have a meaning, if any, only in contrast with restricted selling and buying, with the fettered traders of the Middle Ages, but have no meaning when opposed to the Communistic abolition of buying and selling, of the bourgeois conditions of production, and of the bourgeoisie itself.

You are horrified at our intending to do away with private property. But in your existing society, private property is already done away with for nine-tenths of the population; its existence for the few is solely due to its non-existence in the hands of those nine-tenths. You reproach us, therefore, with intending to do away with a form of property, the necessary condition for whose existence is, the non-existence of any property for the immense majority of society.

In one word, you reproach us with intending to do away with your property. Precisely so; that is just what we intend.

From the moment when labour can no longer be converted into capital, money, or rent, into a social power capable of being monopolised, i.e., from the moment when individual property can no longer be transformed into bourgeois property, into capital, from that moment, you say, individuality vanishes.

You must, therefore, confess that by 'individual' you mean no other person than the bourgeois, than the middle-class owner of property. This person must, indeed, be swept out of the way, and made impossible.

Communism deprives no man of the power to appropriate the products of society; all that it does is to deprive him of the power to subjugate the labour of others by means of such appropriation.

It has been objected that upon the abolition of private property all work will cease, and universal laziness will overtake us.

According to this, bourgeois society ought long ago to have gone to the dogs through sheer idleness; for those of its members who work, acquire nothing, and those who acquire anything, do not work. The whole of this objection is but another expression of the tautology: that there can no longer be any wage labour when there is no longer any capital.

All objections urged against the Communistic code of producing and appropriating material products, have, in the same way, been urged against the Communistic modes of producing and appropriating intellectual products. Just as, to the bourgeois, the disappearance of class property is the disappearance of production itself, so the disappearance of class culture is to him identical with the disappearance of all culture.

That culture, the loss of which he laments, is, for the enormous majority, a mere training to act as a machine.

But don't wrangle with us so long as you apply, to our intended abolition of bourgeois property, the standard of your bourgeois notions of freedom, culture, law, etc. Your very ideas are but the outgrowth of the conditions of your bourgeois production and bourgeois property, just as your jurisprudence is but the will of your class made into a law for all, a will, whose essential character and direction are determined by the economical conditions of existence of your class.

The selfish misconception that induces you to transform into eternal laws of nature and of reason, the social forms springing from your present mode of production and form of property–historical relations that rise and disappear in the progress of production–this misconception you share with every ruling class that has preceded you. What you see clearly in the case of ancient property, what you admit in the case of feudal property, you are of course forbidden to admit in the case of your own bourgeois form of property.

7. Law, Rationalism and Capitalism
by Max Weber

From *(i)* The Protestant Ethic and the Spirit of Capitalism [*first published in* Archiv für Sozialwissenschaft und Sozialpolitik, *1904–5*] *London, George Allen and Unwin (1967) translated by T. Parsons, pp. 13–27 and 180–2; (ii)* The Theory of Social and Economic Organization, *New York, The Free Press (1968) translated by A, M, Henderson and T. Parsons, pp. 152 and 324–64; (iii)* On Law in Economy and Society, *Cambridge, Mass., Harvard University Press (1969) translated by E. Shils and M. Rheinstein, pp. 33–40; (iv)* ibid., *pp. 61–4, 198–204, and 315–18, [taken from parts of* Wirtschaft und Gesellschaft, *first published posthumously 1922, but written 1910–20*].

(i) Rationalism in the West

A product of modern European civilization, studying any problem of universal history, is bound to ask himself to what combination of circumstances the fact should be attributed that in Western civilization, and in Western civilization only, cultural phenomena have appeared which (as we like to think) lie in a line of development having universal significance and value. [In other parts of the world] Institutions of higher education of all possible types, even some superficially similar to our universities, or at least academies, have existed (China, Islam). But a rational, systematic, and specialized pursuit of science, with trained and specialized personnel, has only existed in the West in a sense at all approaching its present dominant place in our culture. Above all is this true of the trained official, the pillar of both the modern State and of the economic life of the West. He forms a type of which there have heretofore only been suggestions, which have never remotely approached its present importance for the social order. Of course the official, even the specialized official, is a very old constituent of the most various societies. But no country and no age has ever experienced, in the same sense as the modern Occident, the absolute and complete dependence of its whole existence, of the political, technical, and economic conditions of its life, on a specially trained *organization* of officials. The most important functions of the everyday life of society have come to be in the hands of technically, commercially, and above all legally trained government officials.

In fact, the State itself, in the sense of a political association with a rational, written constitution, rationally ordained law, and an administration bound to rational rules or laws, administered by trained officials, is known, in this combination of characteristics, only in the Occident, despite all other approaches to it.

And the same is true of the most fateful force in our modern life, capitalism. The impulse to acquisition, pursuit of gain, of money, of the greatest possible amount of money, has in itself nothing to do with capitalism. This impulse exists and has existed among waiters, physicians, coachmen, artists, prostitutes, dishonest officials, soldiers, nobles, crusaders, gamblers, and beggars. One may say that it has been common to all sorts and conditions of men at all times and in all countries of the earth, wherever the objective possibility of it is or has been given.

Now, however, the Occident has developed capitalism both to a quantitative extent, and (carrying this quantitative development) in types, forms, and directions which have never existed elsewhere... The Occident has developed a form of capitalism which has appeared nowhere else: the rational capitalistic organization of (formally) free labour. Only suggestions of it are found elsewhere... [All other] peculiarities of Western capitalism have derived their significance in the last analysis only from their association with the capitalistic organization of labour. Even what is generally called commercialization, the development of negotiable securities and the rationalization of speculation, the exchanges, etc., is connected with it. For without the rational capitalistic organization of labour, all this, so far as it was possible at all, would have nothing like the same significance, above all for the social structure and all the specific problems of the modern Occident connected with it. Exact calculation–the basis of everything–is only possible on a basis of free labour.

Now the peculiar modern Western form of capitalism has been, at first sight, strongly influenced by the development of technical possibilities. Its rationality is to-day essentially dependent on the calculability of the most important technical factors. But this means fundamentally that it is dependent on the peculiarities of modern science, especially the natural sciences based on mathematics and exact and rational experiment. On the other hand, the development of these sciences and of the technique resting upon them now receives important stimulation from these capitalistic interests in its practical economic application ... But the *technical* utilization of scientific knowledge, so important for the living conditions of the

mass of people, was certainly encouraged by economic considerations, which were extremely favourable to it in the Occident.
But this encouragement was derived from the peculiarities of the
social structure of the Occident. We must hence ask, from *what* parts
of that structure was it derived, since not all of them have been of
equal importance?

Among those of undoubted importance are the rational structures
of law and of administration. For modern rational capitalism has
need, not only of the technical means of production, but of a
calculable legal system and of administration in terms of formal
rules. Without it adventurous and speculative trading capitalism and
all sorts of politically determined capitalisms are possible, but no
rational enterprise under individual initiative, with fixed capital and
certainty of calculations. Such a legal system and such
administration have been available for economic activity in a
comparative state of legal and formalistic perfection only in the
Occident. We must hence inquire where that law came from. Among
other circumstances, capitalistic interests have in turn undoubtedly
also helped, but by no means alone nor even principally, to prepare
the way for the predominance in law and administration of a class of
jurists specially trained in rational law. But these interests did not
themselves create the law. Quite different forces were at work in this
development. And why did not the capitalistic interests do the same
in China or India? Why did not the scientific, the artistic, the
political, or the economic development there enter upon that path of
rationalization which is peculiar to the Occident?

It is a question of the specific and peculiar rationalism of Western
culture. Now by this term very different things may be understood
. . . It is hence our first concern to work out and to explain genetically
the special peculiarity of Occidential rationalism, and within this
field that of the modern Occidental form. Every such attempt at
explanation must, recognizing the fundamental importance of the
economic factor, above all take account of the economic conditions.
But at the same time the opposite correlation must not be left out of
consideration. For though the development of economic rationalism
is partly dependent on rational technique and law, it is at the same
time determined by the ability and disposition of men to adopt
certain types of practical rational conduct. When these types have
been obstructed by spiritual obstacles, the development of rational
economic conduct has also met serious inner resistance. The magical

and religious forces, and the ethical ideas of duty based upon them, have in the past always been among the most important formative influences on conduct.

One of the fundamental elements of the spirit of modern capitalism, and not only of that but of all modern culture: rational conduct on the basis of the idea of the calling, was born–that is what this discussion has sought to demonstrate–from the spirit of Christian asceticism. . . The essential elements of the attitude which [I have termed] the spirit of capitalism are the same as what we have just shown to be the content of the Puritan worldly asceticism. . .

The Puritan wanted to work in a calling; we are forced to do so. For when asceticism was carried out of monastic cells into everyday life, and began to dominate worldly morality, it did its part in building the tremendous cosmos of the modern economic order. This order is now bound to the technical and economic conditions of machine production which to-day determine the lives of all the individuals who are born into this mechanism, not only those directly concerned with economic acquisition, with irresistible force. Perhaps it will so determine them until the last ton of fossilized coal is burnt. In Baxter's view the care for external goods should only lie on the shoulders of the 'saint like a light cloak, which can be thrown aside at any moment'. But fate decreed that the cloak should become an iron cage.

Since asceticism undertook to remodel the world and to work out its ideals in the world, material goods have gained an increasing and finally an inexorable power over the lives of men as at no previous period in history. To-day the spirit of religious asceticism–whether finally, who knows?–has escaped from the cage. But victorious capitalism, since it rests on mechanical foundations, needs its support no longer.

No one knows who will live in this cage in the future, or whether at the end of this tremendous development entirely new prophets will arise, or there will be a great rebirth of old ideas and ideals, or, if neither, mechanized petrification, embellished with a sort of convulsive self-importance. For of the last stage of this cultural development, it might well be truly said: 'Specialists without spirit, sensualists without heart; this nullity imagines that it has attained a level of civilization never before achieved.'

But this brings us to the world of judgments of value and of faith, with which this purely historical discussion need not be burdened.

The next task would be rather to show the significance of ascetic rationalism, which has only been touched in the foregoing sketch, for the content of practical social ethics, thus for the types of organization and the functions of social groups from the conventicle to the State.

(ii) Types of Legitimate Authority and Administration

Power, Authority, and Imperative Control:
'Power' *(Macht)* is the probability that one actor within a social relationship will be in a position to carry out his own will despite resistance, regardless of the basis on which this probability rests.

'Imperative control' *(Herrschaft)* is the probability that a command with a given specific content will be obeyed by a given group of persons ... It thus does not include every mode of exercising 'power' or 'influence' over persons. The motives of obedience to commands in this sense can rest on considerations varying over a wide range from case to case; all the way from simple habituation to the most purely rational calculation of advantage. A criterion of every true relation of imperative control, however, is a certain minimum of voluntary submission; thus an interest (based on ulterior motives or genuine acceptance) in obedience...

It is an induction from experience that no system of authority voluntarily limits itself to the appeal to material or affectual or ideal motives as a basis for guaranteeing its continuance. In addition every such system attempts to establish and to cultivate the belief in its 'legitimacy'. But according to the kind of legitimacy which is claimed, the type of obedience, the kind of administrative staff developed to guarantee it, and the mode of exercising authority, will all differ fundamentally. Equally fundamental is the variation in effect. Hence, it is useful to classify the types of authority according to the kind of claim to legitimacy typically made by each. In doing this it is best to start from modern and therefore more familiar examples.

The Three Pure Types of Legitimate Authority:
There are three pure types of legitimate authority. The validity of their claims to legitimacy may be based on:

1. Rational grounds–resting on a belief in the 'legality' of patterns of normative rules and the right of those elevated to authority under such rules to issue commands (legal authority).

2. Traditional grounds–resting on an established belief in the sanctity of immemorial traditions and the legitimacy of the status of those exercising authority under them (traditional authority); or finally,

3. Charismatic grounds–resting on devotion to the specific and exceptional sanctity, heroism or exemplary character of an individual person, and of the normative patterns or order revealed or ordained by him (charismatic authority).

In the case of legal authority, obedience is owed to the legally established impersonal order. It extends to the persons exercising the authority of office under it only by virtue of the formal legality of their commands and only within the scope of authority of the office. In the case of traditional authority, obedience is owed to the *person* of the chief who occupies the traditionally sanctioned position of authority and who is (within its sphere) bound by tradition. But here the obligation of obedience is not based on the impersonal order, but is a matter of personal loyalty within the area of accustomed obligations. In the case of charismatic authority, it is the charismatically qualified leader as such who is obeyed by virtue of personal trust in him and his revelation, his heroism or his exemplary qualities so far as they fall within the scope of the individual's belief in his charisma.

Legal Authority: The Pure Type with Employment of a Bureaucratic Administrative Staff:
The effectiveness of legal authority rests on the acceptance of the validity of the following mutually inter-dependent ideas.

1. That any given legal norm may be established by agreement or by imposition, on grounds of expediency or rational values or both, with a claim to obedience at least on the part of the members of the corporate group. This is, however, usually extended to include all persons within the sphere of authority or of power in question–which in the case of territorial bodies is the territorial area–who stand in certain social relationships or carry out forms of social action which in the order governing the corporate group have been declared to be relevant.

2. That every body of law consists essentially in a consistent system of abstract rules which have normally been intentionally established. Furthermore, administration of law is held to consist in

the application of these rules to particular cases; the administrative process in the rational pursuit of the interests which are specified in the order governing the corporate group within the limits laid down by legal precepts and following principles which are capable of generalized formulation and are approved in the order governing the group, or at least not disapproved in it.

3. That thus the typical person in authority occupies an 'office'. In the action associated with his status, including the commands he issues to others, he is subject to an impersonal order to which his actions are oriented.

4. That the person who obeys authority does so, as it is usually stated, only in his capacity as a 'member' of the corporate group and what he obeys is only 'the law'.

5. In conformity with point 3, it is held that the members of the corporate group, in so far as they obey a person in authority, do not owe this obedience to him as an individual, but to the impersonal order. Hence, it follows that there is an obligation to obedience only within the sphere of the rationally delimited authority which, in terms of the order, has been conferred upon him.

The purest type of exercise of legal authority is that which employs a bureaucratic administrative staff. Only the supreme chief of the organization occupies his position of authority by virtue of appropriation, of election, or of having been designated for the succession. But even *his* authority consists in a sphere of legal 'competence'. The whole administrative staff under the supreme authority then consists, in the purest type, of individual officials who are appointed and function according to the following criteria:

(1) They are personally free and subject to authority only with respect to their impersonal official obligations.

(2) They are organized in a clearly defined hierarchy of offices.

(3) Each office has a clearly defined sphere of competence in the legal sense.

(4) The office is filled by a free contractual relationship. Thus, in principle, there is free selection.

(5) Candidates are selected on the basis of technical qualifications. In the most rational case, this is tested by examination or guaranteed by diplomas certifying technical training, or both. They are *appointed,* not elected.

(6) They are remunerated by fixed salaries in money, for the most part with a right to pensions.

(7) The office is treated as the sole, or at least the primary, occupation of the incumbent.

(8) It constitutes a career. There is a system of 'promotion' according to seniority or to achievement, or both. Promotion is dependent on the judgment of superiors.

(9) The official works entirely separated from ownership of the means of administration and without appropriation of his position.

(10) He is subject to strict and systematic discipline and control in the conduct of the office ...

Experience tends universally to show that the purely bureaucratic type of administrative organization–that is, the monocratic variety of bureaucracy–is, from a purely technical point of view, capable of attaining the highest degree of efficiency and is in this sense formally the most rational known means of carrying out imperative control over human beings. It is superior to any other form in precision, in stability, in the stringency of its discipline, and in its reliability. It thus makes possible a particularly high degree of calculability of results for the heads of the organization and for those acting in relation to it. It is finally superior both in intensive efficiency and in the scope of its operations, and is formally capable of application to all kinds of administrative tasks.

The primary source of the superiority of bureaucratic administration lies in the role of technical knowledge which, through the development of modern technology and business methods in the production of goods, has become completely indispensable. In this respect, it makes no difference whether the economic system is organized on a capitalistic or a socialistic basis. Indeed, if in the latter case a comparable level of technical efficiency were to be achieved, it would mean a tremendous increase in the importance of specialized bureaucracy.

Though by no means alone, the capitalistic system has undeniably played a major role in the development of bureaucracy. Indeed, without it capitalistic production could not continue and any rational type of socialism would have simply to take it over and increase its importance. Its development, largely under capitalistic auspices, has created an urgent need for stable, strict, intensive, and calculable administration. It is this need which gives bureaucracy a crucial role in our society as the central element in any kind of large-scale administration. Only by reversion in every field–political, religious, economic, etc.–to small-scale organization would it be possible to any considerable extent to escape its influence. On the one hand, capitalism in its modern stages of development strongly tends to foster the development of bureaucracy, though both capitalism and bureaucracy have arisen from many different historical sources. Conversely, capitalism is the most rational economic basis for bureaucratic administration and enables it to develop in the most rational form, expecially because, from a fiscal point of view, it supplies the necessary money resources.

Traditional Authority:

A system of imperative co-ordination will be called 'traditional' if legitimacy is claimed for it and believed in on the basis of the sanctity of the order and the attendant powers of control as they have been handed down from the past, 'have always existed'. The person or persons exercising authority are designated according to traditionally transmitted rules. The object of obedience is the personal authority of the individual which he enjoys by virtue of his traditional status. The organized group exercising authority is, in the simplest case, primarily based on relations of personal loyalty, cultivated through a common process of education. The person exercising authority is not a 'superior', but a personal 'chief'.

His administrative staff does not consist primarily of officials, but of personal retainers. Those subject to authority are not 'members' of an association, but are either his traditional 'comrades' or his 'subjects'. What determines the relations of the administrative staff to the chief is not the impersonal obligation of office, but personal loyalty to the chief.

Obedience is not owed to enacted rules, but to the person who occupies a position of authority by tradition or who has been chosen for such a position on a traditional basis. His commands are legitimized in one of two ways: (a) partly in terms of traditions which themselves directly determine the content of the command and the objects and extent of authority. In so far as this is true, to overstep the traditional limitations would endanger his traditional status by undermining acceptance of his legitimacy. (b) In part, it is a matter of the chief's free personal decision, in that tradition leaves a certain sphere open for this. This sphere of traditional prerogative rests primarily on the fact that the obligations of obedience on the basis of personal loyalty are essentially unlimited.

It is impossible in the pure type of traditional authority for law or administrative rules to be deliberately created by legislation. What is actually new is thus claimed to have always been in force but only recently to have become known through the wisdom of the promulgator. The only documents which can play a part in the orientation of legal administration are the documents of tradition; namely, precedents.

Charismatic Authority:

The term 'charisma' will be applied to a certain quality of an individual personality by virtue of which he is set apart from ordinary men and treated as endowed with supernatural, superhuman, or at least specifically exceptional powers or qualities. These are such as are not accessible to the ordinary person, but are regarded as of divine origin or as exemplary, and on the basis of them the individual concerned is treated as a leader. In primitive circumstances this peculiar kind of deference is paid to prophets, to people with a reputation for therapeutic or legal wisdom, to leaders in the hunt, and heroes in war. It is very often thought of as resting on magical powers. How the quality in question would be ultimately judged from any ethical, aesthetic, or other such point of view is naturally entirely indifferent for purposes of definition. What is alone important is how the individual is actually regarded by those subject to charismatic authority, by his 'followers' or 'disciples'.

1. It is recognition on the part of those subject to authority which is decisive for the validity of charisma. This is freely given and guaranteed by what is held to be a 'sign' or proof, originally always a miracle, and consists in devotion to the corresponding revelation, hero worship, or absolute trust in the leader. But where charisma is genuine, it is not this which is the basis of the claim to legitimacy. This basis lies rather in the conception that it is the *duty* of those who have been called to a charismatic mission to recognize its quality and to act accordingly. Psychologically this 'recognition' is a matter of complete personal devotion to the possessor of the quality, arising out of enthusiasm, or of despair and hope.

2. If proof of his charismatic qualification fails him for long, the leader endowed with charisma tends to think his god or his magical or heroic powers have deserted him. If he is for long unsuccessful, above all if his leadership fails to benefit his followers, it is likely that

his charismatic authority will disappear. This is the genuine charismatic meaning of the 'gift of grace'.

3. The corporate group which is subject to charismatic authority is based on an emotional form of communal relationship. The administrative staff of a charismatic leader does not consist of 'officials'; at least its members are not technically trained. It is not chosen on the basis of social privilege nor from the point of view of domestic or personal dependency. It is rather chosen in terms of the charismatic qualities of its members. The prophet has his disciples; the war lord his selected henchmen; the leader, generally, his followers.

Charismatic authority is thus specifically outside the realm of everyday routine and the profane sphere. In this respect, it is sharply opposed both to rational, and particularly bureaucratic, authority, and to traditional authority, whether in its patriarchal, patrimonial, or any other form. Both rational and traditional authority are specifically forms of everyday routine control of action; while the charismatic type is the direct antithesis of this. Bureaucratic authority is specifically rational in the sense of being bound to intellectually analysable rules; while charismatic authority is specifically irrational in the sense of being foreign to all rules. Traditional authority is bound to the precedents handed down from the past and to this extent is also oriented to rules. Within the sphere of its claims, charismatic authority repudiates the past, and is in this sense a specifically revolutionary force. It recognizes no appropriation of positions of power by virtue of the possession of property, either on the part of a chief or of socially privileged groups. The only basis of legitimacy for it is personal charisma, so long as it is proved; that is, as long as it receives recognition and is able to satisfy the followers or disciples. But this lasts only so long as the belief in its charismatic inspiration remains ...

In its pure form charismatic authority has a character specifically foreign to everyday routine structures. The social relationships directly involved are strictly personal, based on the validity and practice of charismatic personal qualities. If this is not to remain a purely transitory phenomenon, but to take on the character of a permanent relationship forming a stable community of disciples or a band of followers or a party organization or any sort of political or hierocratic organization, it is necessary for the character of charismatic authority to become radically changed. Indeed, in its pure form charismatic authority may be said to exist only in the process of originating. It cannot remain stable, but becomes either traditionalized or rationalized, or a combination of both.

(iii) Law and Economic Activity

Sociology is a discipline searching for empirical regularities and types. In so far as it is concerned with legal guaranties and those normative conceptions on which they depend as the motives underlying their creation, interpretation, and application, its interest is thus of a special kind. They are to be considered as consequences as well as, and more so, as causes or concomitant causes of certain regularities . . .

This discussion has been restricted to a consideration of the broad relations between law and economic activity. Summing up, we may now make the following statements:

(1) Law (in the sociological sense) guarantees by no means only economic interests but rather the most diverse interests ranging from the most elementary one of protection of personal security to such purely ideal goods as personal honor or the honor of the divine powers. Above all, it guarantees political, ecclesiastical, familial, and other positions of authority as well as positions of social pre-eminence of any kind which may indeed be economically conditioned or economically relevant in the most diverse ways, but which are neither economic in themselves nor sought for preponderantly economic ends.

(2) Under certain conditions a 'legal order' can remain unchanged while economic relations are undergoing a radical transformation. In theory, a socialist system of production could be brought about without the change of even a single paragraph of our laws, simply by the gradual, free contractual acquisition of all the means of production by the political authority. This example is extreme; but, for the purpose of theoretical speculation, extreme examples are most useful. Should such a situation ever come about–which is most unlikely, though theoretically not unthinkable–the legal order would still be bound to apply its coercive machinery in case its aid were invoked for the enforcement of those obligations which are characteristic of a productive system based on private property. Only, this case would never occur in fact.

(3) The legal status of a matter may be basically different according to the point of view of the legal system from which it is considered. But such differences (of legal classification) need not have any relevant economic consequences provided only that on those points which generally are relevant economically, the *practical* effects are the same for interested parties. This not only is possible, but it actually happens widely, although it must be conceded that any variation of legal classification may engender some economic consequences somewhere. Thus totally different forms of action would have been applicable in Rome depending on whether the 'lease' of a mine were to be regarded legally as a lease in the strict sense of the term, or as a purchase. But the practical effects of the difference for economic life would certainly have been very slight.

(4) Obviously, any legal guaranty is directly at the service of economic interests to a very large extent. Even where this does not seem to be, or actually is not, the case, economic interests are among the strongest factors influencing the creation of law. For, any authority guaranteeing a legal order depends, in some way, upon the consensual action of the constitutive social groups, and the formation of social groups depends, to a large extent, upon constellations of material interests.

(5) Only a limited measure of success can be attained through the threat of coercion supporting the legal order. Owing to a number of external circumstances as well as to its own peculiar nature, this applies especially to the economic sphere. It would be quibbling, however, to assert that the law cannot 'enforce' any particular economic conduct, on the ground that we would have to say, with regard to all its means of coercion, that *coatus tamen voluit* ['Although coerced, it was still his will'–eds]. For this is true, without exception, of all coercion which does not treat the person to be coerced simply as an inanimate object. Even the most drastic means of coercion and punishment are bound to fail where the subjects remain incalcitrant. In a broad mass such a situation would always mean that its members have not been educated to acquiescence. Such education to acquiescence in the law of the time and place has, as a general rule, increased with growing pacification. Thus it should seem that the chances of enforcing economic conduct would have increased, too. Yet, the power of law over economic conduct has in many respects grown weaker rather than stronger as compared with earlier conditions. The effectiveness of maximum price regulations,

for example, has always been precarious, but under present-day conditions they have an even smaller chance of success than ever before.

Thus the measure of possible influence on economic activity is not simply a function of the general level of acquiescence towards legal coercion. The limits of the actual success of legal coercion in the economic sphere rather arise from two main sources. One is consti- tuted by the limitations of the economic capacity of the persons affected. There are limits not only to the stock itself of available goods, but also to the way in which that stock can possibly be used. The second source of the limitation of successful legal coercion in the economic sphere lies in the relative proportion of strength of private economic interests on the one hand and interests promoting conformance to the rules of law on the other. The inclination to forgo economic opportunity simply in order to act legally is obviously slight, unless circumvention of the formal law is strongly disapproved by a powerful convention, and such a situation is not likely to arise where the interests affected by a legal innovation are widespread. Besides, it is often not difficult to disguise the circum- vention of a law in the economic sphere . . .

From the purely theoretical point of view, legal guaranty *by the state* is not indispensable to any basic economic phenomenon. The protection of property, for example, can be provided by the mutual aid system of kinship groups. Creditors' rights have sometimes been protected more efficiently by a religious community's threat of ex- communication than by political bodies. . . .

'Conceptually' the 'state' thus is not indispensable to any economic activity. But an economic system, especially of the modern type, could certainly not exist without a legal order with very special features which could not develop except in the frame of a 'statal' legal order. Present-day economic life rests on opportunities acquired through contracts. It is true, the private interests in the obligation of contract, and the common interest of all property holders in the mutual protection of property are still considerable, and individuals are still markedly influenced by convention and usage even today. Yet, the influence of these factors has declined due to the disintegration of tradition, i.e., of the tradition-determined relationships as well as of the belief in their sacredness. Furthermore, class interests have come to diverge more sharply from one another than ever before. The tempo of modern business communication requires a promptly and predictably functioning legal system, i.e., one which is guaranteed by the strongest coercive power. Finally, modern economic life by its very nature has destroyed those other associations which used to be the bearers of law and thus of legal guaranties. This has been the result of the development of the market. The universal predominance of the market consociation requires on the one hand a legal system the functioning of which is *calculable* in accordance with rational rules. On the other hand, the constant expansion of the market consociation has favored the monopolization and regulation of all 'legitimate' coercive power by *one* universal coercive institution through the disintegration of all particular status-determined and other coercive structures, which have been resting mainly on economic monopolies.

(iv) Legal Thought and Legal Training

Categories of Legal Thought:

The mode in which the current basic conceptions of the various fields of law have been differentiated from each other has depended largely upon factors of legal technique and of political organization. Economic factors can therefore be said to have had an indirect influence only. To be sure, economic influences have played their part, but only to this extent: that certain rationalizations of economic behavior, based upon such phenomena as a market economy or freedom of contract, and the resulting awareness of underlying, and increasingly complex conflicts of interests to be resolved by legal machinery, have influenced the systematization of the law or have intensified the institutionalization of political society. We shall have occasion to observe this time and again. All other purely economic influences merely occur as concrete instances and cannot be formulated in general rules. On the other hand, we shall frequently see that those aspects of law which are conditioned by political factors and by the internal structure of legal thought have exercised a strong influence on economic organization. In the following paragraphs, we shall deal briefly with the most important conditions by which the formal characteristics of law, i.e. lawmaking and lawfinding, have been influenced. We shall be especially interested in observing the extent and the nature of the rationality of the law, and, quite particularly, of that branch of it which is relevant to economic life, viz., private law.

A body of law can be 'rational' in several different senses, depending on which of several possible courses legal thinking takes toward rationalization. Let us begin with the apparently most elementary thought process, viz., generalization, i.e., in our case, the reduction of the reasons relevant in the decision of concrete individual cases to one or more 'principles', i.e., legal propositions. This process of reduction is normally conditional upon a prior or concurrent analysis of the facts of the case as to those ultimate components which are regarded as relevant in the juristic valuation. Conversely, the elaboration of ever more comprehensive 'legal propositions' reacts upon the specification and delimitation of the potentially relevant characteristics of the facts. The process both depends upon, and promotes, casuistry. However, not every well-developed method of casuistry has resulted in, or run parallel to, the development of 'legal propositions of high logical sublimation'. Highly comprehensive schemes of legal casuistry have grown up upon the basis of a merely paratactic association analogy of extrinsic elements.

In our legal system the analytical derivation of 'legal propositions' and the decision of specific cases go hand in hand with the synthetic work of 'construction' of 'legal relations' and 'legal institutions', i.e. the determination of which aspects of a typical kind of communal or consensual action are to be regarded as *legally* relevant, and in which logically consistent way these relevant components are to be regarded as *legally* co-ordinated, i.e. as being in 'legal relationships'. Although this latter process is closely related to the one previously described, it is nonetheless possible for a very high degree of sublimation in analysis to be correlated with a very low degree of constructional conceptualization of the legally relevant social relations. Conversely, the synthesis of a 'legal relationship' may be achieved in a relatively satisfactory way despite a low degree of analysis, or occasionally just because of its limited cultivation.

This contradiction is a result of the fact that analysis gives rise to a further logical task which, while it is compatible with synthetic construction, often turns out to be incompatible with it in fact. We refer to 'systematization', which has never appeared but in late stages of legal modes of thought. To a youthful law, it is unknown. According to present modes of thought it represents an integration of all analytically derived legal propositions in such a way that they constitute a logically clear, internally consistent, and, at least in theory, gapless system of rules, under which, it is implied, all conceivable fact situations must be capable of being logically subsumed lest their order lack an effective guaranty. Even today not every body of law (e.g. English law) claims that it possesses the features of a system as defined above and, of course, the claim was even less frequently made by the legal systems of the past; where it was put forward at all, the degree of logical abstraction was often extremely low. In the main, the 'system' has predominantly been an external scheme for the ordering of legal data and has been of only minor significance in the analytical derivation of legal propositions and in the construction of legal relationships. The specifically modern form of systematization, which developed out of Roman law, has its point of departure in the logical analysis of the meaning of the legal propositions as well as of the social actions. The 'legal relationships' and casuistry, on the other hand, often resist this kind of manipulation, as they have grown out of concrete factual characteristics.

In addition to the diversities discussed so far, we must also consider the differences existing as to the technical apparatus of legal practice; these differences to some extent associate with, but to some extent also overlap, those discussed so far. The following are the possible type situations:

Both lawmaking and lawfinding may be either rational or irrational. They are 'formerly irrational' when one applies in lawmaking or lawfinding means which cannot be controlled by the intellect, for instance when recourse is had to oracles or substitutes therefor. Lawmaking and lawfinding are 'substantively irrational' on the other hand to the extent that decision is influenced by concrete factors of the particular case as evaluated upon an ethical, emotional, or political basis rather than by general norms. 'Rational' lawmaking and lawfinding may be of either a formal or a substantive kind. All formal law is, formally at least, relatively rational. Law, however, is 'formal' to the extent that, in both substantive and procedural matters, only unambiguous general characteristics of the facts of the case are taken into account. This formalism can, again, be of two different kinds.

It is possible that the legally relevant characteristics are of a tangible nature, i.e. that they are perceptible as sense data. This adherence to external characteristics of the facts, for instance, the utterance of certain words, the execution of a signature, or the performance of a certain symbolic act with a fixed meaning, represents the most rigorous type of legal formalism. The other type of formalistic law is found where the legally relevant characteristics of the facts are disclosed through the logical analysis of meaning and where, accordingly, definitely fixed legal concepts in the form of highly abstract rules are formulated and applied. This process of 'logical rationality' diminishes the significance of extrinsic elements and thus softens the rigidity of concrete formalism. But the contrast to 'substantive rationality' is sharpened, because the latter means that the decision of legal problems is influenced by norms different from those obtained through logical generalization of abstract interpretations of meaning.

The norms to which substantive rationality accords predominance include ethical imperatives, utilitarian and other expediental rules, and political maxims, all of which diverge from the formalism of the 'external characteristics' variety as well as from that which uses logical abstraction. However, the peculiarly professional, legalistic, and abstract approach to law in the modern sense is possible only in the measure that the law is formal in character. In so far as the absolute formalism of classification according to 'sense-data characteristics' prevails, it exhausts itself in casuistry. Only that abstract method which employs the logical interpretation of meaning allows the execution of the specifically systematic task, i.e., the collection and rationalization by logical means of all the several rules recognized as legally valid into an internally consistent complex of abstract legal propositions.

Our task is now to find how the various influences which have participated in the formation of the law have influenced the development of its formal qualities. Present-day legal science, at least in those forms which have achieved the highest measure of methodological and logical rationality, i.e., those which have been produced through the legal science of the Pandectists' Civil Law, proceeds from the following five postulates: viz., first, that every concrete legal decision be the 'application' of an abstract legal proposition to a concrete 'fact situation'; second, that it must be possible in every concrete case to derive the decision from abstract legal propositions by means of legal logic; third, that the law must actually or virtually constitute a 'gapless' system of legal propositions, or must, at least, be treated as if it were such a gapless system; fourth, that whatever cannot be 'construed' legally in rational terms is also legally irrelevant; and fifth, that every social action of human beings must always be visualized as either an 'application' or 'execution' of legal propositions, or as an 'infringement' thereof. However, for the moment we shall not concern ourselves with these theoretical postulates, but shall rather investigate certain general formal qualities of the law which are important for its functioning . . .

The Legal Honoratiores and the Types of Legal Thought

For the development of a professional legal training and, through it, of specifically legal modes of thinking two different lines are possible. The first consists in the empirical training in the law as a craft; the apprentices learn from practitioners more or less in the course of actual legal practice. Under the second possibility law is taught in special schools, where the emphasis is placed on legal theory and 'science', that is where legal phenomena are given rational and systematic treatment.

1. A fairly pure illustration of the first type is represented by the guildlike English method of having law taught by the lawyers. During the medieval period a sharp distinction was made between advocate and attorney. The need for an advocate was due to the peculiarities of procedure before the popular assemblies; the attorney emerged when procedure began to be rationalized in the royal courts with their jury trial and the increasing evidentiary importance of the record. In France the verbal formalism which grew out of the strict application of the accusatorial principle in the procedure before the popular assembly, gave rise to the need of an *avant-rulier* (*avant-parlier*). The legal maxim *fautes volent exploits* ['*errors destroy the acts*' – eds.] *and the formalistic effect of the* words spoken compelled the layman to seek the assistance of an *avant rulier* or 'prolocutor' who, upon the party's request, would be assigned to him by the judge from among the judgment-finders, and who would publicly 'speak for', and in the name of, the party the words required for the progress of the case . . . His position was thus quite different from that of the attorney (*avoue, Anwalt, procurator, solicitor*), who assumed the technical tasks of preparing the case and obtaining the evidence. But the attorney could not assume these functions until procedure had undergone a considerable degree of rationalization. Originally an attorney in the modern sense was not possible at all. He could not function as the 'representative' of the party until procedural representation had been made possible, as in

England and France, by the development of the royal law ... With
the coming to the fore of rational modes of procedure, the old
'prolocutors' disappeared. But a new aristocracy of legal
honoratiores came into being, consisting of counsels, serjeants, and
barristers, i.e. of those admitted to represent, and plead for, litigants
before the royal courts.

The practicing barristers lived together in communal fashion in
the corporate and closed guildhouses. The judges were exclusively
chosen from among them and continued to share the communal life
with them. 'Bar' and 'bench' were two functions of the corporate and
later highly exclusive legal profession; in the Middle Ages its
members came largely from the nobility and admission to the guild
was regulated with an ever increasing measure of autonomy. There
was a four-year novitiate, connected with instruction at the guild
school; the call to the bar conferred the right to plead; for the rest,
training was purely practical. The profession insisted on the maintenance of the code of etiquette, especially with regard to the
observance of minimum fees, all fees, however, to be paid voluntarily and not to be actionable. The lecture courses in the Inns were
only introduced as the result of the competitive struggle with the
universities. As soon as the monopoly was achieved, the lectures
began to decline, to be ultimately discontinued altogether.
Thereafter, training was purely empirical and practical and led, as in
the craft guilds, to pronounced specialization.

This kind of legal training naturally produced a formalistic treatment of the law, bounded by precedent and analogies drawn from
precedent. Not only was systematic and comprehensive treatment of
the whole body of the law prevented by the craftlike specialization of
the lawyers, but legal practice did not aim at all at a rational system
but rather at a practically useful scheme of contracts and actions,
oriented towards the interests of clients in typically recurrent
situations. The upshot was the emergence of what had been called in
Roman law 'cautelary jurisprudence', as well as of such practical
devices as procedural fictions which facilitated the disposition of
new situations upon the pattern of previous instances.

From such practices and attitudes no rational system of law could
emerge nor even a rationalization of the law as such because the
concepts thus formed are constructed in relation to the material, and
concretely experienceable events of everyday life, are distinguished
from each other by external criteria, and extended in their scope, as
new needs arise, by means of the techniques just mentioned. They are

not 'general concepts' which would be formed by abstraction from concreteness or by logical interpretation of meaning or by generalization and subsumption; nor were these concepts apt to be used in syllogistically applicable norms. In the purely empirical conduct of legal practice and legal training one always moves from the particular to the particular but never tries to move from the particular to general propositions in order to be able subsequently to deduce from them the norms for new particular cases ...

No rational legal training or theory can ever arise in such a situation. Wherever legal education has been in the hands of practitioners, especially attorneys, who have made admission to practice a guild monopoly, an economic factor, namely, their pecuniary interest, brings to bear a strong influence upon the process not only of stabilizing the official law and of adapting it to changing needs in an exclusively empirical way but also of preventing its rationalization through legislation or legal science. The lawyers' material interests are threatened by every interference with the traditional forms of procedure, and every interference menaces that situation in which the adaptation of the scheme of contracts and actions to both the formal norms and the needs of the interested parties is left exclusively to the legal practitioners. The English lawyers, for example, were largely successful in preventing both a systematic and rational type of lawmaking and a rational legal education, such as exists in the Continental universities; the relationship between 'bar' and 'bench' is still fundamentally different in the English-speaking countries from what it is on the Continent. In particular, the interpretation of newly made laws lay, and still lies, in the hands of judges who have come from the bar ...

2. Modern legal education in the universities represents the purest type of the second way of legal training. Where only law-school graduates are admitted to legal practice, the universities enjoy a monopoly of legal education ... The legal concepts produced by academic law teaching bear the character of abstract norms, which, at least in principle, are formed and distinguished from one another by a rigorously formal and rational logical interpretation of meaning. Their rational, systematic character as well as their relatively small degree of concreteness of content easily result in a far-reaching emancipation of legal thinking from the every-day needs of the public. The force of the purely logical legal doctrines let loose, and a legal practice dominated by it, can considerably reduce the role played by considerations of practical needs in the formation of the

law ... The differences between continental and common law methods of legal thought have been produced mostly by factors which are respectively connected with the internal structure and the modes of existence of the legal profession as well as by factors related to differences in political development. The economic elements, however, have been determinative only in connection with these elements. What we are concerned with here is the fact that, once everything is said and done about these differences in historical developments, modern capitalism prospers equally and manifests essentially identical economic traits under legal systems containing rules and institutions which considerably differ from each other at least from the juridical point of view ... Indeed, we may say that the legal systems under which modern capitalism has been prospering differ profoundly from each other even in their ultimate principles of formal structure ...

All in all, the Common Law thus presents a picture of an administration of justice which in the most fundamental formal features of both substantive law and procedure differs from the structure of continental law as much as is possible within a secular system of justice, that is, a system that is free from theocratic and patriminial powers. Quite definitely, English lawfinding is not, like that of the Continent, 'application' of 'legal propositions' logically derived from statutory texts.

These differences have had some tangible consequences both economically and socially; but these consequences have all been isolated single phenomena rather than differences touching upon the total structure of the economic system. For the development of capitalism two features have been relevant and both have helped to support the capitalistic system. Legal training has primarily been in the hands of the lawyers from among whom also the judges are recruited, i.e., in the hands of a group which is active in the service of propertied, and particularly capitalistic, private interests and which has to gain its livelihood from them. Furthermore and in close connection with this, the concentration of the administration of justice at the central courts in London and its extreme costliness have amounted almost to a denial of access to the courts for those with inadequate means. At any rate, the essential similarity of the capitalist development on the Continent and in England has not been able to eliminate the sharp contrasts between the two types of legal systems. Nor is there any visible tendency towards a transformation of the English legal system in the direction of the Continental under the impetus of the capitalist economy. On the contrary, wherever the two kinds of administration of justice and of legal training have had the opportunity to compete with one another, as for instance in Canada, the Common Law way has come out on top and has overcome the continental alternative rather quickly. We may thus conclude that capitalism has not been a decisive factor in the promotion of that form of rationalization of the law which has been peculiar to the continental West ever since the rise of Romanist studies in the medieval universities.

8. Law, Evolution and Society
by Emile Durkheim

From (i) The Division of Labor in Society [*1893*] *New York, The Free Press (1968) translated by G. Simpson, pp. 39–129; (ii)* 'Two Laws of Penal Evolution' [*1901*] *in* Economy and Society *(1973) vol. 2, no. 3, pp. 278–308, translated by T. A. Jones and A. T. Scull.*

(i) The Division of Labor and Types of Law

The division of labor is not of recent origin, but it was only at the end of the eighteenth century that social cognizance was taken of the principle, though, until then, unwilling submission had been rendered to it. To be sure, several thinkers from earliest times saw its importance; but Adam Smith was the first to attempt a theory of it. Nowadays, the phenomenon has developed so generally it is obvious to all. We need have no further illusions about the tendencies of modern industry; it advances steadily towards powerful machines, towards great concentrations of forces and capital, and consequently to the extreme division of labor. But the division of labor is not peculiar to the economic world; we can observe its growing influence in the most varied fields of society. For example the political, administrative, and judicial functions are growing more and more specialized ... The recent speculations in the philosophy of biology have ended by making us see in the division of labor a fact of a very general nature, which the economists, who first proposed it, never suspected.

Such a fact evidently cannot be produced without profoundly affecting our moral constitution; for the development of man will be conceived in two entirely different ways, depending on whether we yield to the movement or resist it . . . Briefly, is the division of labor, at the same time that it is law of nature, also a moral rule of human conduct; and, if it has this latter character, why and in what degrees?

We are thus led to ask if the division of labor . . . in contemporary societies where it has developed as we know, would not have as its function the integration of the social body to assure unity. (The word *function* is used in two quite different senses. Sometimes it suggests a system of vital movements, without reference to their consequences; at others it expresses the relation existing between these movements and corresponding needs of the organism . . . It is in this second sense that we shall use the term. To ask what is the function of the division of labor is, to seek for the need which it supplies.) It is legitimate to suppose . . . that great political societies can maintain themselves in equilibrium only thanks to the specialization of tasks, that the division of labor is the source, if not unique, at least principal, of social solidarity. If this hypothesis were proved, the division of labor would play a role much more important than that which we ordinarily attribute to it. It would serve not only to raise societies to luxury, desirable perhaps, but superfluous; it could be a condition of their existence. Through it, or at least particularly through it, their cohesion would be assured; it would determine the essential traits of their constitution. But before seeing whether this common opinion is well founded, we must verify the hypothesis that we have just given forth concerning the role of the division of labor. Let us see if, in effect, in the societies in which we live, it is from this that social solidarity essentially derives.

But social solidarity is a completely moral phenomenon which, taken by itself, does not lend itself to exact observation nor indeed to measurement. To proceed to this classification and this comparison, we must substitute for this internal fact which escapes us an external index which symbolizes it and study the former in the light of the latter.

This visible symbol is law. In effect, despite its immaterial character, wherever social solidarity exists, it resides not in a state of pure potentiality, but manifests its presence by sensible indices. Where it is strong, it leads men strongly to one another, frequently puts them in contact, multiplies the occasions when they find themselves related. To speak correctly, considering the point our investigation has reached, it is not easy to say whether social solidarity produces these phenomena, or whether it is a result of them, whether men relate themselves because it is a driving force, or whether it is a driving force because they relate themselves. However it is not, at the moment, necessary to decide this question; it suffices to say that the two orders of fact are linked and vary at the same time and in the same sense. The more solidary the members of a society are, the more they sustain diverse relations, one with another, or with the group taken collectively, for if their meetings were rare, they would depend upon one another only at rare intervals, and then tenuously. Moreover, the number of these relations is necessarily proportional to that of the juridical rules which determine them. Indeed, social life, especially where it exists durably, tends inevitably to assume a definite form and to organize itself, and the law is nothing else than this very organization in so far as it has greater stability and precision. The general life of society cannot extend its sway without juridical life extending its sway at the same time and in direct relation. We can thus be certain of finding reflected in law all the essential varieties of social solidarity.

The objection may be raised, it is true, that social relations can fix themselves without assuming a juridical form. ... Instead of being regulated by law, they are regulated by custom. Law, then, reflects only part of social life and furnishes us with incomplete data for the solution of the problem. Moreover it often happens that custom is not in accord with law. ... This opposition, however, crops up only in quite exceptional circumstances. This comes about when law no longer corresponds to the state of existing society, but maintains itself, without reason for doing so, by the force of habit. ... Thus conflict ensues. But it arises only in rare and pathological cases which cannot endure without danger. Normally, custom is not opposed to law, but is, on the contrary, its basis. It happens, in truth, that on such a basis nothing may rear its head. Social relations ensue which convey a diffuse regulation which comes from custom; but they lack importance and continuity, except in the abnormal cases of which we were just speaking. If, then, there are types of social solidarity which custom alone manifests, they are assuredly secondary;

law produces those which are essential and they are the only ones we need to know.

Our method has now been outlined. Since law reproduces the principal forms of social solidarity, we have only to classify the different types of law to find therefrom the different types of social solidarity which correspond to it. It is now probable that there is a type which symbolizes this special solidarity of which the division of labor is the cause. That found, it will suffice, in order to measure that part of the division of labor, to compare the number of juridical rules which express it with the total volume of law.

For this task, we cannot use the distinctions utilized by the jurisconsults. Created for practical purposes, they can be very useful from this point of view, but science cannot content itself with the empirical classifications and approximations. ... To proceed scientifically, we must find some characteristic which, while being essential to juridical phenomena, varies as they vary. Every precept of law can be defined as a rule of sanctioned conduct. Moreover, it is evident that sanctions change with the gravity attributed to precepts, the place they hold in the public conscience, the role they play in society. It is right, then, to classify juridical rules according to the different sanctions which are attached to them.

They are of two kinds. Some consist essentially in suffering, or at least a loss, inflicted on the agent. They make demands on his fortune, or on his honour, or on his life, or on his liberty, and deprive him of something he enjoys. We call them repressive. They constitute penal law. It is true that those which are attached to rules which are purely moral have the same character, only they are distributed in a diffuse manner, by everybody indiscriminately, whereas those in penal law are applied through the intermediary of a definite organ; they are organized. As for the other type, it does not necessarily imply suffering for the agent, but consists only of *the return of things as they were*, in the re-establishment of troubled relations to their normal state, whether the incriminated act is restored by force to the type whence it deviated, or is annulled, that is, deprived of all social value. We must then separate juridical rules into two great classes, accordingly as they have organized repressive sanctions or only restitutive sanctions. The first comprises all penal law; the second civil law, commercial law, procedural law, administrative and constitutional law, after abstraction of the penal rules which may be found there.

Mechanical Solidarity

The link of social solidarity to which repressive law corresponds is the one whose break constitutes a crime ... In effect, the only common characteristic of all crimes is that they consist ... in acts universally disapproved of by members of each society ... that is, that crime shocks sentiments which, for a given social system, are found in all healthy consciences.

The totality of beliefs and sentiments common to average citizens of the same society form a determinate system which has its own life; one may call it the *collective or common conscience*. No doubt, it has not a specific organ as a substratum; it is, by definition, diffuse in every reach of society. Nevertheless, it has specific characteristics which make it a distinct reality. It is, in effect, independent of the particular conditions in which individuals are placed. Moreover, it does not change with each generation, but, on the contrary, it connects successive generations with one another. It is, thus, an entirely different thing from particular consciences, although it can be realized only through them. ... We can then say that an act is criminal when it offends strong and defined states of the collective conscience. ... In other words, we must not say that an action shocks the common conscience because it is criminal, but rather that it is criminal because it shocks the common conscience. We do not reprove it because it is crime, but it is a crime because we reprove it.

Crime is not simply the disruption even of serious interests; it is an offence against an authority in some way transcendent. But, from experience, there is no moral force superior to the individual save collective force. There is, moreover, a way of checking up on the result at which we have just arrived. What characterizes crime is that it determines punishment. If, then, our definition of crime is exact, it ought to explain all the characteristics of punishment. We shall proceed to this verification. But first we must find out what these characteristics are.

In the first place, punishment consists of a passionate reaction. This character is especially apparent in less cultivated societies. In effect, primitive peoples punish for the sake of punishing, make the culpable suffer particularly for the sake of making him suffer and without seeking any advantage for themselves from the suffering which they impose. The proof of this is that they seek neither to strike back justly nor to strike back usefully, but merely to strike back. It is thus that they punish animals which have committed a wrong act, or even inanimate beings which have been its passive instrument. When punishment is applied only to people, it often extends further than the culpable and reaches the innocent, his wife, his children, his neighbors, etc. That is because the passion which is the soul of punishment ceases only when exhausted. If, therefore, after it has destroyed the one who has immediately called it forth, there still remains force within it, it expands in quite mechancial fashion. . . .

But today, it is said, punishment has changed its character; it is no longer to avenge itself that society punishes, it is to defend itself. The pain which it inflicts is in its hands no longer anything but a methodical means of protection. It punishes, not because chastisement offers it any satisfaction for itself, but so that the fear of punishment may paralyze those who contemplate evil. This is no longer choler, but a reflected provision which determines repression. The preceding observations could not then be made general; they would deal only with the primitive form of punishment and would not extend to the existing form. But to justify such a radical distinction between these two sorts of punishment, it is not enough to state them in view of their employment of different ends. The nature of a practice does not necessarily change because the conscious intentions of those who apply it are modified. It might, in truth, still play the same role as before, but without being perceived. . . .

It is an error to believe that vengeance is but useless cruelty. It is very possible that, in itself, it consists of a mechanical and aimless reaction, in an emotional and irrational movement, in an unintelligent need to destroy; but, in fact, what it tends to destroy was a menace to us. It consists, then, in a veritable act of defense, although an instinctive and unreflective one. . . . Today, since we better understand the end to be attained, we better know how to utilize the means at our disposal; we protect ourselves with better means and, accordingly, more efficiently. . . . We thus reach the conclusion that the essential elements of punishment are the same as of old.

In truth, punishment has remained, at least in part, a work of vengeance. It is said that we do not make the culpable suffer in order to make him suffer; it is none the less true that we find it just that he suffer. Perhaps we are wrong, but that is not the question. We seek, at the moment, to define punishment as it is or has been, not as it ought to be. It is certain that this expression of public vindication which finds its way again and again into the language of the courts is not a word taken in vain. In supposing that punishment can really serve to protect us in the future, we think that it ought to be above all an *expiation* of the past. The proof of this lies in the minute precautions we take to proportion punishment as exactly as possible to the severity of the crime; they would be inexplicable if we did not believe that the culpable ought to suffer because he has done evil and in the same degree. In effect, this gradation is not necessary if punishment is only a means of defense. We can thus say that punishment consists in a passionate reaction of graduated intensity.

But whence comes this reaction, From the individual or from society? Everybody knows that it is society that punishes, but it might be held that this is not by design. What puts beyond doubt the social character of punishment is that, once pronounced, it cannot be lifted except by the government in the name of society. If it were a satisfaction given to particular persons, they would always be the judges of its remission. We cannot conceive of a privilege imposed unless its beneficiary could renounce it. If it is society alone that employs the repression, that is because it is attacked when individuals are, and the attack directed against it is repressed by punishment.

But the above characteristics appertain quite as well to diffuse repression which follows simply immoral actions as they do to legal repression. What distinguishes legal repression is, we have said, that it is organized; but in what does this organization consist?

When we think of penal law as it functions in our own societies, we consider it as a code where very definite punishments are attached to equally definite crimes. This planned organization does not, however, constitute punishment, for there are societies where punishment exists without being fixed in advance. It is not, then, in the regulation of punishments that the distinctive organization of this type of repression consists. It is, moreover, not in the institution of criminal procedure. The only organization which meets us everywhere that there is punishment properly so called is that resident in the establishment of a tribunal. In whatever manner it is composed, whether it comprises all the people, or only a select number, whether or not it follows a regular procedure as much in the instruction of the affair as in the application of the punishment, because the infraction, instead of being judged by each, is submitted to the consideration of a constituted body, because the collective reaction has a definite organ as an intermediary, it ceases to be diffuse; it is organized. The organization will be more complete the moment it exists.

Punishment consists, then, essentially in a passionate reaction of graduated intensity that society exercises through the medium of a body acting upon those of its members who have violated certain rules of conduct.

Thus we see what type of solidarity penal law symbolizes. Everybody knows that there is a social cohesion whose cause lies in a certain conformity of all particular consciences to a common type which is none other than the psychic type of society. The case is the same with punishment. Although it proceeds from a quite mechanical reaction, from movements which are passionate and in great part nonreflective, it does play a useful role.... It does not serve, or else only serves quite secondarily, in correcting the culpable or in intimidating possible followers.... Its true function is to maintain social cohesion intact, while maintaining all its vitality in the common conscience.

The result is this: there exists a social solidarity which comes from a certain number of states of conscience which are common to all the members of the same society. This is what repressive law materially represents, at least in so far as it is essential. The part that it plays in the general integration of society evidently depends upon the greater or lesser extent of the social life which the common conscience embraces and regulates. The greater the diversity of relations wherein the latter makes its action felt, the more also it creates links which attach the individual to the group; the more, consequently, social cohesion derives completely from this source and bears its mark. But the number of these relations is itself proportional to that of the repressive rules. In determining what fraction of the juridical system penal law represents, we, at the same time, measure the relative importance of this solidarity

Organic Solidarity

The very nature of the restitutive sanction suffices to show that the social solidarity to which this type of law corresponds is of a totally different kind. What distinguishes this sanction is that it is not expiatory, but consists of a simple *return in state*. Sufferance proportionate to the misdeed is not inflicted on the one who has violated the law or who disregards it; he is simply sentenced to comply with it. If certain things were done, the judge reinstates them as they would have been. He speaks of law; he says nothing of punishment.

Neglect of these rules is not even punished diffusely. The pleader who has lost in litigation is not disgraced, his honor is not put in question. We can even imagine these rules being other than they are without feeling any repugnance.... As these prescriptions do not correspond to any sentiment in us, ... they have no roots in the majority of us.... This is proof that the rules with a restitutive sanction either do not totally derive from the collective conscience, or are only feeble states of it.

This characteristic is, indeed, made manifest by the manner of its functioning. While repressive law tends to remain diffuse within society, restitutive law creates organs which are more and more specialized: consular tribunals, councils of arbitration, administrative tribunals of every sort. Even in its most general part, that which pertains to civil law, it is exercised only through particular functionaries: magistrates, lawyers, etc., who have become apt at this role because of very special training. But although these rules are more or less outside the collective conscience, they are not interested solely in individuals. If this were so, restitutive law would have nothing in common with social solidarity, for the relations that it regulates would bind individuals to one another without binding them to society. They would simply be happening in private life, as friendly relations are. But society is far from having no hand in this sphere of juridical life. It is true that, generally, it does not intervene of itself and through its own movements; it must be solicited by the interested parties. But, in being called forth, its intervention is none the less the essential cog in the machine, since it alone makes it function. It propounds the law through the organ of its representatives.

Since rules with restitutive sanctions are strangers to the common conscience, the relations that they determine are not those which attach themselves instinctively everywhere. That is to say, they are established immediately, not between the individual and society, but between restricted, special parties in society whom they bind.... But these relations can take two very different forms: sometimes they are negative and reduce themselves to pure abstraction; sometimes they are positive and cooperative. To the two classes of rules which determine these, there correspond two sorts of social solidarity which we must distinguish.

The negative relation which may serve as a type for the others is the one which unites the thing to the person. Things to be sure, form part of society just as persons, and they play a specific role in it. Thus it is necessary that their relations with the social organism be determined. We may then say that there is a solidarity of things whose nature is quite special and translates itself outside through juridical consequences of a very particular character.

The jurisconsults distinguish two kinds of rights: to one they give the name real; to the other, that of personal. The right of property the pledge, pertains to the first type; the right of credit to the second. What characterizes real rights is that they give a preferential and successoral right. Thus the right that I have in the thing excludes anyone else from coming to usurp what is mine. . . . But for this to come about, it is necessary for the bond of law to unite me directly and without the mediation of any other person to the thing determinate of my juridical personality. The privileged situation is, then, the consequence of the solidarity proper to things. On the other hand, when the right is personal, the person who is obliged to me can, in contracting new obligations, give me co-creditors whose right is equal to mine, and although I may have as security all the goods of my debtor, if he alienates them, they come out of my security and patrimony. The reason for this is that there is no special relation between these goods and me, but between the person of their owner and my own person.

Thus we see what this real solidarity consists of; it directly links things to persons, but not persons among themselves. In a strict sense, one can exercise a real right by thinking one is alone in the world, without reference to other men. Consequently, since it is only through the medium of persons that things are integrated in society, the solidarity resulting from this integration is wholly negative. It does not lead wills to move towards common ends, but merely makes things gravitate around wills in orderly fashion. Because real rights are thus linked, they do not cause conflicts; hostility is precluded, but there is no active coming together, no consensus. From the preceding, it is easy to determine what part of restitutive law this solidarity corresponds to: it is the body of real rights. But from the definition which has been given of them, it comes about that the law of property is the most perfect example of them.

In short, the rules relative to real rights and to personal relations which are established in their turn form a definite system which has as its function, not to attach different parts of society to one another, but, on the contrary, to put them outside one another, to mark clearly the barriers which separate them. They do not correspond to a positive social link. The very expression of negative solidarity which we have used is not perfectly exact. It is not a true solidarity, having its own existence and its special nature, but rather the negative side of every species of solidarity. The first condition of total coherence is that the parties who compose it should not interfere with one another through discordant movements. But this external accord does not make for cohesion; on the contrary, it supposes it. Negative solidarity is possible only where there exists some other of a positive nature, of which it is at once the result and the condition.

If, from restitutive law, we take away the rules of which we have just spoken, what remains constitutes a system no less definite, which comprises domestic law, contract-law, commercial law, procedural law, administrative law and constitutional law. The relations which are regulated by it are of a totally different character from the preceding ones; they express a positive union, a co-operation which derives, in essentials, from the division of labor.

The contract is, *par excellence,* the juridical expression of co-operation. There are, to be sure, contracts of benevolence, where only one of the parties is bound . . . they are very rare, for it is very exceptional for acts of kindness to come under legal surveillance. As for the other contracts, which constitute the great majority, the obligations to which they give rise are correlative or reciprocal obligations, or events already effectuated. The involvement of one party results either from involvement assumed by the other, or from some service already rendered by the latter. But this reciprocity is possible only where there is cooperation, and that, in its turn, does not come about without the division of labor. . . . Thus it is clear that exchange always presupposes some division of labor more or less developed. It is true that the contracts of which we have just been speaking still have a somewhat general character. But one must not forget that law deals only in generalities, in the great lines of social relations, those which are found identical in the different spheres of collective life. Thus, each of these types of contract implies a multitude of others, more particular, of which it is the common imprint and which it regulates in one sweep, but where the relations established are between very special functions. This specialization of function is, indeed, more immediately apparent in the commerical code which regulates, pre-eminently, the contracts special to business: contracts between commission-agents and principal, between carrier and shipper, etc., etc. . . .

Procedural law–which takes care of criminal, civil or commercial procedure–plays the same role in the juridical scheme. The sanctions of juridical rules of all sorts can be applied only thanks to the interplay of a certain number of functions, of magistrates, of defense counsel etc., etc. Procedure fixes the way in which they must come into play and relate themselves. It announces what they must be and what part each plays in the general life of the organ.

[In summary] the relations governed by co-operative law with restitutive sanctions and the solidarity which they express, result from the division of social labour. . . . Which is to say that we can equally measure the degree of concentration at which society has arrived in accordance with the division of social labor according to the development of co-operative law with restitutive sanctions.

(ii) Two Laws of Penal Evolution

The variations through which punishment has passed in the course of history are of two sorts, quantitative and qualitative. The laws governing each of these are, of course, different.

I. *The Law of Qualitative Change*
The intensity of punishment is the greater the more closely societies approximate to a less developed type–and the more the central power assumes an absolute character.

It is relatively easy to determine whether one social type is more or less advanced than another: one has only to see whether they are more or less complex and, as to the extent of similar composition, whether they are more or less organized. This hierarchy of social types, moreover, does not imply that succession of societies takes a unilinear form. . .

The second factor which we have distinguished must concern us at more length. We say that government power is absolute when it encounters among the other social functions nothing which serves to counterbalance it and to limit it effectively. In reality, the complete absence of all such limitations is nowhere to be found: one might even say that it is inconceivable. Traditions and religious beliefs act as brakes on even the strongest governments ... But this factual limitation may be in no sense legally required of the government which submits to it; although it exercises a certain amount of care in the exercise of its prerogatives, it is not held back by written or by customary law. In such a case, it exercises a power which we may term absolute.

One can characterize an absolute government in yet another way. . . . [Now], the more the relations of the supreme power with the rest of society have a unilateral character, in other words the more these relationships resemble those which unite the possessor with the thing concerned, the more absolute is the government. Conversely, the more completely bilateral [e.g. contractual] are its relations with other social groups, the less absolute it is.

Therefore, what makes the central authority more or less absolute in character, is the degree to which all counterweights organized with a view to restraining it are missing. One can therefore foresee that this kind of power structure comes into being when all the directive functions of society are more or less completely brought together into one and the same hand. . . . . The person who wields such an authority finds himself possessed of a power which frees him from any collective restraint, and which to some extent means that he only takes into account himself and his own whims and can impose his own wishes. This hypercentralization releases a social force *sui generis* which is of such intensity that it dominates all the others and holds them in thrall. And this does not simply amount to a *de facto* dominance, but is seen as being as of right.

This special kind of political organization is not, therefore, a consequence of the fundamental nature of the society, but rather depends on unique, transitory, and contingent factors. This is why these two causes of the evolution of punishment–the nature of social types and of the government organ–must be carefully distinguished. For being independent, they act independently of one another, on occasion even in opposite directions. For example, it happens that, in passing from a primitive type of society to other more advanced types, we do not see punishment decreasing as we might have expected, because the organization of government acts at the same time to neutralize the effects of social organization. Thus the process is a very complex one.

II *The Law of Qualitative Change*
Deprivation of liberty, and of liberty alone, varying in time according to the seriousness of the crime, tends to become more and more the normal means of social control.

Primitive societies almost completely lack prisons. . . . [whereas in modern societies] . . . the death penalty has been utilised less and less frequently; it has even disappeared completely from some legal codes, to such an extent that virtually the whole field of punishment is now found to consist in the suppression of liberty for limited periods of time or for life.

III *Explanation of the Second Law*
It is easy to understand why imprisonment is not present in relatively under-developed societies; it does not serve any need. In these societies responsibility is collective; when a crime is committed, it is not only the guilty party who pays penalty or reparation. . . . Under these conditions, there is no reason to arrest and hold under guard the presumed author of an act. . . . Furthermore, the moral and legal independence, which characterizes each familial group at this time, serves to restrain the demand that one of its members be handed over in this way on mere suspicion. But to the extent that society is centralized, these elementary groups lose their autonomy and become merged with the total mass, and responsibility becomes individual. Consequently, some measures are necessary to prevent punishment being evaded by the flight of those who have earned it and, as the least offensive to established morality, imprisonment makes it appearance.

However, this explanation is incomplete. To explain an institution, it is not enough to establish that when it appeared it served some useful end; for just because it was desirable it does not follow that it was possible. In addition, one must discover how the necessary conditions for the realization of that goal came into existence. As the social horizon extends, as collective life, instead of being dispersed in a multitude of small centres where it can only be weak, is concentrated in a more limited number of places, it becomes at the same time more intense and more continuous. Because this sphere assumes greater importance, so the dwelling places of those who direct are transformed. They are enlarged, they are organized in terms of the wider and more permanent functions which are laid upon them. . . . The conditions for the creation of the prison are now present. . . . Thus, at the very time when the establishment of a place of detention was becoming useful in consequence of the progressive disappearance of collective responsibility, buildings were arising which could be utilized for this purpose.

As to the juridical development of this new punishment from the time of its formation onward, it can be accounted for by combining the precedings considerations with the law relating to the progressive weakening of punishment. In practice, this weakening takes place from top to bottom of the penal code. In general, it is the most serious punishment which are the first to be affected by this regression, that is to say, which are the first to grow milder, then to disappear. . . . It follows from this that lesser punishments must be developed to fill the gaps which this regression produces. . . . Now the various modes of imprisonment are the last punishments to develop. . . . For this reason the future was reserved for them.

Thus, the qualitative changes in punishment are in part dependent on the simultaneous quantitative changes it undergoes.

IV *Explanation of the First Law*
Without it being necessary to go in detail into the proofs which justify the distinctions, we think that it will be readily conceded that all acts deemed criminal in every known society may be divided into two basic categories: those which are directed against collective things (whether ideal or material, it matters not) of which the principal kinds are offences against public authority and its representatives, the mores, traditions and religion; and those which only injure the individual (murders, thefts, violence and fraud of all types). . . . The first may be called religious criminality because outrages against religion are the most essential part of it, and because crimes against tradition or chiefs of state have always had a more or less religious character; the second, one might term human criminality. Now these two kinds of criminality differ profoundly because the collective sentiments which they offend are not of the same type. As a result, repression cannot be the same for the one as for the other.

The collective sentiments which are contradicted and offended by the criminality characteristic of primitive societies are collective, as it were, in a double sense. Not only have they the collectivity as their subject, so that they are found in the majority of individual consciences, but more than that *they have collective things as their object*. . . . In the case of crimes which violate these sentiments and which consist of the neglect of special obligations, these cannot fail to appear to us as directed against these transcendent beings, since they do indeed strike at them. It is because of this that they appear exceptionally odious; for an offence is the more revolting when the person offended is higher in nature and dignity than the offender. . . . The sympathy which men experience for one of their kind, especially one disgraced by an offence, cannot restrain the effects of the reverential fear which they feel for divinity. In the face of a power which is so much greater than him, the individual appears so insignificant that his sufferings lose their relative importance and become a negligible quantity. It is otherwise with collective sentiments which have the individual as their object; for each of us is an individual. . . . Consequently the conditions of repression are no longer the same as in the first case. . . . The moral scandal which the criminal act constitutes is, therefore, less severe, and consequently does not call for such violent repression.

Seeing as, in the course of time, crime is reduced more and more to offences against persons alone, religious forms of criminality decline, it is inevitable that punishment on the average should become weaker. . . . But a reciprocal influence must be noted, for as human criminality gains ground, it reacts in its turn on religious criminality and, so to speak, assimilates it. If it is offences against persons which constitute the principal crimes today, offences against collective things nevertheless still exist. However, these collective things themselves tend to lose more and more that religiosity which formally marked them. . . . As a result, crimes directed against these collectives partake of the characteristics of those which directly injure individuals; and punishments which are aimed at the former themselves become milder.

We may now return to the second factor of penal evolution, which we have up to now left out of account; namely the nature of the means of government. In truth, the constitution of an absolute power necessarily has the effect of raising the one who wields it above the rest of humanity, making of him something superhuman; the more so as the power with which he is armed is more unlimited . . . From that moment, this religiosity cannot fail to have its usual effects on punishment . . . From this stems the exceptional position that the penal law assigns to crimes of *lese-majesty* among all peoples subjected to an absolutist government . . . Thus the gravity of most crimes is heightened by degrees; consequently the average intensity of punishment is extraordinarly increased.

Conclusions

Understood in this way, the law we have just described takes on a quite different significance ... This allows us to avoid an error to which the immediate observation of the facts might have led. Seeing with what regularity repression seems weaker the farther one goes in evolution, one might believe that the movement is destined to continue without end; in other words, that punishment is tending towards zero. Now, such a consequence would be in contradiction with the true sense of our law. In that the cause which has determined this regression would not produce its attenuating effects indefinitely ... The moment must come ... when offences against the person will fill the whole of criminal law, or what remains of the other offences will be considered as no more than an appendage of the previous sort. Then the movement of retreat will cease. For there is no reason to believe that human criminality must in its turn regress as have the penalties which punish it. Rather, everything points to its gradual development; that the list of acts which are defined as crimes of this type will grow, and that their criminal character will be accentuated.

II Debates and Developments — The Twentieth Century

1. Introduction

The sociology of law during this century has continued to explore the issues and approaches suggested by the classical writers. This should hardly occasion surprise since, as we have noted, the conflicts and tensions which attended the birth pangs of the new societies in continental Europe produced writers who were able to discern the truly fundamental questions about law and the ordering of society. The classical writers did not, however, produce final answers to the problems they raised. Indeed they argued vociferously with each other. Their 'answers' are controversial and contraverted. Indeed any closure of debate is inherently unlikely within our subject because, as many of the writers in this chapter illustrate, there is no conceptual agreement about the 'facts' to be explained. Discussion of what 'law' is, what 'society' is, what 'order' is, involves the use of terms that gain conceptual clarity only within a theory. This theory dependence is, of course, common to all social science, but within the sociology of law it gains especial prominence. In doing sociology of law men are engaged in trying to understand, and perhaps also change, the fabric of the social world that orders their very existence. We cannot help but feel passionate about such an objective, and our motives for approaching it are likely to invoke powerful moral sentiments about what we believe a just society should be like. Over such profound beliefs men disagree, sometimes violently; their beliefs will shape the questions they think a sociology of law should ask, and the methods by which they should be answered. The debates and arguments therefore have continued, and are likely to go on doing so.

The styles and emphases in this continuing debate have varied as much as they did in the nineteenth century. In this section we have attempted to represent some of the major trends.

We have already suggested that British sociology has been largely devoid of major theoretical initiatives. Yet if we consider the social sciences in Britain as a whole we may say there has been one notable exception to this general state. British anthropology, perhaps because of the impetus of imperial and post-imperial connections, and perhaps also because of its institutional isolation from the dead hand of British sociological pragmatism, has made significant contributions to the contemporary sociology of law. British anthropology has taken as one of its themes the social nature of law, and we have represented this tradition with two excerpts, by Bronislaw Malinowski and Max Gluckman. Their significance, however, is not simply that they represent this British tradition; they also demonstrate how the problems raised by the classical theorists are of universal human relevance.

In Europe, as one might expect, we find a direct continuance of issues raised by the classical writers, frequently informed by an intimate knowledge of that tradition. This continuity is represented below by the work of Karl Renner, Eugen Ehrlich and Leon Petrazycki. In the United States the continuities are not so straight-forward. America developed its own indigenous sociological tradition – independent from and often largely uninformed by the work of the classical European theorists. The great 'schools' of American sociology, such as that associated with Chicago, may have developed close parallels to European work, but they largely stand as a monument to original developments. On the other hand, some direct continuities are to be found, most notably in the work of Talcott Parsons. Parsons was responsible for introducing many English readers to the classical European tradition both by incorporating them in his own developmental theories of social order, and by translating some of them into English. We therefore include brief excerpts from Parsons' work, and that of his student Bredemeier. Other later American work, such as that of Philip Selznick, reproduced below, takes up, and re-examines, themes of the classical tradition.

However in the United States there also existed a utilitarian pragmatism as powerful as that in England. Roscoe Pound attempted over a period of sixty years, beginning early in the century, to create a 'sociological jurisprudence', which would push the social study of law into immediate questions of practical reformism. We reprint the manifesto. His arguments help to bolster socio-legal studies that are concerned with social engineering yet largely uninterested in the social forces that shape and constrain that very possibility. Such an approach remains influential and important to this day on both sides of the Atlantic.

This section concludes with the work of three writers chosen to reflect the fact that contemporary work in the sociology of law, in many different ways and with many different styles, still continues to worry about the problems that we inherited from the classical tradition. This is manifested in searching criticism of prior writings, concern about the role of researcher in relation to policy issues and exploring the possibilities of learning from or learning about others by first understanding the nature of their beliefs in law.

2. Law and Custom
by Bronislaw Malinowski

From Crime and Custom in Savage Society, *London, Kegan Paul (1926) pp. 51–68.*

If we designate the sum total of rules, conventions, and patterns of behaviour as the body of custom, there is no doubt that the native feels a strong respect for all of them, has a tendency to do what others do, what everyone approves of, and, if not drawn or driven in another direction by his appetites or interests, will follow the biddings of custom rather than any other course. The force of habit, the awe of traditional command and a sentimental attachment to it, the desire to satisfy public opinion – all combine to make custom be obeyed for its own sake. In this the 'savages' do not differ from the members of any self-contained community with a limited horizon, whether this be an Eastern European ghetto, an Oxford college, or a Fundamentalist Middle-West community. But love of tradition, conformism and the sway of custom account but to a very partial extent for obedience to rules among dons, savages, peasants or Junkers.

[T]here are among the Trobrianders a number of traditional rules instructing the craftsman how to apply his trade. The inert and uncritical way in which these rules are obeyed is due to the general 'conformism of savages' as we might call it. But in the main these rules are followed because their practical utility is recognized by reason and testified by experience.... There are also norms pertaining to things sacred and important, the rules of magical rite, funerary pomp and such like. These are primarily backed up by supernatural sanctions and by the strong feeling that sacred matters must not be tampered with. By an equally strong moral force are maintained certain rules of personal conduct towards near relatives, members of the household and others towards whom strong sentiments of friendship, loyalty, or devotion are felt, which back up the dictates of the social code.

This brief catalogue is not an attempt at classification, but is mainly meant to indicate clearly that, besides the rules of law, there are several other types of norm and traditional commandment which are backed up by motives or forces, mainly psychological, in any case entirely different from those which are characteristic of law in that community.... The rules of law stand out from the rest in that they are felt and regarded as the obligations of one person and the rightful claims of another. They are sanctioned not by a mere psychological motive but by a definite social machinery of binding force, based ... upon mutual dependence and realized in the equivalent arrangement of reciprocal services, as well as in the combination of such claims into strands of multiple relationship. The ceremonial manner in which most transactions are carried out, which entails public control and criticism, adds still more to their binding force.

We may therefore ... dismiss the view that 'group sentiment' or 'collective responsibility' is the only or even the main force which ensures adhesion to custom and which makes it binding and legal ... the savage is neither an extreme 'collectivist' nor an intransigent 'individualist' – he is, like man in general, a mixture of both.

It results also from the account here given that primitive law does not consist exclusively or even chiefly of negative injunctions, nor is all savage law criminal law ... If we have to provide the rules described ... with some modern, hence necessarily inappropriate label, - they must be called the body of 'civil law' of the Trobriand is - landers.

'Civil law', the positive law governing all the phases of tribal life, consists then of a body of binding obligations, regarded as a right by one party and acknowledged as a duty by the other, kept in force by a specific mechanism of reciprocity and publicity inherent in the structure of their society. These rules of civil law are elastic and possess a certain latitude. They offer not only penalties for failure, but also premiums for an overdose of fulfilment. Their stringency is ensured through the rational appreciation of cause and effect by the natives, combined with a number of social and personal sentiments such as ambition, vanity, pride, desire of self-enhancement by display, and also attachment, friendship, devotion and loyalty to their kin.

It scarcely needs to be added that 'law' and 'legal phenomena' ... do not consist in any independent institutions. Law represents rather an aspect of their tribal life, one side of their structure, than any independent, self-contained social arrangements. Law dwells not in a special system of decrees, which foresee and define possible forms of non-fulfilment and provide appropriate barriers and remedies. Law is the specific result of the configuration of obligations, which makes it impossible for the native to shirk his responsibility without suffering for it in the future. ...

The fundamental function of law is to curb certain natural propensities, to hem in and control human instincts and to impose a non-spontaneous, compulsory behaviour - in other words to ensure a type of co-operation which is based on mutual concessions and sacrifices for a common end. A new force, different from the innate, spontaneous endowment must be present to perform this task. ... [T]he force of custom, the glamour of tradition, if it stood alone, would not be enough to counteract the temptations of appetite or lust or the dictates of self-interest ... [T]he fundamental rules safeguarding life, property, and personality form the class which might be described as 'criminal law' - very often over-emphasized by anthropologists and falsely connected with the problem of 'government' and 'central authority' and invariably torn out of its proper context of other legal rules. For - and here we come at last to the most important point - there exists a class of binding rules which control most aspects of tribal life, which regulate personal relations between kinsmen, clansmen and tribesmen, settle economic relations, the exercise of power and of magic, the status of husband and wife, and of their respective families. These are the rules of the Melanesian community which correspond to our civil law . . . There must be in all societies a class of rules too practical to be backed up by religious sanctions, too burdensome to be left to mere good will, too personally vital to individuals to be enforced by any abstract agency. This is the domain of legal rules, and I venture to foretell that reciprocity, systematic incidence, publicity and ambition will be found to be the main factors in the binding machinery of primitive law.

3. The Judicial Process and Reasonable Men
by Max Gluckman

From The Judicial Process among the Barotse, *Manchester, Manchester University Press (1955), pp. 17–24.*

Among the Barotse before the coming of the White man, practically all goods and services were held and disposed of in face-to-face relationships established by relative social position. A man was thrust into one set of these relationships, that of the kinship system, by birth: as he matured, these relationships were extended by his and his kinsfolk's marriages. The other set of relationships was defined by the political structure and his links in it were dictated by its authorities. He could satisy almost all his wants in these two sets of relationships.

The implications of this situation affect both the procedure and purpose of courts, and every doctrine of Lozi jurisprudence. In general terms, their courts aim at the same ends as courts in highly developed societies; the regulation of established and the creation of new relationships, the protection and maintenance of certain norms of behaviour, the readjustment of disturbed social relationships, and the punishing of offenders against certain rules. Their jurisprudence shares with other legal systems many basic doctrines: right and duty and injury; the concept of the reasonable man; the distinctions between statute and custom and between statute and equity or justice; responsibility, negligence, and guilt; ownership and trespass; etc. I shall establish the existence of these doctrines and examine how their particular character in Barotseland is determined by their setting within a social system in which most of the relationships between groups and individuals, and between these and land and chattels, are defined by position in the nation, in a village, and in kinship groupings.

In all societies men and women co-operate or struggle with one another in activities, organized or informal, which are directed to various ends. Sociologists classify these purposes as sexual, procreative, economic, educational, recreational, religious, political, and so on. The interactions between persons to serve each of these purposes constitute systems of social ties which are contained within the total social system and mutually influence one another. In more differentiated societies a person is linked to a variety of different persons, with many of whom his relationship is formally confined to a single interest, as, for example, that of a labourer with his employer, a bus traveller with the conductor, a housewife with a shopkeeper, even an invalid with a doctor or a churchgoer with a priest. It is chiefly in our simple family that we find the mixed ties that are typical of Barotse society. There nearly every social relationship serves many interests. Men live in villages with their kinsmen or quasi-kinsmen, and by virtue of kinship ties they acquire their rights and obligations. With his kin a man holds land and chattels; he produces goods in co-operation with them and shares with them in consuming these; he depends on them for insurance against famine, illness, and old age; he forms with them religious communities tending the same ancestors; they are responsible for the main part of his education; he seeks his recreation with them. He even ascribes the misfortunes which befall him to punishment inflicted on him by his ancestors for quarrelling with his kin, or to his kin's sorcery directed against him. He will be dominantly associated with the kin in whose village he resides. The family village is a group of kin which is defined by allegiance to a headman, a senior kinsman; the members of such a village are associated together by more important legal ties than those which link them to kin in other villages. Some Lozi live in royal villages, whose headmen are queens, princes, princesses, or councillors, with people of other kin-groups and even tribes. Then their bonds with their fellow-villagers are quasi-kinship bonds. This total set of relationships constitutes the village-kinship system. Its importance is shown in the widely extended system of classificatory kinship nomenclature, which groups distance kin with a few categories of close relatives – a system which all simple societies have.

But the village is also a basic political unit. The headman is related to his villagers by political as well as kinship bonds. By birth and by residence in a village a man acquires his civic status and is linked to a number of overlords. These political relationships also subsume a variety of ties. The state is not merely a political organization to maintain internal law and order and to wage defensive or aggressive war. As a subject, a man has the right to ask land from his king, and he works for and may beg help from his king. The nation is a religious community dependent on the king's ancestors for good fortune.

The network of links by which a man is attached to the king through councillors and stewards is intricate, but it usually originates in his headman, who occupies a crucial position in interlocking the political and kinship systems.

Political relationships are single-interest linkages far more than kinship relationships are, but the two sets of bonds are closely identified in their simplicity and common values. A chief is regarded as the parent of his people: he is called 'father and mother'. Every lord is a father to his underlings, and every father is a lord over his dependants. Therefore Lozi constantly use political terms like chief and councillor, as well as specific titles of councillors, in kinship relations, and use kinship terms like father, mother, child, brother, in political relations. This identification expresses the manner in which face-to-face personal relations dominate Lozi life.

As we shall have constantly to refer to the consistency of Lozi law with these relationships which serve many interests, I propose, for brevity, to call them *multiplex* relationships. I require also a term to cover the structure of relationships in which a person tends to occupy the same position relative to the same set of other persons in all networks of purposive ties – economic, political, procreative, religious, educational. Professor Radcliffe-Brown has suggested I call this an *uncomplicated* structure, in contrast to Bouglé's defining our own social structure as *complicated*, since it links us with many different persons in various systems of ties. 'Complicated' and 'uncomplicated' are relative in their connotation. Lozi social structure is uncomplicated when compared with our own; but it is complicated when compared with, say, Andamanese or Bushman structure. Degree of complication therefore defines relatively the degree of congruence in the links between the positions of persons in various systems of ties which make up the total social system.

But it is of fundamental importance to know that each Lozi man or woman is involved in more than one of these sets of multiplex ties. He or she belongs to several sets. Some of these sets of ties are of the same kind: a Lozi has rights in several different villages and several different kinship groupings. Villages and kinship groupings overlap but are distinctive and thus are examples of the different types of groupings of which a Lozi is a member. He is also linked in established relationships with neighbours and blood-brothers and friends, and in several different sets of political relationships and groups through stewards, councillors, and members of the royal family, and with fellow-tribesmen. This multiple membership of diverse groups and in diverse relationships is an important source of quarrels and conflict; but it is equally the basis of internal cohesion in any society.

With this brief survey of the structure of Lozi society, we may glance in a summary way at the problems we shall be considering. Most Lozi relationships are multiplex, enduring through the lives of individuals and even generations. Each of these relationships is part of an intricate network of similar relationships. Inevitably, therefore, many of the disputes which are investigated by Lozi kutas arise not in ephemeral relationships, involving single interests, but in relationships which embrace many interests, which depend on similar related relationships, and which may endure into the future. This, at least, is usually the desire of the parties and the hope and desire of the judge and unbiased onlookers. The Lozi disapprove of any irremediable breaking of relationships. For them it is a supreme value that villages should remain united, kinsfolk and families and kinship groups should not separate, lord and underling should remain associated. Throughout a court hearing of this kind the judges try to prevent the breaking of relationships, and to make it possible for the parties to live together amicably in the future. Obviously this does not apply in every case, but it is true of a large number, and it is present in some degree in almost all cases. Therefore the court tends to be conciliating; it strives to effect a compromise acceptable to, and accepted by, all parties. This is the main task of the judges. The task is related to the nature of the social relationships out of which spring the disputes that come before them. In order to fulfil their task the judges constantly have to broaden the field of their enquiries, and consider the total history of relations between the litigants, not only the narrow legal issue raised by one of them. Since the kuta is an administrative body, as well as a law-court, it may take varied action to achieve its aim, or convert a 'civil suit' into a 'criminal hearing' in the public interest. The result is that in cases of this sort the court's conception of 'relevance' is very wide, for many facts affect the settlement of the dispute. This applies particularly to cases between blood-kin and between fellow-villagers. The relationship of husband and wife is more ephemeral, and in disputes between them the court concentrates more on the immediately relevant facts. When a contract between strangers, or an injury by a man on a stranger, is involved, the court narrows its range of relevance yet further.

Lozi, like all Africans, appear to be very litigious. Almost every Lozi of middle age can recount dispute after dispute in which he has been involved: most of these have been debated in family and village 'courts' but many have also gone to political courts. Many Lozi are ever ready to rush to court where they dispute with great bitterness and determination. In cases where they clearly cannot win, they will proceed from court to court. Their bitterness must be understood from the way in which a dispute provoking a lawsuit precipitates ill-feeling about many trifling incidents in the past both between the parties and among their kin, incidents which may go back over many years. Men may sue knowing they will lose, but that they thus bring to the kuta a kinsman who has slighted them and who will be rebuked. Or a man will commit an offence to induce another to sue him, with the same end in view.

The kuta should not achieve a reconciliation without blaming those who have done wrong. The litigants in coming to court have appealed for a public hearing of their grievances, and these are examined against the norms of behaviour expected of people. The judges therefore upbraid all the parties where they have departed from these norms: judgements are sermons on filial, parental, and brotherly love. This is not inappropriate since the kuta is the central administrative chapter for national religious affairs. People involved indirectly, as well as the litigants themselves, are admonished on how to behave.

When we assemble the norms which are stated in this exemplary way, we shall see that they form that figure which is so prominent in all legal systems – the reasonable man. This figure is also used by the judges as the basis of their cross-examination to arrive at the truth. The reasonable man in Lozi society is highly specified, in accordance with the specific social positions which the parties occupy. Following up this point we shall find many disputes, apparently over gardens or chattels, are in fact suits by the plaintiff to have the kuta state that the defendant has not behaved reasonably in accordance with the norms of their relationship.

It will have already emerged from this summary account, that in assessing whether behaviour is reasonable the judges lay blame on those who have erred. Implicit in the reasonable man is the upright man, and moral issues in these relationships are barely differentiated from legal issues. This is so even though the Lozi distinguish 'legal' rules which the kuta has power to enforce or protect, from 'moral' rules it has not power to enforce or protect. But the judges are reluctant to support the person who is right in law, but wrong in justice, and may seek to achieve justice by indirect, and perhaps administrative, action.

In the course of this account of Lozi trials we shall also cover a number of other problems. I indicate a few here. First, since almost all a man's relationships exist in his positions in the political and kinship systems, a litigant in many cases arising from these multiplex relationships comes to court not as a right-and-duty bearing *persona*, but in terms of his total social personality. That is, in most disputes a person is not involved merely as buyer, seller, lessor, lessee, landowner, the injured party and the wrongdoer – briefly, the plaintiff and the defendant, the complainant and the accused – but he is involved as an individual in specific relationships with a whole set of other people. In administering the law the judges consider these total relationships, not only the relations between right-and-duty bearing units. But concepts of these units exist as nuclei for the substantive law.

I conclude this section of the analysis by surveying the relation of the judicial process to 'law' as a whole among the Lozi, and find that it is in essence similar to that process in Western law. The judges have to apply certain normative rules to a particular set of circumstances in dispute. These rules, known somewhat vaguely as 'the law' are contained in customary usages; in statutes; in institutions common to all tribes of the region and in some institutions which they believe are common to all humanity and derive from God; in general equity and justice; in judicial precedent; and in the regular processes of the natural world (in our sense). Customary usage – ritual and secular – is one of the sources of Lozi law, as it has been in all systems; and the Lozi have the same other sources as those other systems.

Theoretically, this total body of law is known and certain and the judges are supposed only to pronounce it, abide by it, and apply it. However, since the law has only recently and barely begun to be recorded, the judges do not make a systematic survey of all the sources and decide what rules are applicable. Generally they tend to form a moral and equitable judgment on the case and then state – and amend – the law to accord with this judgment. Often they cannot do this, and must abide by some well-known statutory law or customary rule. But especially in cases between kinsmen, they are generally able to satisfy their ethical view of the facts. This process emerges notably in the fact that judges refer less often to judicial precedents in previous disputes, than to precedents of people behaving morally in circumstances similar to those of the case they are trying.

This process of judicial reasoning begins with the pleadings of the parties and the judges' examination of the evidence, which at every point is evaluated against moral norms. Nevertheless, the process is controlled by logical reasoning, which proceeds from premises of fact and premises of law ('reasons' as the Lozi call them) to certain conclusions, and the Lozi have a developed vocabulary to evaluate the skill or clumsiness of judicial analyses. Judges also try to develop the law by reasoning by analogy and logical development to meet new situations. Thus they employ Cardozo's methods of philosophy, evolution, and tradition. They also employ his so-called 'method of sociology' by which they import equity, social welfare and public policy, into their applications of the law. They are able to do so because the main certainty of the law consists in certain general principles whose constituent concepts are 'flexible' – as law itself, right and duty, good evidence, negligence, reasonableness. The judges' task is to define these concepts for a particular set of circumstances, and in this process of specification they introduce into judgment through the flexible concepts all sorts of social values and prejudices, and indeed personal prejudices and values.

Finally, I conclude by making bold to submit that Western jurists, in maintaining or attacking the myth of law's certainty, have not fully explored the flexible 'uncertainty' of legal concepts; and have particularly failed to arrange these concepts in order either of flexibility or of moral implication. I suggest that this ordering is necessary if we are to understand the relation between law and ethics; for I see the judicial process as the attempt to specify legal concepts with ethical implications according to the structure of society, in application to the great variety of circumstance of life itself. In this process the judges are able to develop the law to cope with social changes.

4. Legal Forms and Social Reality
by Karl Renner

From The Institutions of Private Law and their Social Functions [1904] London, Routledge and Kegan Paul (1949) pp. 55–9, 105–22, 252–3.

Our inquiry is not concerned with positive legal analysis, the systematic exposition of legal institutions, a field which has been amply covered by others. Nor are we investigating the problems of the creation of law. We shall refrain from analysing the questions as to how the norms originate which make up the legal institutions, how a legal norm grows from its economic background, and what are the economic causes of the creation of legal norms. This field, it is true, has not been cultivated, but we shall keep away from it. We propose to examine only the economic and social effect of the valid norm as it exists, so long as the norm does not change. Those acquainted with socialist literature will at once perceive that we have taken as our subject the mutual relations between law and economics. The traditional Marxist school conceives the economic relations as the substructure and the legal institutions as the superstructure. 'Substructure' and 'superstructure' are metaphors, borrowed from architecture; it is obvious that they serve only to illustrate the connection, not to define it in exact terms. This superstructure, according to Marx's well-known formula, comprises not only law but also ethics and culture, in fact every ideology. This terminology must therefore apply to many facts other than those relevant to the law, whose structures are completely different and must be separately defined. The relation between the philosophy of an age and the economic substructure of that age is obviously determined by key concepts quite different from those of legal norm, exercise of a right and the like. We must desist, therefore, from attempting to give a general exposition of the Marxist concept of superstructure. We must recognize that each of these social phenomena, which in their general aspects are quite aptly illustrated by Marx's metaphor, requires a specific investigation. We attempt this investigation in regard to law.

It is a mere platitude to say that laws can influence economy sufficiently to change it and can therefore be considered as causes of economic results. Marx, of course, was the last person to deny this. 'The influence of laws upon the conservation of the relations of distribution and consequently their influence upon production must be specifically determined.' (*Neue Zeit*, p. 744). Laws are made with the intention of producing economic results, and as a rule they achieve this effect. Social life is not so simple that we can grasp it, open it and reveal its kernel like a nut, by placing it between the two arms of a nutcracker called cause and effect. Although he was much occupied with legal problems, Marx never found time to 'determine the influence of the laws' yet he saw the problem clearly as proved in particular by the following methodological hint: 'The really difficult point to be discussed here, however, is how the relations of production as relations of the law enters into a disparate development. An instance is Roman civil law in its relations to modern production' (*ibid.*, p. 779). We make use of this hint in the formulation of our problem: (1) Law which continues unchanged in relation to changing economic conditions; (2) changed economic conditions in relation to the new norms of the new law. Our study, however, will be concerned with the first part of the problem only.

Every economic process which in theory is an isolated unit is only part of the whole process of social production and reproduction. If the economic function is related to this whole, it becomes the social function of the legal institution. If we regard a social order as static and confine our attention to a certain moment of history, then the legal norms and the economic process merely appear as mutually conditioned and subservient to one another. Within the economic structure economic process and legal norms appear as the same thing; the former seen as an external, technical-natural event, the latter as an inherent relation of wills, seen from the point of view of individual will-formation. We call the external, technical-natural process the substratum of the norm. This sounds very plausible. But we can no more study the laws of gravity from a stone in a state of rest than we can learn the arts of cooking from the cook who was pricked by the Sleeping Beauty's spindle. All that we can observe is that in a state of rest legal and economic institutions, though not identical, are but two aspects of the same thing, inextricably interwoven. We must define and describe this co-existence.

This observation, however, only stresses the fact that they are mutually determined. We must study the process in its historical sequence, the gradual transition of a social order from a given stage to the next. The inherent laws of development can only be revealed if the events are seen in motion, in the historic sequence of economic and legal systems. If we examine two consecutive periods, chosen at random, we may obtain results which, though they apply to these particular periods of transition, cannot claim to be generally valid. To decide the function of the law in general, we have to study inductively all social orders as they appear in the course of history, from the most primitive to the most highly developed. By this method we obtain the general categories of the social order and at the same time the general functions of the law. This procedure is legitimate in spite of the fact that every individual stage of development has its specific nature and is subject to its peculiar laws . . . The right of ownership, *dominion*, is a person's all embracing legal power over a tangible object. It is a right, i.e. a power conferred upon a subject (person) by the law. This right is absolute, the imperatives upon which it is based are addressed to all persons without exception and claim their respect. Its content is the power to dispose of the object and this power is all embracing. The owner in his capacity as owner may dispose in any manner: he may, for instance, use the object, consume it, destroy it or abandon it. Ownership is not, therefore an aggregate of individual rights, it implies unlimited possibilities of disposal. . . . The subject matter of the property norm is generally an occupied item of nature, a corporeal thing. In its natural form it is technically subservient to man. Insofar as it is not ready to be consumed, it is at first raw material or working tool, and in this form it enters the process of production. The character mask of the property subject is that of a person owning material goods. At the stage of simple commodity production the owner is at the same time a worker who enjoys the benefit of his labour. All economic character masks which later become distinct from one another, are still united within the same individual ... Journeymen and apprentices used to live in the master's household. Their relation was in the nature of a subjection determined by public law, on the lines of the Germanic *patria potestas*, which served the purposes of education, training and mastery of the craft, and whose function therefore was to ensure the continuity of the working population. This relationship was abolished by the mere force of facts; it was replaced by the private contracts of *do ut facias*. The old regulation of labour is dissolved, and for a while there is no new regulation.

But the property object (*res*) as it develops into and assumes the functions of capital, itself inaugurates a process of education for the owner no less than for the disposed.

> We saw in a former chapter, that a certain minimum amount of capital was necessary, in order that the number of labourers simultaneously employed ... might suffice to liberate the employer himself from manual labour, convert him from a small master into a capitalist, and thus formally to establish a capitalist production ... We also saw that, at first, the subjection of labour to capital was only a formal result of the fact that the labourer, instead of working for himself, works for and consequently under the capitalist. By the co-operation of numerous wage labourers, the sway of capital develops into a requisite for carrying on the labour process itself, into a real requisite of production. That a capitalist should command on the field of production, is now as indispensable as that a general should command on the field of battle ... The work of directing, superintending and adjusting, becomes one of the functions of capital, from the moment that labour under the control of capital, becomes co-operative. Once a function of capital it acquires special characteristics. [*Capital*, 1, pp. 320–1]

What is the essence of this power of command? It is based on contract. But so was the relation of the feudal lord to his vassal, yet this was essentially of a public nature. An element of domination is without doubt implied in this system of superordination and subordination, and in spite of the formal contract it remains essentially a system of power.

The question is whether this control is still in essence the Germanic medieval *mundium*, that reflection of paternal power. Is it established in favour of the ruled or of the ruling, is it a government of protection or of exploitation? What are its essential features?

> The directing motive, the end and aim of capitalist production, is to extract the greatest amount of surplus value, and consequently to exploit labour power to the greatest possible extent ... The control exercised by the capitalist is not only a special function, due to the nature of the social labour process, and peculiar to that process, but it is, at the same time, a function of the exploitation of a social labour process, and is consequently rooted in the unavoidable antagonism between the exploiter and the living and labouring raw material he exploits ... moreover the co-operation of wage labourers is entirely brought about by the capital that employs them. Their union into one single productive body and the establishment of a connection between their individual functions, are matters foreign and external to them, are not their own act, but the act of the capital that brings and needs them together. Hence the connection existing between their various labour appears to them, ideally, in the shape of a pre-conceived plan of the capitalist, in the shape of the powerful will of another, who subjects their activity to his aims. [*ibid.*, pp. 321–2].

In the eyes of the law the property subject is related to the object only, controlling matter alone. But what is control of property in law, becomes in fact man's control of human beings, of the wage labourers, as soon as property has developed into capital. The individual called owner sets the tasks to others, he makes them subject to his commands and, at least in the initial stages of capital development, supervises the execution of his commands. The owner of a *res* imposes his will upon *personae*, autonomy is converted into heteronomy of will.

Capital extends its scale, it expands beyond the sphere of the capitalist's personal control. 'Just as at first the capitalist is relieved from actual labour ... so now he hands over the work of direct and constant supervision ... to a speical kind of wage labourer ... the work of supervision becomes their established and exclusive function' (*ibid.*, p. 322).

We see that the right of ownership thus assumes a new social function. Without any change in the norm, below the threshold of collective consciousness, a *de facto* right is added to the personal absolute domination over a corporeal thing. This right is not based upon a special legal provision. It is the power of control, the power to issue commands and to enforce them. The inherent urge of capital to beget constantly further capital provides the motive for this *imperium*.

This power of control is a social necessity, but at the same time it is profitable to the owners – it establishes a rule not for the purpose of protection but for the purpose of exploitation, of profit.

The subordination of the workers which at the same time effects their mutual co-ordination, is a corresponding phenomenon. Is this co-ordination also based on contract? The workers are not asked whether their neighbour appeals to them, yet they are forced into close proximity and in this way they become united into an association of workers. What is it that brings about this passive association of the workers? What is it that correlates their functions and shapes them into a unified productive body? There is no doubt that these workers who contribute partial operations form a compulsory association according to all rules of legal doctrine.

This association receives its individuality from the capital that collects the workers in one place and keeps them there. Just as the law is the norm for the citizens, so the plan, the plan of production, is the abstract and impersonal norm for this compulsory association, supported by the ultimate and most concrete authority of the capitalist, the power of an alien will. Supervision is delegated to special functionaries, and thus relations of superordination and subordination are made into an organic whole.

Thus the institution of property leads automatically to an organization similar to this state. Power over matter begets personal power. 'It is not because he is a leader of industry that a man is a capitalist; on the contrary he is a leader of industry because he is a capitalist. The leader of industry is an attribute of capital, just as in feudal times the functions of general and judge were attribute of landed property' (*ibid.*, p. 323). We see that even at the first stage of capitalism, that of co-operation, the old microcosm is replaced by a new one which derives its unity from capital, which here is the aggregate of the technical means of production, i.e. objects of owner-ship. These new organizations bring about a gradual transformation of man and matter, without any norm imposed by the state ...

At this stage it is useful to realise the original implications of the institution of property: it is not a mere order of goods. It is just in respect of the deliberate planned social distribution of goods that it first abdicates. It merely protects him who has possessions by virtue of an unassailable title but it does not distribute goods according to a plan. Contrast with this the law of property of the feudal epoch. How richly diversified was its catalogue of *jura in rem*. The property law of bourgeois society leaves the order of the goods to the goods themselves. It is only thus that they become commodities in capital, only thus that they organize themselves and accumulate in accordance with the specific laws of capital circulation. At this stage we see already that the synonymous and anarchical regulation of 'goods' becomes control over men in their capacity as potential labour. We also see that in our time this factual regulation of 'goods' presumes to dictate the social regulation of power and labour. We see further that this regulation of power and labour remains concealed to the whole of bourgeois legal doctrine which is aware of nothing but its most formal, general and extraneous limitations, vis its foundation on a contract of employment.

Wage labour is a relation of autocracy with all the legal characteristics of despotism. The factory is an establishment with its own code with all the characteristics of a legal code. It contains norms of every description, not excluding criminal law, and it establishes special organs and jurisdiction. Labour regulations and the conventions valid within economic enterprises deserve just as well to be treated as legal institutions as the manorial law of the feudal epoch. This too was based upon private rule, upon the will of a Lord, one manorial custom differing from another only in details. Even if this difference had been so fundamental as to exclude all understanding and explanation on a common basis – and this cannot even be imagined – these institutions would still remain an integral part of the legal system of that period. The same applies to factory law, the general regulations of labour in economic enterprises. No exposition of our legal order can be complete without it, it regulates the relations of a large part of the population. . .

New functions accrue to the legal character 'person' who also has the economic character 'proprietor' now he regulates labour, ruling and exploiting. Property, from a mere title to dispose of material objects, becomes a title to power, and as it exercises power in the private interests, it becomes a title to domination. At the same time the free person, the labourer with no property, becomes a subject *sui generis*, as history does not repeat itself. Among all those who have the power and are destined to be his master he may choose the master who most appeals to him, but as a class the subjects are chained to the class of the masters.

We see that property at the stage of simple commodity production endows the worker with the detention of his means of production, making man the master of matter. Now property changes its function without a corresponding change in the law. It gives the legal detention of the means of production to the individuals who do not perform any labour, making them thus masters of labour. Property automatically takes over the function of regulating power and labour, and it becomes a private title to domination. The law endows this non worker with legal detention of the means of production but in any society only the worker can actually hold them, as he must have them in his hands in order to work with them. Thus the law, by means of a complementary institution, the contract of service, takes actual detention away from the owner. The workers may mind the machine but he must pay the price of submitting himself to exploitation. A permanent state of war between the legal and actual potential is thus established ... The prospective employee registers with a labour exchange, which is either a private establishment or run by the state, a municipality or a trade union. He is assigned to a job by rote. This state of affairs is unintelligible in an economy based upon freedom of contract, which can explain it no more than pure science can explain the working of a typewriter which is a technical product. If the worker is accepted, at terms which are fixed beforehand and scarcely mentioned, he goes on the job. Formally based upon contract, the labour relationship is now developed into a 'position' just as property has developed into public utility. If a person occupies a 'position', this means that his rights and duties are closely circumscribed, the 'position' has become a legal institution in character much like the fee of feudal times. The 'position' comprises the claim to adequate remuneration (settled by collective agreement or works rule), the obligation to pay certain contributions (for trade unions and insurance), the right to special benefits (sickness, accident, old age, death) and finally certain safeguards against loss of position or in case of its loss.

What is the meaning of this development from the contract of employment to the position of work and service? The private contract, by means of the complementary institutions of collective agreement, labour exchanges, social insurance and the like, has become an institution of public law. It is still largely determined by the private will of the individuals concerned, yet this influence is continually decreasing and the state element is almost of greater importance than the private element, the collective element more important than the individual element ... The legal institution of property has undergone an extensive development in a relatively short period. It has suffered a drastic transformation which has not, however, been accompanied by noticeable modifications of its legal structure. This fact proves our first thesis, that *fundamental changes in society are possible without accompanying alterations of the legal system.*

A second thesis is also proved, that *it is not the law that causes economic development.* All the examples given above demonstrate that the existence of society as it is, depends on and presupposes a determined, historically conditioned, legal order. The latter, however, has never caused social change. A legal order adapted to a definite historical substratum, simple commodity production, derived its significance from the substratum; its purpose was to hold it together and to stabilise it. But this legal order does not prevent changes in the substratum. The essential character of the social process as preservation and reproduction of the species undergoes continual change while the form of the law is constant. The form of the law is not the *causa causans* which brings about the change. The social function undergoes change unaccompanied by a juridical change of the legal institution.

This seems to imply a third thesis, that *economic change does not change the law,* as it has been our leading assumption that the juridical character of the institutions is constant. Thus our investigation seems to prove that the legal superstructure is absolutely independent of its economic substructure, its substratum; and that changes in the legal system must proceed from other than economic sources. Yet this would be a premature conclusion. A supplementary investigation of the change of norms might show that the economic substratum would eventually transform the law also, though strictly in accordance with forms of creation specific to norms. So our third thesis is valid with a reservation, that *economic change does not immediately and automatically bring about changes in the law.*

How does this change of functions come about? We have seen that
it proceeds steadily, continuously, imperceptibly, like the growth of
grass, according to the law of all organic development. As the
process of growth cannot be understood by a glance at the plant, but
only by study of the whole successive development from germ to
fruit and again to new germ; so the change of functions can be
recognised only at an advanced stage and then only by way of
historical comparison: it can be recognised only when it has
matured. Hence our fourth thesis, that *development by leaps and
bounds is unknown in the social substratum, which knows evolution
only, not revolution.*

5. Intuitive Law

by Leon Petrazycki

From Law and Morality [*1905–7*] *Cambridge, Mass., Harvard University
Press (1955) pp. 6–18, 71–5, 93–6.*

The fundamental method of studying and gaining knowledge of
objects and of phenomena is observation. In studying the objects
and phenomena of the physical and material world, observation
consists in perception with the aid of 'the external senses' (sight,
hearing, smell, taste and touch), and is termed external observation.
In studying phenomena of the spiritual world – psychic phenomena
– observation consists in internal perception of what is taking place
within one's own mind, and is termed internal observation: self
observation or introspection.

There are fields of cognition, where the application of observation
and the success of cognition are obstructed by misunderstanding as
to the actual sphere where the corresponding real phenomena are.
We shall deal *infra* with a special class of psychic processes which
have the peculiar property that external objects seem (to persons
experiencing these processes) to possess particular attributes (not
actually present) or to exist in the external world (where they do not
so exist at all).

In the corresponding fields of cognition, we must avoid the error of accepting as real that which seems to exist in a world external to the person experiencing such processes, and keep in mind that the corresponding real phenomena are to be found in the mind – and only in the mind – of that person. It would be naive to suppose that an epithet 'nice' or 'dear' as applied to another connotes any peculiar qualities of the person to whom such attributes are ascribed: however closely we study that person – examining him from head to foot, and seeking otherwise to find something corresponding to the epithet 'dear' – our search will fail and the meaning of the word 'dear' will remain hidden from us. Only when we turn to a study of the psychic experiences of the persons using these terms can that meaning be explained.

Misunderstandings of this sort are possible – and in fact play a great part – in the sphere of phenomena of modern life. The statement that so-and-so is under such-and-such a moral obligation ordinarily presupposes, as the expression itself shows, that 'moral obligation' is a real phenomenon, found where the man is found to whom that obligation is ascribed. In reality, however, the real phenomenon corresponding to the expression 'moral obligation' is found in an entirely different sphere: in the mind of him who finds that another is under a moral obligation.

This must be kept in mind also in the field of law and the study of law. Suppose we are concerned with the judgement: 'Squire A has a right to obtain from lessee B 5,000 roubles rent'; or 'Lessee B is bound to pay Squire A the 5,000 roubles stipulated in the lease'; or 'Lessee B is bound to pay Squire A the 5,000 roubles stipulated in the lease'. According to legal terminology, there is – as between A and B – the legal relationship of lessor/lessee. Here a legal phenomenon confronts us: where is it? Where can it be found for purposes of study? It would be a mistake to suppose that it is to be found somewhere in space between A and B, or that – if A and B are in a certain province – the legal phenomenon is somewhere in that province, or to suppose that the legal obligation ascribed to lessee B in the judgement aforesaid is something found in him, and that the right to obtain 5,000 roubles is something present – and to be found – in Squire A, in his hands, or in his spirit, or anywhere at all around or in him. The scientific and critical answer to this question can and should be simply this: the legal phenomenon is in the mind of the third person C who supposes that A has a right to receive – and that B is bound to pay – 5,000 roubles.

In precisely the same way, if a learned jurist experiences the judgement: 'lessees are bound to pay lessors the agreed rent upon the expiration of the period of occupancy', we have before us a legal phenomenon; and the learned jurist may take advantage of its presence to observe, study and analyse it. He would, however, be acting under a misapprehension if he thought the corresponding legal phenomenon somewhere in space above or between people, in the 'social milieu', or the like: it occurs within himself – in his own mind – and only there. Legal phenomena consist of unique psychic processes expressed, incidentally, in the unique form of ascribing to different beings (not only to people, but to beings of various other classes, conceived of in the mind), or to certain classes of such beings, 'duties' and 'rights'; so that these beings, so conceived of, are seemingly found in certain peculiar conditions of being bound or of possessing certain objects ('rights'), and the like.

The science of law (and the science of morality where moral obligations, norms and the like are under study) is therefore influenced by the misunderstanding which came to light in our survey of persons as 'nice' or 'dear' in order to find in them corresponding attributes. The content of traditional legal science is tantamount to an optical illusion: it does not see legal phenomena where they actually occur, but discerns them where there is absolutely nought of them – where they cannot be found, observed, or known – that is to say, in a world external to the subject who is experiencing the legal phenomena. We shall see *infra* that this optical illusion has its natural psychological causes, precisely as the optical illusion (in the literal sense of the word) is perfectly natural, when people ignorant of astronomy suppose (as the science of astronomy itself did down to Copernicus) that the sun 'rises' in the morning and revolves around us.

Observation is the fundamental method of studying phenomena – whether of the physical world or of the spiritual world. It is clear from what has already been set out, that legal phenomena occur – and can be found for the purposes of observation – not where optical illusion leads us to suppose they are but much nearer: here, within us; in our consciousness; in the consciousness of him who is experiencing rights and duties at that given second. To be freed from this optical illusion means the elimination of a vast province where legal phenomena are (supposedly) found and can (supposedly) be investigated, as well as of a vast quantity of (supposedly) legal phenomena and their elements. Even with the number of legal phenomena, and of the spheres of their being, thus significantly smaller than those contemplated by the prevailing theory, their number is still not small, even from our point of view: the number of the spheres where legal phenomena are is the same as the number of living creatures capable of experiencing – and in fact experiencing – the corresponding mental states, while the number of legal phenomena is equal to the number of these experiences. Of all the extremely numerous species of beings endowed with psychic life on earth (animals) only one – homo sapiens – is distinguished by the capacity to experience the complicated psychic processes which constitute legal phenomena.

The introspective method – simple and experimental 'self-knowledge' – is the sole means of observation, *and of the immediate and reliable* cognition and study, of legal and moral phenomena. Without it there is *no possibility whatsoever of any knowledge of them at all*. In general, the only categories of psychic phenomena accessible to our cognition are those known to us from the history of our ego – with them we are acquainted because we have ourselves experienced them. The other categories of psychic phenomena are absolutely inaccessible to our cognition. One who did not, through his own psychic experience, know of hunger, thirst, anger, joy and the like would, in general, be incapable of knowing the psychic phenomena, although others know and experience them; hence he could not understand the corresponding behaviour, bodily movements, or speeches of others, and so forth. The same is true as to legal phenomena. A man suffering from an absolute legal idiotism – that is to say, complete inability to have legal experience – could not possibly know what law is, or understand the human conduct evoked thereby. Having heard the word 'law', and seen that much in the human society is done with reference to 'law', he would perhaps fashion his own special interpretation of these expressions and of this conduct: he might suppose that it was a matter of commands laid by the powerful in their own interests upon the weak and defenceless, with appropriate threats in case of disobedience, and that these threatening orders were carried out by the weak for reasons of expediency. This, however, would have absolutely nothing in common with the knowledge of what law actually is.

The misunderstanding as to the whereabouts of legal phenomena, set out above, is not the only obstacle to the formulation of a scientific theory of law: another – even more formidable – is that in jurisprudence (as in the social sciences and the humanities) there is no correct doctrine as to the formation of general concepts. It is commonly assumed that, in order to form the concept 'law', one should make a survey of legal phenomena, compare them with one another, and then with kindred phenomena, and finally select *the* attributes which are common to the law and distinguish law from other phenomena. This is, however, impossible: such surveys and comparisons presuppose knowledge of what are – and what are not – legal phenomena. The proper procedure is to formulate class concepts correctly.

A general or class concept is the *idea* of objects which possess certain attributes or traits. A class consists of all the objects having these traits. Thus the *idea* of white things is a *class concept*, and the *things themselves* comprise a corresponding *class*. Class concepts are by no means limited to things which actually exist: there are class concepts of things entirely imaginary, such as those in geometry, and even class concepts meant to cover real things are not limited to those actually existent but include as well things of the past and of the future possessing the relevant attributes.

[*Editors' note*: Petrazycki goes on to conclude that '*law* – in the sense of a special class of real phenomena – is to be understood as those ethical experiences whose impulsions have an attributive character. All other ethical experiences – those connected with purely imperative impulsions – we shall call moral phenomena'.]

Our concept of law ... denies the real existence of what is held by jurists really to exist in the legal field, and reveals real legal phenomena as a special class of complex psychic processes in a wholly different sphere: that is to say, in the mind of the individual ... the number of everyday cases and the problems of conduct contemplated and determined by official regulation, as compared with the immense quantity thereof anticipated by law (in the sense herein established) is infinitesimal. Particularly in all the innumerable and manifold cases and areas of conduct, which neither are nor can be provided for by official codes of any kind, there is ordinarily some imperative attributive indication in our legal consciousness – where it is a matter of causing any kind of good or evil to another (even though it be a small satisfaction or a trifling unpleasantness) – as to what is due and owing to others from us, or to us from others, or to others from a third person; or that we have a right to do – and that others should endure – it, or the reverse. This includes such elements of conduct as words addressed to others (their content, the means of pronouncing them, the intonation, the gestures, and the pose) or judgements expressed about third persons (of their content and their shades of meaning). If, in their content or in the tone in which they are pronounced, words addressed to others contain anything pleasant or unpleasant for them (as when it is a matter of expressing sympathy, respect, gratitude and the like – or reproaches on some score, censure, irony or derision – or of using a 'dry' and 'cold' tone of scorn in speaking or a contemptuous smile), the legal conscience holds court and adjudges whether or not such conduct is in conformity with the deserts of the other: whether or not the reproach is well founded and merited (so that the person making the reproach had a right to do so) or without foundation (so that the person who suffered it had a right that the former refrain from it, and now has a right that it be recognized as without foundation and retracted). Even artistic, scientific, technical or other criticism of the product of another's creative or other labour is subjected to legal regulations in our sense, since it is in the sphere within which law, as attributive ethical experience, operates.

Furthermore, law in the sense herein established includes not only much that is outside the cognizance of the state and does not enjoy positive official recognition and protection, but also much that encounters an attitude of outright hostility on the part of the state and is to be hunted out and eradicated as contrary and antagonistic to the law officially recognized by the state. Some of these categories of phenomena are of special interest and merit particular attention.

(1) The law of criminal organizations. In these (robber bands, pirates, gangs of thieves and the like), entire systems of imperative attributive norms (of more or less complexity) have been worked out and carried out with unhesitating precision; they define the organization of the gang, distribute obligations and functions among the members, and endow them with corresponding rights (in particular to a definite share of the booty, and otherwise). Insofar as contracts establish actual rights and obligations in criminal organizations the contract rights and obligations (those concerned with helping to commit the crime and being paid a reward therefor, and the like) are ordinarily observed strictly and 'honourably', and the same is true as to contracts concluded by criminal gangs or individual criminals

with outsiders. Such obligations, while entirely without official protection through the courts, are carried out with greater punctiliousness and honour than is true of some obligations which the courts do recognize and enforce, such as the duty to return money borrowed from an acquaintance, or to pay when due the purchase price of things that have been bought.

(2) Law which continues to exist and to operate in the minds of certain strata of the population – certain classes of society, or religious or tribal groups which are component parts of the state – notwithstanding the fact that not merely are the corresponding imperative attributive norms not acknowledged as law from the official point of view: they are eradicated, more or less inexorably, as inadmissible, barbarian, anti-cultural and the like. Notwithstanding the hostile competition of another law (supported by the authority of the state and the force at its disposal), the tribal mind holds tenaciously to certain elements of ancient law, so that – for centuries sometimes – a dual system of law continues to exist, with resulting conflicts and occasional tragedies and the imposition of more or less cruel punishments (from organs of official power which follow the official law and consider it alone 'law') upon persons acting in accordance with the directions of their legal conscience in effectuating rights sacred in their opinion or in fulfilling the sacred legal duty. No significance of any kind attaches either to recognition and protection by the state, or to any acknowledgement of whatso-ever sort by anyone at all, as regards the concept of law here-in established and its extension to the corresponding psychic phenomena. From the point of view of this concept, the countless imperative attributive experiences and the projections thereof are nonetheless law, legal judgements and so forth because they are present in the mind of but one individual and are unknown to anyone else in the world. In general every kind of law and all legal phenomena – including such legal judgements as meet with assent and encouragement from others – represent purely and exclusively individual phenomena from our point of view, and the eventual consent and encouragement on the part of others are irrelevant from the point of view of defining and studying the nature of legal phenomena. This is a necessary conclusion from the psychological theory of law. . .

The essential significance in human life of ethical experience of both the moral and of the legal type is that they: (a) operate as motives of conduct and stimulate to the accomplishment of some actions and to abstention from others (the motivational effect of ethical experiences), and (b) produce certain changes in the mind of individuals and masses, developing and intensifying some habits and propensities and weakening and eradicating others (the pedagogical or educational effect of ethical experiences). Since they are abstract, moral and legal impulsions do not *per se* predetermine the character and direction of conduct and can (having regard to the content of the action and other ideas connected with them) serve as stimuli to the most diverse conduct (including conduct which is socially harmful) and exert an educative influence in the most diverse directions (including directions socially harmful). By virtue, however, of the action of those social psychic processes which evoke the appearance – and define the direction of the development – of ethical impulsive intellectual complexes, the latter, speaking generally, receive such a content – as regards motivation and education – as corresponds with the welfare of society. They act in general in favour of conduct socially desirable and against conduct socially harmful, and educate in the direction of developing and intensifying socially desirable habits and propensities, and of weakening and eradicating those which are socially harmful.

In accordance with its imperative attributive nature, however, the action of law upon human behaviour and the development of the human mind, differs from that of morality (purely imperative ethics) in two important respects.

(1) The attributive nature of the consciousness of legal duty – the consciousness that here is not merely a simple deontological concept of what is due (an obligation which is free in regard to others), but a duty of such a character that the obligation to which we are bound is at the same time owed to another as his due – gives this consciousness a special motivational force, and creates an additional pressure towards the corresponding conduct, not found in morality (where we do not consider as owing from us to others the obligation to which we are bound). *Ceteris paribus*, the attributive or legal consciousness of duty exerts upon conduct a pressure more powerful, and evokes conduct more consistently compliant, than does the purely imperative consciousness of duty (the consciousness of a purely moral duty where there is no right in any other person). That the legal imperative attributive mentality can evoke relatively general and constant observance of the corresponding rules of social

Law and Society

conduct must be recognized as a great advantage of this branch of ethics over the purely imperative morality which has no such motivational force.

(2) The imperative attributive consciousness exerts specific and immediate influence upon our conduct – not only when we experience it as consciousness of our being obligated (of the right of another) but also where we experience it as consciousness of the duty of another with regard to us (of our being endowed with a right as regards that other). Here the urge provoked by the imperative attributive impulsion has the character of an impelling and authoritatively sanctioning stimulus to conduct which corresponds with the content of our right: the corresponding conduct appears to us sanctioned by the higher authority of the attributive norm. And the more intensive the corresponding impulsion, the more powerful the mystic-authoritative character of the attribution, and the more 'sacred' and indubitable our right seems to us, the more powerful is this motivation and the more lively, assured, and decisive is our action.

Motivation originating in consciousness of our right and another's duty we may call active legal motivation, to distinguish it from that originating in consciousness of our legal and moral duty, which we may call passive ethical (legal and moral) motivation. Active ethical motivation manifestly does not exist in the province of morality, it is peculiar to the law in the sense herein established. In general, active legal motivation – side by side with passive motivation – is an essential and necessary factor of social life and social order: without it the latter could not exist as it does now. The present distribution of property, and the corresponding economic order and economic life, are created not only on the basis that members of society respect and observe property rights of others, but also that those others ascribe to themselves corresponding rights and act in conformity therewith.

6. Living Law
by Eugen Ehrlich

From Fundamental Principles of the Sociology of Law [*1912*] *Cambridge, Mass., Harvard University Press (1936) pp. 61-74, 486-93.*

A doctrine which has a great vogue at the present time, and which derives from various sources, seeks to explain the origin of the legal norms, and occasionally also of the other social norms, especially those for morality, by the power of the dominant groups in society, which have established them, and are enforcing them in their own interest. But power over men can be maintained and exercised permanently only by uniting them in associations and prescribing rules of conduct for them within the association, i.e. by organizing them. In this sense the doctrine referred to would be in harmony with that taught here, according to which the social norms are but the order of the human associations.

The question then is by what means do the social associations induce their individual members to obey the norms of the association. There is, certainly, nothing more untenable psychologically than the idea, which has such a vogue, that men refrain from laying violent hands upon other men's property only because they fear the criminal law; that they pay their debts only because they fear that their goods will be levied on. Even at times when penal laws lose their force – as is often the case temporarily in time of war or of domestic disorder – it is always only a very small portion of the population that participates in murder, robbery, theft and plundering; and in times of tranquility most men perform the obligations they have assumed without thinking of levy of execution. From this it does not indeed follow that the great majority of men conform to the norms because they are prompted by an inner impulse; but it does follow that fear of punishment or of levy of execution is not the only consideration that prompts them to do so, quite apart from the fact that there is a sufficiently large number of social norms that threaten the transgressor neither with punishment nor with levy of execution, but which nevertheless are not ineffectual.

Sanction is not a peculiarity of the legal norms. The norms of ethical custom, morality, religion, tact, decorum, etiquette, and fashion would be quite meaningless if they did not exercise a certain amount of coercion. They too constitute the order of the human associations, and it is their specific function to coerce the individual members of the association to submit to the order. All compulsion exercised by the norms is based upon the fact that the individual is never actually an isolated individual; he is enrolled, placed, embedded, wedged, into so many associations that existence outside of these would be unendurable, often even impossible, to him.

All of us then are living within numberless, more or less compactly, occasionally quite loosely, organized associations, and our fate in life will, in the main, be conditioned by the kind of position we are able to achieve within them. It is clear that in this matter there must be a reciprocity of services rendered. It is impossible for the associations to offer something to each of its members unless each individual is at the same time a giver. And in fact all these associations – whether they are organized or un-organized, and whether they are called country, home, residence, religious communion, family, circle of friends, social life, political party, industrial association, or good will of a business – make certain demands in exchange for that which they give; and the social norms which prevail in these communities are nothing more than the universally valid precipitate of the claims which the latter make upon the individual. He therefore who is in need of the support of the circle to which he belongs – and who is not? – does wisely if he conforms, at least in a general way, to its norms. He who refuses to conform to them must face the fact that his conduct will loosen the bonds of solidarity within his own circle. He who persistently refuses obedience has himself loosened the bonds which until now have united him with his associates. He will gradually be deserted, avoided, excluded. Here then in the social association, is the source of the coercive power, the sanction, of all social norms, of law no more than of morality, ethical cutsom, religion, honour, decorum, etiquette, fashion at least as far as the outward observance of the precepts is concerned.

Man therefore conducts himself according to law, chiefly because this is made imperative by his social relations. In this respect the legal norm does not differ from the other norms. The state is not the only association that exercises coercion; there is an untold number of associations in society that exercise it much more forcefully than the state. . .

The reason why the dominant school of legal science so greatly prefers the legal proposition to all other legal phenomena as an object of investigation is that it tacitly assumes that the whole law is found in the legal propositions. It is assumed furthermore that since, at the present time, all legal propositions are to be found in the statutes, where they are readily accessible to anyone, all that is necessary in order to get a knowledge of the law of the present time is to gather the material from the statutes, to ascertain the content of this material by one's own individual interpretation, and to utilize this interpretation for the purposes of juristic literature and judicial decision. Occasionally one meets with the further idea that legal propositions may arise independently of statute. In Germany the usual belief is that they can be found in juristic literature; in France, in judicial decisions. 'Customary law', on the other hand, in the prevailing view, is so unimportant that no effort is being put forth to ascertain its content by scientific method, much less to create methods for its investigation.

To attempt to imprison the law of a time or of a people within the sections of a code is as about as reasonable as to attempt to confine a stream within a pond. The water that is put in the pond is no longer a living stream but a stagnant pool, and but little water can be put in the pond. Moreover, if one considers that the living law had already overtaken and grown away from each one of these codes at the very moment the latter were enacted, and is growing away from them more and more every day, one cannot but realize the enormous extent of this as yet unploughed and unfurrowed field of activity which is being pointed out to the modern legal investigator. It could not be otherwise. The legal propositions are not intended to present a complete picture of the state of the law. The jurist draws them up with a view to existing practical needs, and with a view to what he is interested in for practical reasons.

As a result of the methods employed by modern legal science, the present state of our law is, in a great measure, actually unknown to us. We often know nothing, not only of things that are remote but also things that happen before our very eyes. Almost every day brings some juristic surprise which we owe to a lucky accident, to a peculiar law suit, or to an article in the daily papers. But he who observes life with careful attentiveness knows that these are not isolated occurrences. We are groping in the dark everywhere. And we cannot plead the excuse that the legal historian can avail himself of, i.e. that a bit of the past has been irrecoverably lost. We need but to open our eyes and ears in order to learn everything that is of significance for the law of our time.

In the part of the Austrian code that deals with matrimonial agreements there are four meagre sections which, according to the marginal heading, deal with the matrimonial regime of community of goods. Anyone who has had opportunity of coming into contact with the German peasantry of Austria knows that they live almost exclusively under a matrimonial regime of community of goods. But this matrimonial community of goods, which is the prevailing, freely chosen property regime of the German peasantry in Austria, has nothing in common with the community of goods provided for in the Austrian Civil Code, and the provisions of the Civil Code are never being applied since they are always excluded by a marriage contract formally entered into. What would be the value of a science of law which failed to recognize that the community of goods that the Austrian Civil Code speaks of exists only on paper? What would be the value of a science of law which thinks it is fulfilling its whole task when it ascertains the intent of the law giver, which has been expressed in the above four sections, but does not concern itself with the community of goods, which is based on readily accessible legal documents, and according to which pratically the entire German peasantry of Austria lives?

Again there is the agricultural usufructuary lease. The few provisions contained in the modern codes on the subject, especially in the Austrian and German codes, were for the most part taken from Roman law, and had arisen on the exhausted soil of Italy in the days of the Roman Empire with its system of extensive *latifundia* and an oppressed peasant class. They would be altogether insufficient today. A glance at life will convince us that they are almost never being applied. Their operation is almost always being excluded and they are being replaced by the provisions of contracts of usufructuary lease such as are suitable to modern social and economic conditions, and are being entered into between the lessor and lessee in almost every instance.

The only branch of law the juristic science of which is based not merely incidentally, but throughout, on actual usage is commercial law. The latter has been officially received into juristic science in the form of business custom and usage. The organization of the great landed estate and of the factory, even of the bank, has, to the present day, remained to the jurist a book sealed with seven seals, but the organization of the commercial house he knows, in its main outlines at least, from the Commercial Code. He knows the position of the principal and of the holder of a general power of procurations; of the holder of a mercantile power of agency and of the mercantile employee of the mercantile agent, of the commercial traveller; he knows the significance of the mercantile trade name, of the books of accounts, and of business correspondence. He has a conception of the significance of all these things not only from the economic but also from the legal point of view. And the contract law of modern commercial law has not been taken over from the *corpus iuris*; nor is it a product of the diligent reflection of its authors. What the commercial statutes and commercial codes have to say about buying and selling, about commissions, about forwarding of goods, about the insurance, the freight and the banking business, is actually being practiced somewhere even though, possibly, not always to the extent set forth therein. Likewise many commercial institutions, particularly the Exchange, have been properly furrowed and ploughed by jurists. The fact that much hard work remains to be done in every nook and corner is caused less in this sphere than in others by the lack of understanding and appreciation of the actual realities and more by the difficulties inherent in the subject matter and by its extremely rapid development. The gigantic organization of the production of goods which is taking place before our very eyes in trusts and cartels, all the modern achievements in commerce, the numerous new inventions, lead to new formations at every moment, and open new fields of labour for the jurist.

This then is the *living* law in contradistinction to that which is being enforced in the courts and other tribunals. The living law is the law which dominates life itself even though it has not been posited in legal propositions. The source of our knowledge of the law is, first, the modern legal document; secondly, direct observation of life, of commerce, of customs and usages, and of all associations, not only of those that the law has recognized but also of those that it has overlooked and passed by, indeed even of those that it has disapproved.

7. Law as an Integrative Mechanism
by Harry C. Bredemeier

From 'Law as an integrative mechanism' in W. M. Evan, Law and Sociology, New York, The Free Press (1962) pp. 74–86.

The framework I employ is that developed by Talcott Parsons and his colleagues, particularly as stated in *Economy and Society*. This framework posits four major functional processes to be observed in a social system: adaptation, goal pursuance, pattern maintenance, and integration. Parsons and Smelser have identified adaptation with economic processes, and goal pursuance with political processes. Pattern maintenance processes may very roughly ... be identified with what we ordinarily refer to as socialization. Integrative processes are not so neatly defined with familiar patterns; but I propose to identify them in part with 'the law', that is, with legal processes.

The function of the law is the orderly resolution of conflicts. As this implies 'the law' (the clearest model of which I shall take to be the court system) is brought into operation after there has been a conflict. Someone claims that his interests have been violated by someone else. The court's task is to render a decision that will prevent the conflict – and all potential conflicts like it – from disrupting productive co-operation. In order to do this, the court needs three things – or, in the language of Parsons and his colleagues, the court is dependent upon three kinds of 'inputs'.

In the first place the court needs an analysis of cause and effect relationships. It needs a way of ascertaining both the *past* relationship between the alleged act of the defendant and the alleged injury of the plaintiff, and the probable *future* relationship between the decision and the activities of the defendant and plaintiff (and all persons similarly situated). I suggest that this input comes from the adaptive system, in return for an immediate output of 'organic', as distinguished from 'mechanical', solidarity.

In the second place, as is implied by the phrase 'productive co-operation', the court needs a conception of what the division of labour is *for*; what the goals of the system are, what state of affairs is to be created or maintained by the exercise of power. In other words, it needs standards by which to *evaluate* the conflicting claims and the anticipated effects of a decision on the role structure. I suggest that this is the primary input from the goal pursuance or political system, in exchange for which the court's primary output is 'interpretation' of the meaning in a particular case of the abstract language of legislation, or the even more abstract language of the society's 'ideals'.

Finally, in order to perform its function, the court needs a willingness on the part of potential litigants to *use* the court as a conflict resolving mechanism. This motivation to accept the court and abide by its decisions is an output from the pattern maintenance or socialization system, and the court's immediate return output is what is termed 'justice'.

The Law and Adaptive Processes
Adaptation refers essentially to the production of instrumental facilities for coping with obstacles to the achievement of system goals ... I want to conceive of adaptive structures, at least for Western societies, as those of science and technology.

When the courts receive a signal, in the shape of a law suit, that there has been a clash of interest, the first requirement is 'to understand it'. This means two things. First, it means discovering the factual connection between the alleged harm and the event alleged to have caused it. Second, it means discovering the functional context of the action of the plaintiff and defendant – that is to say, (a) the roles they are performing, (b) the functional significance for the system of these roles, and (c) the necessity (for efficient performance) of playing the roles in the manner in which the litigants had in fact been playing them. These 'discoveries' are made on the basis of certain cognitive generalizations, beliefs, and theories concerning cause and effect relationships; and they are made with the aid of techniques for ascertaining 'truth'. The elaborate equipment and techniques of crime detection in laboratories; the statistics contained in a 'Brandeis-type' brief; the mortality tables used in calculating potential earning power in order to assess the 'damages' of a death; psychiatric examinations; public opinion polls showing the amount of confusion existing between trademarks or brand names – all these are examples of inputs to the legal system from the adaptive system of society. Not only technique and factual knowledge are involved in this input, but also cognitive theories regarding the necessity of certain kinds of behaviour if certain functions are to be efficiently performed. An important example of such an input is the use by the courts of classical economic theory. In all areas of decision making, the courts (more or less systematically) use as a decision making criterion, the expected impact of a decision on productive efficiency. In tort law, for example, such perennial issues as the distinction among trespassers, licencees and invitees, or the problem of the immunity of governmental agencies or charitable institutions from liability for their negligence, are nearly always debated in the context of the question, 'what will be the impact on people's ability to carry out their responsibility?'

The court utilizes inputs of knowledge . . . to make a decision. The decision, which will of course be binding on all persons in the same class or category as the particular litigants at bar, is an output to the adaptive system of the society. It is an output of *organization* or structure. The decision asserts a set of rights, duties, liabilities, exposures, immunities and privileges that either alter or reinforce the organization of roles and the division of labour. For example, the extension of the protection of the fourteenth amendment to corporations, regarded as 'legal persons', vividly affected the adaptive machinery of the society.

In Durkheim's terminology, the court's integrative contribution to the adaptive system may be regarded as an output of organic solidarity. That is, the court's contribution to adaptation is an imposition of rights and obligations *in the interests of efficient organization*. It is dependent for this, however, on knowledge of what efficient organization *is*, and what can contribute to it.

The Law and the Polity
In modern democratic societies the prototype of the sovereign may be taken to be the legislature. Legislative determination of policy – the actual uses to which the power is put – is one of the primary sources of the law's conception of goals, or standards for evaluating the 'efficiency' of a given or anticipated role structure. The legislature's primary input into the legal system is, in other words, a description of the ideal state of affairs for which social resources are to be mobilized through the exercise of power. The immediate corresponding output of the legal system is the *application* of general policy statements to the specific conflict at hand. This, of course, means that the courts can by no means be passive or mechanical 'implementers' of the legislature policy; the

statute must be interpreted, and its interpretation is a creative act, giving real effect to the abstract language of the legislature. It is an indispensable adjunct to the legislative exercise of power. In return for the output of interpretation, the legal system receives from the polity a secondary input, the sanction of *enforcement*. Judicial decisions become binding on the litigants through the power of the state; and – also to be included in the concept of enforcement – it is by the legislature that the courts are *empowered* to resolve disputes and are given the facilities for doing so: courthouses, judgeships, salaries, and so on.

These interchanges, of course, do not occur in any automatic or inevitable way. The transactions between the legal system and the polity may break down. Courts may 'interpret' the life out of legislative policies; or they may even ignore a statute. In turn, the polity may refuse to enforce legal decisions, and may fail to give any clear direction of public policy as a guide to judicial action. These interchanges are often precariously balanced ... When the exchanges are not completed smoothly, some readjustment is likely to occur, in the first place; and in the second place there will be repercussions in other sub-systems of the society.

The exchange of policy directives for interpretation of such policies is especially susceptible to disruption because the legislature, subject to the influence of whimsical shifts in public opinion and to the private demands of various interests groups, often enact contradictory policies. The court in such cases must choose between different policies of the state ... That the courts must choose between conflicting policies means they have a secondary kind of output to make to the polity in exchange for the secondary input of enforcement. In a sense, the court becomes a legitimator of legislative decisions; and this adds to the polity's dependence on a successful completion of the exchange.

The Law and Pattern Maintenance

Presupposed so far is a third condition necessary if the legal system is to contribute to integration through the resolution of conflicts. This is the obvious fact that conflicts must be brought to the court's attention. People must be motivated to turn to the law for protection of their interests, and this implies that they must feel that the law will in fact give them justice. It is thus in the offer of 'justice' that the legal system makes its major output, in exchange for the input of motivations to accept the court as a problem solving structure. To do the proverbial rushing in, I want to define 'justice' for present purposes simply as a subjective feeling one has got what's coming to him, that one has received his 'due'. This amounts to saying that internalized expectations have been met.

It is perhaps in connection with these interchanges between the legal system and the pattern maintenance system that there are the most familiar breakdowns ... [There is] a feeling that the court's conceptions of legitimate expectations are very different from one's own. And this is likely to be true, partly because of differences between the reference groups of judges and clients, and partly because of the nature of one important mechanism relied upon by the court to ensure conformity to institutionalized expectations. The mechanism I refer to is the doctrine of *stare decisis*, the doctrine that the courts are bound by their own precedents, and that lower courts are bound by the old decisions of higher courts ... The 'certainty and predictability' of the law, so important to acceptance of the law as an integrative mechanism, is sought then, by the law's own moral commitment to precedent. This commitment, though, interferes with another condition necessary for public acceptance of the legal process: a flexibility sufficient to adapt to changed circumstances, new interests, and different dangers and liabilities attendant upon social change ... Changed community sentiments regarding the meaning of 'justice' tend not so readily to be reflected in judicial decisions.

A related aspect of *stare decisis* also contributes to the law's lack of receptivity to new claims. This is the persistence, to some extent, of the doctrine that only those interests will be recognized that were previously recognized. That is to say, new needs for which court protection is sought may be dismissed by the court with the deadly sentence, 'Plaintiff has failed to state a cause of action', which means that he has failed to demonstrate that any court in the past has even been willing to listen to evidence on such a violation of an expectation. The central condition responsible for such dismissal seems to be that the court's *manifest* function is to apply an already existing law; the latent function of resolving disputes *efficiently* is seldom recognized.

Two additional mechanisms by which the court's output of justice may be kept in fairly close balance with community sentiments should, however, be noted. One is the jury system. Although nominally only a 'trier of facts' when the facts are in dispute, the jury probably tries a good many things besides facts behind its closed doors. Without overt changes in the legal doctrines, then, justice – according to the community's views – may nonetheless be served, although, to be sure, in a mysterious and somewhat 'chancy' way. A second such mechanism is the system of communication internal to the legal system itself. I include in this both law schools and the extensive commentaries and criticisms of judicial opinions in law journals ... To the unknown degree to which the journals are considered by the bench and bar, the legal system may be kept in fairly close touch with prevailing community sentiments – depending also, of course, on the degree to which academic jurists are themselves in touch with them.

The fact remains, however, that 'the law' is for many people something to be avoided if at all possible. There is not a very good market for the law's output of justice; and – the other side of the same coin – the law is not widely regarded as the place to take one's conflicts, except as a last resort. A deeper reason for this than any so far considered may be related to the fact that, almost by definition, 50% of the people involved in litigation must have their expectations violated. Someone has to lose ... There are two related characteristics of the law that contribute to making its output of 'justice' unpalatable. One is the fact that the legal system tends to have written into it the assumption that in any dispute one side is right and the other side is wrong. The adversary system is built on this assumption and helps to reinforce it; and the court is ordinarily empowered only to decide a winner and a loser – not to find a way to help the loser adjust to his loss or to avoid in the future the action that led to the loss, or to alter the conditions that led to the loser's behaving as he did. The second difficulty is related to this. An assumption implicit in the operation of the law is that one's rights and obligations have been authoritatively stated, individuals have only one mode of adaptation available to them: acceptance. The assumption in other words is that *learning* is the only response to a deprivation. In fact, of course, there is good reason to believe that learning – that is, a reorganization of the individual's personality system so as smoothly to adapt to the new reality – is not even a very likely response, except under special conditions.

8. Role-Strain and the Law

by Talcott Parsons

From 'The Law and Social Control' *in* W. M. *Evan*, Law and Sociology, *New York, The Free Press (1962) pp. 64–9.*

The severity and difficulty of the problems of conflict between mutually contradictory statutes is well known to lawyers. Anglo-American law relies heavily on the processes of judicial decision and, through these, the accumulation of precedents. But the problem of maintaining the internal consistency of the precedent system, even to a tolerable degree, is formidable. Furthermore, there must be orientation to the authority of the basic constitutional documents, which naturally means continual re-interpretation of them, and to the positive acts of legislation that are continually being produced.

The problems faced by our legal profession in this respect may be compared with two other types of situations. First there is an analogy to the professions concerned with the application of scientific knowledge, such as engineering and medicine. In these cases it is a sociologically central fact that the available knowledge is far from adequate to cover the practical needs. Nevertheless, established scientific knowledge does constitute a highly stable point of reference. Hence the 'authority' of the relevant professional groups for interpretations can always be referred to such established knowledge. This is, moreover, a basis of reference that is steadily growing in stability. The other type of case is very different, namely, that in which there is a fountainhead of authority beyond which there is no appeal. The Roman Catholic Church is perhaps the most conspicuous large-scale example, though the Soviet Communist Party is in certain respects similar. The essential point is that the 'correct doctrine' is assumed not to be dependent on any human will, but to be infallibly specific and definite, with a clearly authorized human agency for its implementation.

As compared with both of these our secular law is considerably looser in its points of reference. The Constitution is considerably less clear cut than the authoritative canons of the church and even the Supreme Court is less 'canonical' than is the papacy. The legal profession, then, has to maintain difficult balances in a tradition that is in itself exceedingly complex, that is applied to very complex and changing conditions, subject to severe pressures from interest groups, authoritatively based only on very general and partly ambiguous documents, and subject to change within considerable limits by the more or less arbitrary and unpredictable 'will of the people'. We know from analysis of a great many such situations that the assumption of responsibility for such functions where within considerable limits no clearly 'right' answers can be attained is a source of strain. We also know that in relation to such strains tendencies to various types of 'deviant' behaviour are likely to develop. One of these is probably yielding to expediency, through financial temptations and other pressures from clients . . . [T]hat the tendency exists to abdicate responsibilities in the service of their own financial 'self-interest' or 'peace' in the face of severe pressure can scarcely be doubted.

A second type of deviation consists in exaggerated legal 'formalism', the tendency to insist on what is conceived to be the 'letter' of the law without due regard to a 'reasonable' balance of considerations. Legal 'technicalities' may of course be, and often are, invoked as tactical weapons in various types of procedures . . . but apart from their instrumental use, undoubtedly there is a tendency in many legal quarters to exaggerate the importance of being formally 'correct' down to the last detail. In psychological terms, the legal profession probably has at least its share, if not more, of 'compulsive personalities' as compared with other occupations. The essential point is that this tendency in the profession is not simply a result of certain types of people 'happening' to be lawyers, but grows out of the situation in which lawyers as a group are placed.

A third type of deviant tendency prominent in the law may be said to be the 'sentimental' exaggeration of the substantive claims of clients or other 'interests' represented by the lawyer. Thus corporation lawyers may often become more lyrical about the rights of 'property' than the main tradition of the law warrants, or labour lawyers about 'human rights' and the like. Or, to take another example, the lawyer who identifies with an injured client to the extent of fighting very hard to get for him what, on cooler considera-tion, look like highly excessive damages, is guilty of 'sentimentality' in this sense. . . .

[T]he member of a profession stands *between* two major aspects of our social structure; in the case of the law, between public authority and its norms and the private individual or group whose conduct or intentions may or may not be in accord with the law. In the case of the physician it is between the worlds of sickness and of health; he himself is defined as not sick, but he participates more intimately with the sick than any other category of well-person. In the case of the teacher it is between the world of childhood – or, on advanced levels, of relative 'untrainedness' – and the full status of being trained. The professions in this sense may, sociologically, be regarded as what we call 'mechanisms of social control'. They either, like the teaching profession, help to 'socialize' the young, to bring them into accord with the expectations of full membership in the society, or like the medical profession bring them *back* into accord when they have deviated. The legal profession may be presumed to do this and two other things: first to forestall deviance by advising the client in ways that will keep him better in line, and also by 'cooling him off'; second, if it comes to a serious case, to implement the procedure by which the socially sanctioned decision about the status of the client is arrived at. . . . [A]nalysis has shown that effective performance of these functions depends on whether the role in which they were performed meets certain broad sociological conditions.

In the first place, in the situations of strain, scope seems to be required for a certain permissiveness for expression of attitudes and sentiments that, in ordinary circumstances, would not be acceptable. If this permissiveness is to operate effectively it must be associated with relief from anxiety. In order to be capable, psychologically, of 'getting things off his chest' a person must be assured that, within certain limits, otherwise ordinary or possible negative sanctions will not operate. In general this implies a protected situation. The confidential character of the lawyer's relation to his client provides just such a situation. The client can talk freely to an understanding and knowledgeable ear without fear of immediate repercussions. What is relayed beyond this confidential relationship is selected through the screen of the lawyer's judgement. To some extent the same kind of thing occurs in other phases of the legal process, notably the hearing by judges of some evidence in chambers.

In the case of the law the situations of strain with which it deals focus to a large extent on conflicts. One of the very important aspects of legal procedure is to provide mechanisms for the 'cooling off' of the passions aroused in such situations. Undoubtedly the private attorney does a great deal of this. Like the physician who helps his client to 'face reality', to confine his claim to what he has a real chance of making 'stand up' in court or in direct negotiation, and to realize and emotionally to accept the fact that the other fellow may have a case too. The element of delay in bringing things to a head, though doubtless often carried too far because of crowding of court calendars and the like, may have a similar function. The important thing here is that a person under strain should have some opportunity for 'tension release' that is treated as institutionally legitimate.

Secondly, it is a feature of the types of situation I am thinking of that there is some assurance of 'support' or 'acceptance' within broader limits than would otherwise be the case. The physician in one sense tends to be particularly 'tolerant' of human beings; he does not judge them morally, but tries to 'help' them as best he can. Certain features of legal practice also seem to fit into this pattern. Although there are expectations that the attorney will not consciously attempt to 'get off' a person he knows to be guilty of a crime, there is on the other hand the presumption that the client is entitled to a 'fair trial' not only in the formal sense, but a hearing from his attorney, and any help within the bounds of reason and professional ethics. The lawyer is not easily shocked in the way the general public may be; he is familiar with the complexities of human living and ready to 'give a break' to the person who has become involved in a difficult situation.

But while the lawyer tends to be both permissive and supportive in his relation with his clients, there is another side to the picture. He is, after all, schooled in the great tradition of the law. As a member of a great profession he accepts responsibility for its integrity, and his position in society focusses that responsibility upon him. His function in relation to clients is by no means only to 'give them what they want' but often to resist their pressures and get them to realize some of the hard facts of their situation, not only with reference to what they can, even with clever legal help, expect to 'get away with' but with reference to what the law will permit them to do. In this sense, then, the lawyer stands as a kind of buffer between the illegitimate desires of his client and the social interest. Here in a sense he 'represents' the law rather than the client. His tendency under certain circumstances to give way to the pressures of client interest is one way in which, as noted above, he can be 'deviant'. But in this connection he can retreat into the formalism of the law as a means of resisting these pressures. From the present point of view the significant point is that *both* these functions are combined in a particular way in the same agency.

9. Legality
by Philip Selznick

From Law, Society and Industrial Justice, *New York, Russell Sage (1969)* pp. 4–17.

If we are to study justice in industry, or in any other specialized institution, we must first be clear that law is found in many settings; it is not uniquely associated with the state. We need a concept of law that is sufficiently general to embrace legal experience within 'private' associations, but not so general as to make law lose its distinctive character or become equivalent to social control. . .

Social science is best served when definitions are 'weak' and concepts are 'strong'. A weak definition is inclusive; its conditions are easily met. A strong concept is more demanding in that, for example, it may identify attributes that are latent as well as manifest, or offer a model of what the phenomenon is like in a fully developed (or deteriorated) state. Accordingly in what follows the word law is used in a way that is general enough to embrace all legal experience, however various or rudimentary. At the same time, law and legal process are understood as pointing to a larger achievement and a greater elaboration. . .

We should see law as endemic in all institutions *that rely for social control on formal authority and rule making.* Laws so understood is analytically distinct from the narrower view of public government, but it is also distinct from the broader idea of social control. The middle ground we seek is occupied by Fuller, for example, when he interprets law as 'the enterprise of subjecting human conduct to the governance of rules'. The phrase 'governance of rules' must be understood as shorthand for a system of order that contains specialized mechanisms for certifying rules as authoritative and for safeguarding rule making and rule applying from the intrusion of other forms of direction and control ... To equate law and the state impoverishes sociological analysis, because the concept of law should be available for the study of any setting in which human conduct is subject to explicit rule making; and when we deny the place of law in specialized institutions *we withhold from the private setting the funded experience of the political community in matters of governance.* To say that law is generic is a necessary first step in applying legal theory to specialized institutions. Our second step invokes the perspective of moral evolution. We want to ask what it means to 'legalize' an institution, that is, to infuse its mode of governance with the aspiration and constraints of a legal order. To do this we should first understand the view that law is intimately associated with the realization of values.

In the discussion of law there is an ever renewed conflict between those who see it as a functional necessity and others who invest it with hope and promise. The former accept law as given, as fact, at best as an instrument of practical problem solving. For the legal idealist, on the other hand, law connotes a larger moral achievement.

When law is conceived as a functional necessity, the focus tends to be on order and control. Law is summoned by elementary urgencies: keep the peace, settle disputes, suppress deviance. Authority pays its way, and redeems its coercive sins, if it can establish tranquility, facilitate co-operative action, and uphold the mores whatever they may be. This might be called the *minimalist* view of what law is and does. For it 'justice' is not a compelling symbol and at an extreme may even be scorned as the refuge of hopelessly muddled men.

It should be noted that order and control are values of a sort. They are certainly 'things prized', and would satisfy almost any minimum definition of value, such as 'the object of any interest'. But order and control are values in a weak sense. They cannot of themselves sustain personal or group identity. They do not readily serve as vehicles of loyalty and commitment.

The alternative is to think of law as instituting a *kind* of order and a *kind* of social control. This approach asks more of the legal system and yields a richer sense of value. The contribution of law to social order is not lost, *but a closer concern for the continuum of means and ends appears.* Where there is fidelity to law, order is not to be purchased at any price. Rather, law imposes limits on social control. For example, the commitment of police to lawfulness is always to some extent a restraint on the means they can use to prevent crime or apprehend criminals. The greater the self-consciousness about law, and the more law is looked to for the vindication of rights, the more apparent is a tension between law and order.

The normative concept of law, or of any similar phenomenon, turns attention from necessity to fulfilment. Instead of concentrating on the minimum functions of law, or on the minimum conditions that signify its emergence, the emphasis shifts to law's civilizing potential. A logically similar problem appears when the idea of 'education' is discussed. A minimalist concept of education is content to equate it with the transmission of skills, including social skills, and of a received tradition. A more expansive and normative view embraces the contribution of education to moral sensibility.

A superficially attractive way of resolving the conceptual ambiguity would restrict law, education, friendship, or literature in minimalist terms, then specify additional attributes that warrant the designation 'good' law, 'good' education, 'good' literature, 'good' friendship, and so forth. This solution has merit, but it is defective if the normative attributes are taken to be merely subjective preferences. For that lends an arbitrary cast to the phenomenon's 'high state' or 'excellence'; as if this were a mere matter of likes and dislikes and had no intrinsic relation to the natural characteristics or the social dynamics of the institution or relationship. Although a definition of law should be spacious and inclusive, it ought to contain a theoretical warrant for treating at least a *strain* toward legal development as objectively grounded. This is accomplished when law is defined as a system of authoritative rules and decision making.

A normative theory of law or friendship specifies *latent* values that inhere in the phenomenon. These values serve as resources for critical evaluation, not from the standpoint of the observer's preference, but in the light of the inner order of the phenomenon, including what the participants are likely to experience as deprivation or satisfaction. . .

The idea that law connotes a special kind of order is implicitly accepted when we pay our respects to 'the rule of law'. In English *a* rule of law is a specific norm or guide to decision. The phrase is meant to be descriptive and value free but *the* rule of law is a more connotative and value laden idea. It refers to aspirations that distinguish a developed legal order from a system of subordination to naked power.

The impulse to create a legal order is, in the first instance, a practical one. From the standpoint of the rulers, power is made more secure when it is legitimate; from the standpoint of the ruled, fears of oppression are allayed. Thus legalization is rooted in the problems of collective life. It is not, in its primitive forms, an expression of social idealism. It is obvious, moreover, that communities survive and even flourish without going very far toward legalization. We do not suppose that the values associated with law must necessarily be realized. Other values, for example, religion or aesthetic values, may define a world more appealing.

To understand what legalization entails for the life of a political community or a specialized institution, however, we should consider its ideal or developed state. In what follows we shall briefly explicate what is meant by 'legality', which we take to be a synonym for 'the rule of law'.

The essential element in the rule of law is the restraint of official power by rational principles of civic order. Where this ideal exists, no power, including the democratic majority, is immune from criticism or entirely free to follow its own bent, however well intentioned it may be. Legality imposes an environment of constraint, of tests to be met, standards to be observed, ideals to be fulfilled. Legality has to do mainly with *how* policies and rules are made and applied rather than with their content.

The effort to see in law a set of standards, an internal basis for criticism and reconstruction, leads us to a true *grundnorm* – the idea that a legal order faithful to itself seeks *progressively to reduce the degree of arbitrariness in positive law and its administration.* By 'positive law' we mean those public obligations that have been defined by duly constituted mechanisms, such as the legislature, court, administrative agency, or referendum. . .

If the reduction of arbitrariness is central to legality, three corollaries may be suggested:

Legality is a variable achievement. A developed legal order is the product of continuing effort and posits values that are always incompletely fulfilled. We can unblushingly speak of more or less legality, meaning nothing more obscure than that some systems of rules, and some modes of decision, are less arbitrary than others. A major topic in legal sociology is the study of empirical conditions that reduce or exacerbate the arbitrary element in making or applying rules. For example, studies of police discretion locate systematic sources of arbitrary decision in the handling of juveniles;

'treatment' is seen as a cover for unsupervised control; the low visibility of decisions in administrative agencies tends to encourage self-serving discretion.

The reduction of arbitrariness cannot be equated with the elaboration of formal rules and procedures. 'Formal justice' equalizes parties and makes decisions predictable; it is therefore a major contribution to the mitigation of arbitrary rule. But legal 'correctness' has its own costs. Like any other technology, it is vulnerable to the divorce of means and ends. When this occurs, legality degenerates into legalism.

Properly understood, the concept of legality is more critical than celebrationist. To say that legality is a variable achievement is to leave room for the conclusion that, at any given time, the system of positive law is 'congealed injustice'. An affirmative approach to legal values need not accept the defensive rhetoric of men in power. On the contrary it offers principles of criticism to evaluate the shortcomings of the existing systems of rules and practices.

Legality extends to administration as well as adjudication. Wherever there is official conduct the possibility of arbitrary decision arises. That conduct may be far removed from rule making or adjudication, at least in spirit or purpose. It may be a practical effort to get a job done. Yet the question of legitimacy – of power exercised *in the light* of governing norms – is always appropriate. Furthermore, the problem of arbitrariness is at issue whenever rights are determined, something that may occur quite incidentally, in the course of administrative decision and policy making. Thus any official decision, whether it be a purchase, a hiring, a development of police power, or any other active effort to accomplish a defined social purpose, may be criticized in the name of legality.

Legality applies to public participation as well as to the conduct of officials. The general public contributes to legality, not only through the quality of democratic decision making, but also insofar as it has the competence, and recognizes the duty, of criticizing authority. To be sure, there must be public respect for law, and appropriate self-restraint, but in a vital legal order something more is wanted than submission to constituted authority. A military establishment places very great emphasis on obedience to lawful commands, yet such a setting is hardly a model of institutionalized legality. So too, a conception of law as the manifestation of awesome authority encourages feelings of deference and is compatible with much arbitrary rule. In a community that aspires to a high order of legality obedience to law is not submissive compliance. The obligation to obey the law is closely tied to the defensibility of the rules themselves and of the official decisions that enforce them.

10. Social Engineering
by Roscoe Pound

From Jurisprudence, *5 vols, St. Paul, Minn.,* West Publishing Company (1959) vol. 1, pp. 350-8.

Sociological jurists seek to enable and to compel law making, whether legislative or judicial or administrative, and also the development, interpretation, and application of legal precepts, to take more complete and intelligent account of the social facts upon which law must proceed and to which it is to be applied. In different parts of the world they are insisting upon some or all of eight points.

(1) *Study of the actual social effects of legal institutions, of legal precepts, and of legal doctrines.* What Kantorowicz said a generation ago still holds true: 'Advise one . . . to read a section of the German civil code in the following way: let him ask himself with respect to each statement . . . what harms would social life undergo if instead of this statement the opposite were enacted. And then let him turn to all textbooks, commentaries, monographs, and reports of decisions and see how many questions of this sort he will find answered and how many he will find even put. . . For instance, we only know that the civil code governs five forms of matrimonial property regime, but we have not the least suggestion in what numerical relation and in what geographical sub-divisions the several forms occur now in social life.' Ehrlich in his seminar for living law was the pioneer in this connection.

(2) *Sociological study in preparation for law making.* The accepted scientific method in preparing for law making has been to study other legislation analytically. Comparative legislation has been

taken to be the best foundation for wise law making. Comparative legislation by comparison of legislative texts is still advocated by leading authorities ... but it is not enough to compare the texts of the laws and to consider the abstract justice of their content. It is even more important to study their social operation and the effects which they produce in action.

(3) *Study of the means of making legal precepts effective in action.* This subject has been neglected in the past. The analytical school was interested only in the logical consistency of the rule with the content of other rules. It considered that the state must give the rule effect by force. If it did not the trouble was not with the rule but with the state or its executive. The historical school assumed that the rule had evolved spontaneously from the life of the people and hence the working would take care of itself. If it did not, that merely proved that experience had not been rightly formulated. The philosophical school in the last century considered that the abstract justice of the rule gave it efficacy. Hence one need only ask how far its content was abstractly just. If it was not, there was no matter if the rule did fail of effect. Sociological jurists insist that we must look at law functionally. We must inquire how it operates, since the life of law is in its application and enforcement. It is imperative to have serious scientific study of how to make our huge annual output of legislation and judicial law making effective in action.

(4) *Study of juridical method: psychological study of the judicial, administrative, legislative and juristic process as well as philosophical study of the ideals.* This is one of the main items in the Realist programme. But studies of how judges, law makers, and jurists actually develop legal materials as grounds of decision, as the basis of statutes and as the basis of doctrines, of what determines their starting points, their choice of materials, and the direction of their reasoning from analogy, need to be made from more than one standpoint.

(5) *A sociological legal history: that is, study not merely of how doctrines have evolved, considered solely as legal materials, but study also of what social effects the doctrines of the law have produced in the past, and how they have produced them.* Legal history has dealt with precepts and doctrines in connection with political rather than in connection with social history. Historical

jurists in the nineteenth century commonly distinguished the external history of a legal system from its internal history, meaning thereby a distinction between its institutions as political institutions and its doctrines looked at from a historical philosophical standpoint. Sociological jurists call for a legal history which shall show us: (1) how or how far the law of the past grew out of the social, economic, and psychological conditions; (2) how it accommodated itself to them; (3) how far we can proceed today on the basis of the law of the past or in disregard of it with well grounded expectations of producing the results desired . . .

(6) *Recognition of the importance of individualized application of legal precepts – of reasonable and just solution of individual cases.* This has been sacrificed too often in the immediate past in the attempt to bring about an impossible degree of certainty. What is called for is study of a system of individualization of application. This involves study of the relation between the judicial process and the administrative process.

(7) *In common law countries, a Ministry of Justice.* In America, our so-called Departments of Justice are but offices for legal advice to state officers, for representation of the state in its civil litigation, and for advocacy in criminal causes – chiefly in the courts of review. In the federal government, the Department of Justice is more. There is a well organized prosecuting bureau. But nowhere is it adequately organized to study the functioning of our legal institutions, the application and enforcement of law, the cases in which and reasons for which it fails to do justice, or to do complete justice, the new situations which arise continually and the means of meeting them, what legislation achieves its purpose and what does not and why, and thus to give expert and intelligent guidance to those who frame and those who administer our laws. In the rural, agricultural society of the past, the judiciary committees of the two houses of the legislature could do efficiently so much of this as was needed. Today, even if our crowded legislative sessions allowed the time, no legislative committee is competent to do the highly specialized work required. In consequence, commissions are provided from time to time to study particular subjects. But their work is not co-ordinated, there is no continuity in what they do, and the whole process is wasteful, expensive, and ineffective. In practice in the United States much of the preparation for legislation is done by private foundations and

voluntary associations. A large part is done also by business and trade associations framing and pressing measures in their own interest. The results are apt to take the form of partial tinkering with subjects requiring comprehensive treatment or to be one-sided and partial.

(8) *Finally, the end, towards which the foregoing points are but some of the means, is to make effort more effective in achieving the purpose of legal order.*

11. Understanding Legal Thinking
by Vilhelm Aubert

From 'The Structure of Legal Thinking' in Legal Essays in Honour of Frede Castberg, *Oslo, Universitetsforlaget (1963) pp. 41–53.*

Natural science, the biological sciences of man, and to a large extent even the social sciences, psychology and sociology, attempt to establish invariant relationships between phenomena. The independent as well as the dependent variables in these schemes of thought are, as far as possible, classified in general categories. This aspect of scientific procedure can properly be termed 'economy of thought', an economy which is bought at the cost of some lack of realism in the description of the unique event. In spite of the cost, the ideal within these branches of science appears to be represented by the laws of Newtonian physics, whereby an enormous number of events are made predictable, although not in their detailed appearance, by the establishment of a few simple and generalizable initial conditions. Many statements in legal debates, in the doctrinal literature and in court records, might make one believe that this ideal is also sought after in the realm of law. One of the most frequently reiterated purposes of the legal system is to promote the predictability of the consequences of actions, predictability in interaction between citizens, and more specifically, predictability of official behaviour. . . . A certain distinction must be drawn between the thinking in practical legal work and in the scholarly work of the doctrinal jurists. Obviously, those who are engaged in making decisions on current problems, whether on general policies or on particular cases, may have to adopt *ad hoc* solutions and formulations, without being able to consider thoroughly whether these decisions fit perfectly in a scheme of generalization developed to maximize predictability. For it is quite clear that predictability is not the sole aim of law. The doctrinal jurist, working on a scholarly basis, may concentrate more systematically on the task of establishing general relationships between operative facts and legal consequences. Nevertheless, the same factors which counteract a maximizing of this trend in practical legal work will also counteract the maximizing of predictability and generality in scholarly expositions. A doctrinal jurist who goes too far in the direction of scientific systematization, will inevitably become less realistic, in the sense that his theories become insensitive to the variations and nuances which characterize the law in action. Or, to be more precise: the loss in realism will become too great to warrant the advantages inherent in his overly neat system. For his 'consumers' deal with particulars on which they must not be misled, even if they should get the right advice on the average.

There are aspects of legal ethics which make it inadvisable for the practical lawyer to go wrong in specific cases, even if he turns out to be right on the average. The physician, no doubt, faces the same difficulty, but the problem seems to be even more pointed in law. Thus, the doctrinal jurist must to a large extent be true to the scientific deficiencies of practical legal thinking even in his own scholarly expositions, so as not to mislead his readers into overlooking the hard-to-systematize nuances and loop-holes of the law in action, or into disregarding the unexpected and the possibility of modifying the status quo. It is an interesting example of a field of social study where the scientific discipline is to some extent bound by the structure of thinking among the subject of his study: the practical jurists.

We may now raise the question whether this deficiency in practical legal thinking with respect to the goal of thought economy and maximal generality of propositions is merely a result of inadequate time of preparation, insufficient information, etc. In other words, is this particular kind of deficiency really considered a deficiency, to be overcome as far as possible? To some extent, yes. But a closer inspection, especially of the activities of the courts, may lead one to believe that there are strong reasons why the judges should not want to make their own behavior maximally predictable. If that is so, it will also have consequences for legislation as well as for doctrinal expositions on a scholarly basis. The literature style of judicial opinion is definitely closer to the humanist tradition of the story-teller than to the rigorously systematic exposition of the natural scientist. It is quite obvious that much that could be done to standard-ize and make uniform the verdicts of the courts has been left undone. Why is that so? To explain it by sloppiness, lack of attention and interest seems inappropriate, considering the amount of care which otherwise goes into legal policy and juridical work. Neither does it seem adequate to explain it simply by the irrelevancy of being more systematic and more cumulative. From certain points of view such a development would be eminently relevant and highly desirable. We are thus led to believe that there are positive reasons why legal decisions are made less predictable than would be dictated by necessity. Some of these reasons are fairly obvious. Next to predict-ability, there is another goal of legal systems, the achievement of concrete justice in individual cases. To combine the need for predict-ability with the need for individual justice requires either super-human omniscience or a willingness to limit justice to simple, abstract criteria.

If the style of legal decisions had been such as to make for a maximum of clarity and generality, there would be a constant danger that the verdict, although considered just in individual cases, would raise expectations with respect to the outcome in new cases, which could not be fulfilled without violating considerations of concrete justice. It is possible, nay likely, that the optimum combination of predictability and justice has not been reached, and that the courts could move toward more predictability without violating justice. But here we must consider the inadequate informa-tion and foresight available to the courts in these very complex matters which pertain to the future. In such a situation, where the consequences of the verdicts are necessarily hard to predict, the safest strategy for the judge is to hide some of his footprints, so as not to commit himself and other judges beyond the minimum necessary. In other words: because he lacks omniscience, and because he is under pressure not to make just decisions more difficult in the future, he must show caution in making his and his colleagues' behavior predictable.

In the realm of law any prediction has a normative tinge; it implies a demand that expectations should be fulfilled. The system, of legal thought must in a certain sense be kept open. It must not be submitted to any rigorous test of falsification, for falsification would mean something more than that a theory was wrong. It would mean that responsible legal agents had made wrong or even illegal decisions. This may be one of the most profound reasons behind the apparent difference between legal and scientific thinking, with respect to the handling of generality and predictability. For the scientist the crux of his method is to make predictions that can, occasionally, be proven false.[1] Such falsification is no disproof of his merit as a scientist. On the contrary, it proves that he is willing to submit himself to the rigors of confrontation with reality, one of his supreme obligations. The supreme obligation of the judge, however, is to avoid wrong decisions while always being willing to decide. If he were to arrange his materials and pronounce the grounds of his verdicts in the same fashion as the scientist, he would submit himself and his colleagues to the obvious possibility of falsification. But such disproof would detract from his merit as a judge, and imply that basic canons of the legal ethics had been violated in individual cases. Faced with this severe dilemma, the judge will naturally tend to individualize to some extent, to present the case as unique in certain *relevant* respects. This is his line of defense in the exposed position in which he is being held responsible for predictions derived from his decisions. He behaves in this respect similarly to anybody in a position of power. It is inherent in the status of those in power, that their interests make it advantageous to avoid becoming completely predictable.

... When we say that law is nonscientific, nothing is implied concerning its intellectual quality. The statement does not mean that law is less systematic, less rigorously thought through, or in any way less demanding as a discipline than, say, the natural sciences. What we mean is that its structure is different, in part, because its purposes and functions differ.

The problem of causality arises especially in criminal law and in the law of torts. If somebody is charged with the liability for somebody's loss, through destruction of economic value, the question arises whether the loss is caused by his actions. In jurisprudence there has been much controversy concerning the proper meaning of this question. Some have based their arguments upon conceptions of causality supposedly derived from the natural sciences. Others have tended more toward a normative view, emphasizing the over-all reasonableness or unreasonableness of the charge. In concrete cases, however, all seem to put major emphasis upon what 'a reasonable person' could have been expected to foresee as a consequence of his action, provided he proceeded with proper caution and care. This means, in effect, that the legal decision-maker and the legal scholar are exempt from making original studies to establish relationships of cause and effect that could not already have been anticipated by laymen involved in the events. Even causal relationships that are fairly well established by science, may be considered irrelevant if it cannot be considered imprudent of the individual not to have been aware of them. To sum up, it may be said that law is not unconcerned with causal relationships, but their delimitation and sometimes their interpretation are narrowly defined by normative considerations. The function of legal thought in relation to such causal problems is purely passive and receptive. Therefore, the usual methods applied in the causal sciences have not profoundly affected the structure of legal thinking and decision-making ... Law is nonprobabilistic in several senses. A legal decision does not find that something probably happened, but that a certain fact must be considered as established or as not established. It does not say that a specific decision is right, or that a rule is valid law with a certain degree of probability. The decision is, in the final analysis, either right or wrong, a rule is valid or invalid ... A legal decision-maker in the end will have to decide in favor of one single version of what happened as *the* truth. This might seem odd, unrealistic and unjust in cases where there has been very great doubt concerning the facts, where one is close to a point of equal probability for and against an event having taken place. In such cases a simple rule to the effect that the most probable version should be the basis of the verdict, would not only contradict certain other normative considerations, but would give clear expression to the view that law builds upon probabilities and not upon certainties. In the face of grave doubt there is, of course, no way of completely denying this. The interesting point is, however, that procedural law, rather than encouraging frank statements on degrees of probability, has devised rules of evidence which tend to obscure the exact degree of uncertainty.

1. Karl Popper, *The Logic of Scientific Discovery*, London, Hutchinson (1959) pp. 78–9; Michael Polanyi, *Personal Knowledge*, London, Routledge and Kegan Paul (1958) pp. 120ff, 177, 309ff.

12. Law and Conflict
by W. J. Chambliss and R. B. Seidman

From Law, Order and Power, *Reading, Mass., Addison-Wesley (1971) pp. 3–46.*

Most courses in law schools, and virtually every course in high school that touches on the law, continue to assume that the prescriptions of the American Constitution, the common law, and the statutes, are descriptions of the real world. How many courses taught in law schools utilize carefully done empirical studies of the social dynamics of legal controls? How many undergraduate courses in law taught in political science departments rely to any significant degree on empirical studies of the law in action? In high school the Pollyanna perspective is even worse: the 'ought' defined by law is blindly taught as the 'is'. As a result the teaching of the law is usually the perpetuation of a myth.

The central myth about the legal order in the United States is that the normative structures of the written law represent the actual operation of the legal order. This is a myth that is based on the assumption that in the main, except for legislators, officials lack discretion to create law; in applying it, they merely carry out its dictates. 'Ours is a government of laws, not of men.'

A corollary to this myth is the notion, less well articulated but nevertheless widely prevalent, that despite the existence of sharp conflicts between interest groups in the society, the State itself, as represented by the courts and the police, as well as by other elements, provides a value neutral framework within which the struggle can take place. The legislature, of course, is not itself value neutral, but the framework of elections is thought to be so. The legislature is therefore conceived of as an arena within which groups reflecting the power configurations of society itself can peacefully resolve their conflicts. The police are seen as carrying out the laws which the legislature enacts, the courts as deciding which side of a dispute is telling the truth and then fairly and impartially applying the law and meting out the sanction required by the law itself.

This myth of the operation of the law is given the lie daily. We all know today that the blacks and the poor are not treated fairly or equitably by the police. We know that judges have discretion and in fact make policy (as the Supreme Court did in the school desegregation cases). We know that electoral laws have been loaded in the past in favour of rural elements, that the electoral process is loaded in favour of the rich, that the average Presidential candidate is not a poor man, that one-fifth of the Senators of the United States are millionaires. Yet the myth persists. These aberrations are thought to be merely temporary biases. The framework is nevertheless 'on the whole' impartial and neutral. Predetermined rules are believed to ordain decisions of government, not the value loaded discretion of police, judges, or bureaucrats.

It is our contention that, far from being primarily a value neutral framework within which conflict can be peacefully resolved, the power of the State is itself the principal prize in the perpetual conflict that is society. The legal order – the rules which the various law making institutions in the bureaucracy that is the State lay down for the governance of officials and citizens, the tribunals, official and unofficial, formal and informal, which determine whether the rules have been breached, and the bureaucratic agencies which have enforced the law – is in fact a self-serving system to maintain power and privilege. In a society sharply divided into haves and have-nots, poor and rich, blacks and whites, powerful and weak, shot with a myriad of special interest groups, not only is the myth false because of imperfections in the normative system: it is *inevitable* that it be so.

Two models of society

Two very general models of society purport to answer the question whether society is based on a value consensus or a value antagonsm. This question is crucial to our discussion. If society represents a value consensus, then the whole problem raised earlier disappears. The State of course must represent that value consensus. The only legal problem, then, is to ensure that individual role occupants do not substitute their own deviant motivations for the values of the polity. If, on the other hand, society is not based on value consensus at every point, then the issue which we have raised is sharply poised.

 Thus it is argued on the one hand that, even if society is racked by conflict, the State is itself value neutral. No matter how antagonistic toward one another the several groups and strata in the society may be, on this much they must agree: the peaceful settlement of conflict is better than violence and open warfare. The State, in this view, represents the entire population, but only to a limited degree. Every specific law or activity of the State is value loaded, but the machinery by which the State comes to the decision to create and enforce any particular law is itself value neutral, permitting conflict to work itself out peacably.

On the other hand, conflict theorists argue that even so limited a conception of the value free character of the State is false. State power is the most important weapon in the unceasing struggle that takes place beneath the more or less smooth and peaceful facade masking social reality. Whoever is in control of the State uses it in his own interest. Since his own interest requires the exclusion of his antagonists from participation in decision making, even the processes by which the struggle for State power is carried on are warped in favour of one contending group or another.

The first question that must be answered, therefore, is whether society is in fact based on a value consensus or a value antagonism. In many discussions of the problem, the answer is assumed. Roscoe Pound, for example, whose writings on Jurisprudence did an enormous service in advancing the whole concept of social engineering through law, urged that in a democratic society, the values of the law ought to respond to the values of those to whom it applied. He therefore urged that the claims and demands made upon the legal system be catalogued, the values subsuming them synthesised and then used to determine the serial order in which these claims and demands should be paid. It is a system which is based on the assumption that there is in every society a basic consensus of values reflected in the totality of social demands.

Exactly that claim has been made by Talcott Parsons and the entire school of sociology of which he is the outstanding exponent. Parsons bases his model on four principle assertions:

1. Every society is a relatively persisting configuration of elements.
2. Every society is a well-integrated configuration of elements.
3. Every element in a society contributes to its functioning.
4. Every society rests upon the consensus of its members.

Given such a consensus the only problem for the legislator is to determine what in fact the values of the society are just as Pound urged.

In opposition to this model, Ralf Dahrendorf and others have urged a conflict model. This model takes a diametrically opposed position on every point:

1. Every society is at every moment subject to change; social change is ubiquitous.
2. Every society experiences at every moment social conflict; social conflict is ubiquitous.
3. Every element in a society contributes to its change.
4. Every society rests on constraint of some of its members by others.

Dahrendorf asserts that it is impossible empirically to choose between these two sets of assumptions. 'Stability and change, integration and conflict, function and "dysfunction", consensus and constraint are, it would seem, two equally valid aspects of every imaginable society.' Like the dual theories of light, each model may be useful to explain specific aspects of social process.

When applied to the study of the legal order, Dahrendorf's claim that one cannot choose between the value consensus and conflict models is not very persuasive. Indeed the empirical studies [we report here] make it quite clear that the value consensus model is not only incapable of accounting for the shape and character of the legal system, but it even fails to raise the most fundamental and socio-logically relevant questions about the law. The conflict model by contrast while having many shortcomings and not providing a complete answer to the questions raised by the study of law, is none-theless much more useful as a heuristic model for analysing legal systems ...

The literature on the conflict models of law and society is far smaller than the literature which assumes that the State exercises power in the impartial interest of the entire population. The reason for this relative paucity appears easy enough to discover. Juris-prudential theory has always been more than a disinterested search for truth. It is a legitimizing weapon of the highest order. The class of jurisprudents as a whole has not been noticably overloaded with revolutionaries.

Indeed the very fact that the literature defining conflict models is so sparse should give pause. Jurisprudential models denying value choice by the State have been proposed in every era, and they all try to justify the existing State. Natural law theories justified feudalism as divinely ordained and therefore in the interests of all of us;

Hobbes justified the Stuart monarchy, von Savigny the German state, Austin the Victorian state. Few people, looking backward, would assert that any of these states were in fact value neutral. Theories claiming that the existing twentieth century liberal democratic state is uniquely value neutral require careful analysis, less they, too, be mere ideologies for legitimizing the existing law and State. What legitimacy, after all, could better protect the State than that grounded on the common belief that the State equitably represents the interests of all - white and black, rich and poor, draftee and citizen - by providing a neutral framework that protects us all from authoritarianism and anarchy alike?

13. Morals and Order
by Jack D. Douglas

From The American Social Order, *New York, The Free Press (1971)* pp. 15–19, 75–8.

One of the basic assumptions of common sense in the earlier centuries of Western societies, and very probably in all reasonably simple societies, was *the assumption that the moral rules and other meanings of the society are absolute.* There are at least six basic properties to this assumption of absoluteness concerning any social meanings (i.e., ideas, beliefs, feelings, values, etc.). First, the meanings are assumed to be completely *homogeneous* (or the same) for everyone (or, at least, for all normal, adequate persons). There can be no variability or relativity of morality, beliefs, etc. Second, the meanings are assumed to be *unproblematic*, so that everyone can be assumed to know without question or uncertainty what is right or wrong at all times and for all situations. Third, the meanings are assumed to be *external* to the individual, independent of his own will, so that they in no way depend on him for their existence or meaning. Fourth, the meanings are assumed to be *necessary*: there can be no escaping them or choosing not to invoke them. Fifth, the meanings are assumed to be a *necessary part of reality*, derived from the very substance of Being or God. Sixth, the meanings are assumed to be *timeless* or eternal. They are always the same; they do not change or go into abeyance.

These assumptions have been made not only by men acting from common sense, but, more importantly, by officials seeking to control the members of Western societies in accord with their own morality. This *official moral absolutism* and its consequences will be discussed later but it is important to note here that official control agencies in Western societies take a more absolute view of morality than do most men of common sense in these same societies. For reasons to be discussed later, the officials themselves do in fact violate the supposedly absolute morality for the obstensible purpose of enforcing it, and they necessarily reinterpret it as their situations change; however, this does not prevent them from acting *as if* the morality they are enforcing is absolute. Official moral absolutism is important for our purposes here because the sociologists from the eighteenth century up the twentieth century were sometimes official agents of control and, more often, were engaged in helping officials to find better ways to 'solve social problems', which largely meant enforcing the supposedly absolute morality. The traditional sociological perspective on deviance, then, was largely developed within an official context, so that the sociologists tended more strongly than most men of common sense to assume the absolutism of morals, beliefs, and other social meanings.

These early sociologists unquestioningly accepted the official assumption that there was something necessarily 'immoral' about such actions as suicide, divorce, or theft; they implicitly assumed that the meanings of such terms as 'moral', 'immoral', 'crime', and 'suicide' could be taken for granted. These assumptions led them and succeeding generations of sociologists to adopt a theoretical perspective on these forms of behavior that assumed such behavior must be studied *as violations of moral rules* and that the meanings of these social categories, including 'moral rule' itself, are unproblematic. These theoretical assumptions have had far-reaching consequences for sociological studies of social rules and social order; and repudiation of these assumptions has been one of the most important reasons for the creative developments in recent years in the field of deviance and in the theory of social order.

In relatively simple, homogeneous, and stable societies the

members of the society generally *take it for granted* that their many social meanings are right and adequate. To them it is 'obvious' that reality has one and only one meaning; it is also obvious that any man of 'good will' with 'adequate senses' will 'see' the meaning of things in just the way any such member of that society sees them.

The members of simple societies have little reason to see things differently. Most of their communications are with other members of the little society in which experiences have been largely homogenous. Such an *absolutist view* of one's way of life probably makes the group more successful in its attempts to compete with other groups and to preserve itself. Most contacts with other groups involve actual or potential conflict, which tends to encourage an absolutist view of one's 'way of life' and a view of one's way as obviously superior to that of the enemy 'barbarians', the inferior outsiders. Also, most records of events are simply transmitted personal memories, which is the form of recording that is most subject to reconstruction to fit the demands of any current social situation.

We must, of course, be careful not to fall victim to the same tendency to accept a polarized view of the 'barbarians'. There have probably always been primitive philosophers, marginal men, diplomats with dual allegiances, and cynical politicians who questioned the rules of their societies; but there is a real difference in the frequencies and degrees to which members of different societies take their social meanings for granted and as absolute. Generally, *the more simple, homogeneous, closed, stable and internally unconflictful a social group, the more the tendency of its members to take their social meanings for granted and as absolute.* The converse seems equally true: *the more complex, variegated, open, changing and internally conflictful a social group, the more the tendency of its members to see their social meanings as problematic and relative.*

Even when members of a society come to see tastes, motives, and beliefs as relative and subjective, even as legitimately varying for different groups, individuals and situations, they resist seeing social rules as similarly relative. There are no doubt many reasons for the tenacity of this belief in the absoluteness and universality of social rules. Rules are seen as basic or ultimate: they form much of the basis on which the accepted differences in motives, tastes, and beliefs are regulated or coordinated. Because of this, any questioning of the rules is generally seen as posing a threat to the ordering of one's social life and, thus, arouses deep anxieties.

... When sociologists knowingly or unknowingly commit themselves to the kind of practical activity implicit in the nature of official information on deviance (or any other phenomena), then they are committing themselves to *doing official action.* Allowing one's theories to be predetermined in this way by the nature of the official information used defeats the whole purpose of science. I do not mean by this to argue that we must seek some kind of 'absolute' knowledge that is free of all predetermination by the nature of methods and the nature of values. We now have every reason to believe that this kind of absolute knowledge is impossible. As I have argued before, we must recognize that all knowledge is to some degree situation-bound, that all knowledge can at best be *useful-knowledge* because it does implicitly assume certain properties of the information used and certain general goals. *But it is of crucial importance that one seek to control and to minimize such effects and to make his knowledge of society as generally or universally useful as possible.* Only when one does this is he doing science, as opposed to more immediately practical, situation-bound kinds of activity.

The kind of theory based on official information, especially on official statistics on deviance, is of little value or is actually dangerous to most of us. This is true partly because it makes the theory so situation-bound, so completely dependent on assuming the perspectives and goals of official organizations in our society, the generality of the knowledge involved is exceedingly limited. In a complex society such as ours it is very difficult for policy makers to honestly know what is going on in all of the important parts of the society, nonetheless to understand the complex relations among these parts. For this reason, anyone who would be an effective policy maker (i.e., who will in fact run the society so that people become more rather than less satisfied) must have some highly reliable and valid information. In addition, in a society changing so rapidly as ours, any effective policy maker must have generalizable rather than situation-bound information, because only the former will allow him to anticipate the nature of *future* possible states of society. Situation-bound information on the so-called 'status-quo' will necessarily distort any such futuristic, policy-oriented thought and decisions based on it will produce more or less unhappy results. The need for generalizable information constitutes the real social justification of social science. Committing ourselves to the official perspectives and goals implicit in official information necessarily prevents our reaching such social science.

But it is also true that *official-knowledge* produced by social scientists can be *dangerous-knowledge* because it provides a powerful rhetoric to the officials that they use in achieving their goals, which generally consist of a further standardization of life. This in turn has the effect of making their mathematical information more reliable and valid as a description of the society, so that the more effective they are in achieving their social goals, the more they are able to provide an *ex post facto validation* of their kind of *official-knowledge*. The officials have understood well the power of this mathematical rhetoric, and, as I have already argued, this is a basic reason for creating and using the official statistics in the first place. The imprimatur of the scientific disciplines on one's side is even more important as a rhetorical device. Then it is not merely the officials, who are suspect in any society that values individual freedoms, but it is also the 'scientists' who support the official policies and general perspectives. The rhetorical power of this 'expert' status is great and growing in our increasingly technological society, so it is valuable to officials to have the experts on their side, quite independently of any truly scientific information they might have.

In our world today the officially-controlled mass society and the official-statistical knowledge of 'social problems' are necessarily interdependent. Each can exist only to the extent that the other does; to create one makes the other possible. For social scientists to create such official statistical 'knowledge' is, then, to make official control more possible. In addition, since the sociologists disavow control of such knowledge by selling it through the consulting relationship, they make it almost completely amenable to the specific goals of the officials in control.

If sociologists are to fulfill their purpose of creating scientific knowledge of social phenomena, such as moral phenomena, then they must remain free of all of the basic assumptions of official information, the implicit goals of such information, and of the organizations which create it. They must, instead, construct their own information about the phenomena, controlling the methods used to get the observations on which such information is ultimately based. Above all, they must control these observations in such a way as to have the least possible effect on the observations. *We must be as true as possible to the phenomena we are studying.* Only in this way can we possibly build a valid science of human beings and human society. If we cannot or do not remain as true to the phenomena as possible, then we can only do pseudo-science which can be used to control human beings, but not to make them freer.

III The Maintenance of Order

1. Introduction

Law attempts to create order. It holds out an ideal of how an ordered society should function, and deploys this ideal in justifying its over-arching right to be the final arbitrator of what order is, and how it may be achieved and protected. Societies based on what Weber called 'legal domination' grant this central role to law in the creation of an orderly society.

However the ideal of law is rarely, if ever, achieved. Law as a complex institution, and as a projected vision, is itself dependent upon some degree of pre-existing social order. The actual operation of law takes place in a real world whose inequalties of power and prestige it cannot easily transcend. Frequently its aims and obligations are compromised by the exigencies of effectiveness, and its implementation is constrained by what is (believed to be) pragmatically possible.

The sociology of law studies how law actually operates. Yet the relationship between actual operation and ideals is of interest, since it may crucially affect whether law is granted legitimacy. In studying legal actuality we are concerned to understand how far men do orientate their actions according to legal dictates, or to other, more or less independent, influences. In addition we seek to discover how far non-legal institutions are as powerful, or even more powerful, than law in guaranteeing obedience. Finally we must examine critically how far the structures and institutions of society, such as power or class, can invade the law and subvert its ideals. This may be because law is weak, because it is truly a refraction of those other forces, or because its structure cannot prevent invasion.

159

Ultimately we must understand the extent to which law creates or maintains an ordered society, and the extent to which it is itself a product of order developed or achieved elsewhere in society. This section explores some of the dimensions and aspects of law's relationship to ordered action. The complexity of the relationship is recognized in the writings excerpted, but ways in which that complexity may be unravelled and understood are suggested.

2. The Architecture of the Legal System
by Marc Galanter

From 'Why the "Haves" Come Out Ahead: Speculations on the Limits of Legal Change', Law and Society Review (1974) vol. 9, pp. 95–114.

I would like to try to put forward some conjectures about the way in which the basic architecture of the legal system creates and limits the possibilities of using the system as a means of redistributive (that is, systemically equalizing) change. Our question, specifically, is under what conditions can litigation be redistributive, taking litigation in the broadest sense of the presentation of claims to be decided by courts (or court-like agencies) and the whole penumbra of threats, feints, and so forth, surrounding such presentation. . .

Most analyses of the legal system start at the rules end and work down through institutional facilities to see what effect the rules have on the parties. I would like to reverse that procedure and look through the other end of the telescope. Let's think about the different kinds of parties and the effect these differences might have on the way the system works.

Because of differences in their size, differences in the state of the law, and differences in their resources, some of the actors in the society have many occasions to utilize the courts (in the broad sense) to make (or defend) claims; others do so only rarely. We might divide our actors into those claimants who have only occasional recourse to the courts (one-shotters or OS) and repeat players (RP) who are engaged in many similar litigations over time.[1] The spouse in a divorce case, the auto-injury claimant, the criminal accused are OSs; the insurance company, the prosecutor, the finance company are RPs. Obviously this is an oversimplification; there are inter- mediate cases such as the professional criminal. So we ought to think of OS–RP as a continuum rather than as a dichotomous pair. Typically, the RP is a larger unit and the stakes in any given case are smaller (relative to total worth). OSs are usually smaller units and the stakes represented by the tangible outcome of the case may be high relative to total worth, as in the case of the injury victim or the criminal accused. Or, the OS may suffer from the opposite problem: his claims may be so small and unmanageable (the shortweighted consumer or the holder of performing rights) that the cost of enforcing them outruns any promise of benefit.

Let us refine our notion of the RP into an 'ideal type' if you will–a unit which has had and anticipates repeated litigation, which has low stakes in the outcome of any one case, and which has the resources to pursue its long-run interests. (This does not include every real-world repeat player; that most common repeat player, the alcoholic derelict, enjoys few of the advantages that may accrue to the RP. His resources are too few to bargain in the short run or take heed of in the long run.) An OS, on the other hand, is a unit whose claims are too large (relative to his size) or too small (relative to the cost of remedies) to be managed routinely and rationally.

We would expect an RP to play the litigation game differently from an OS. Let us consider some of his advantages:

(1) RPs, having done it before, have advance intelligence; they are able to structure the next transaction and build a record. It is the RP who writes the form contract, requires the security deposit, and the like.

(2) RPs develop expertise and have ready access to specialists. They enjoy economies of scale and have low start-up costs for any case.

(3) RPs have opportunities to develop facilitative informal relations with institutional incumbents.

(4) The RP must establish and maintain credibility as a combatant. His interest in his 'bargaining reputation' serves as a resource to establish 'commitment' to his bargaining positions. With no bargaining reputation to maintain, the OS has more difficulty in convincingly committing himself in bargaining.[2]

(5) RPs can play the odds. The larger the matter at issue looms for OS, the more likely he is to adopt a minimax strategy (minimize the probability of maximum loss). Assuming that the stakes are relatively smaller for RPs, they can adopt strategies calculated to maximize gain over a long series of cases, even where this involves the risk of maximum loss in some cases.

(6) RPs can play for rules as well as immediate gains. First, it pays an RP to expend resources in influencing the making of the relevant rules by such methods as lobbying. (And his accumulated expertise enables him to do this persuasively.)

(7) RPs can also play for rules in litigation itself, whereas an OS is unlikely to. That is, there is a difference in what they regard as a favorable outcome. Because his stakes in the immediate outcome are high and because by definition OS is unconcerned with the outcome of similar litigation in the future, OS will have little interest in that element of the outcome which might influence the disposition of the decision-maker next time around. For the RP, on the other hand, anything that will favorably influence the outcomes of future cases is a worthwhile result. The larger the stake for any player and the lower the probability of repeat play, the less likely that he will be concerned with the rules which govern future cases of the same kind. Consider two parents contesting the custody of their only child, the prizefighter vs. the IRS for tax arrears, the convict facing the death penalty. On the other hand, the player with small stakes in the present case and the prospect of a series of similar cases (the IRS, the adoption agency, the prosecutor) may be more interested in the state of the law. . .

Of course it is not suggested that the strategic configuration of the parties is the sole or major determinant of rule-development. Rule-development is shaped by a relatively autonomous learned tradition, by the impingement of intellectual currents from outside, by the preferences and prudences of the decision-makers. But courts are passive and these factors operate only when the process is triggered by parties. The point here is merely to note the superior opportunities of the RP to trigger promising cases and prevent the triggering of unpromising ones. It is not incompatible with a course of rule-development favoring OSs (or, as indicated below, with OSs failing to get the benefit of those favorable new rules).

In stipulating that RPs can play for rules, I do not mean to imply that RPs pursue rule-gain as such. If we recall that not all rules penetrate (i.e. become effectively applied at the field level) we come to some additional advantages of RPs.

(8) RPs, by virtue of experience and expertise, are more likely to be able to discern which rules are likely to 'penetrate' and which are likely to remain merely symbolic commitments. RPs may be able to concentrate their resources on rule-changes that are likely to make a tangible difference. They can trade off symbolic defeats for tangible gains.

(9) Since penetration depends in part on the resources of the parties (knowledge, attentiveness, expert services, money), RPs are more likely to be able to invest the matching resources necessary to secure the penetration of rules favorable to them.

It is not suggested that RPs are to be equated with 'haves' (in terms of power, wealth and status) or OSs with 'have-nots'. In the American setting most RPs are larger, richer and more powerful than are most OSs, so these categories overlap, but there are obvious exceptions. RPs may be 'have-nots' (alcoholic derelicts) or may act as champions of 'have-nots' (as government does from time to time); OSs such as criminal defendants may be wealthy. What this analysis does is to define a position of advantage in the configuration of contending parties and indicate how those with other advantages tend to occupy this position of advantage and to have their other advantages reinforced and augumented thereby. This position of advantage is one of the ways in which a legal system formally neutral as between 'haves' and 'have-nots' may perpetuate and augment the advantages of the former.

We may think of litigation as typically involving various combinations of OSs and RPs. We can then construct a matrix such as Figure 1 and fill in the boxes with some well-known if only approximate American examples. (We ignore for the moment that the terms OS and RP represent ends of a continuum, rather than a dichotomous pair.)

On the basis of our incomplete and unsystematic examples, let us conjecture a bit about the content of these boxes:

Box I: OS vs. OS
The most numerous occupants of this box are divorces and insanity hearings. Most (over 90 per cent of divorces, for example) are uncontested. A large portion of these are really pseudo-litigation,

FIGURE 1
*A taxonomy of litigation by strategic
configuration of parties*

| | | Initiator, Claimant | |
		One-Shotter	Repeat Player
Defendant	**One-Shotter**	Parent v. Parent (Custody) Spouse v. Spouse (Divorce) Family v. Family Member (Insanity Commitment) Family v. Family (Inheritance) Neighbor v. Neighbor Partner v. Partner OS vs OS I	Prosecutor v. Accused Finance Co. v. Debtor Landlord v. Tenant IRS v. Taxpayer Condemnor v. Property Owner RP vs OS II
	Repeat Player	Welfare Client v. Agency Auto Dealer v. Manufacturer Injury Victim v. Insurance Company Tenant v. Landlord Bankrupt Consumer v. Creditors Defamed v. Publisher OS vs RP III	Union v. Company Movie Distributor v. Censorship Board Developer v. Suburban Municipality Regulatory Agency v. Firms of Regulated Industry RP vs RP IV

that is, a settlement is worked out between the parties and ratified in the guise of adjudication. When we get real litigation in Box I, it is often between parties who have some intimate tie with one another, fighting over some unsharable good, often with overtones of 'spite' and 'irrationality'. Courts are resorted to where an ongoing relationship is ruptured; they have little to do with the routine patterning of activity. The law is invoked *ad hoc* and instrumentally by the parties. There may be a strong interest in vindication, but neither party is likely to have much interest in the long-term state of the law (of, for instance, custody or nuisance). There are few appeals, few test cases, little expenditure of resources on rule-development. Legal doctrine is likely to remain remote from everyday practice and from popular attitudes.

Box II: RP vs. OS

The great bulk of litigation is found in this box–indeed every really numerous kind except personal injury cases, insanity hearings, and divorces. The law is used for routine processing of claims by parties for whom the making of such claims is a regular business activity. Often the cases here take the form of stereotyped mass processing with little of the individuated attention of full-dress adjudication. Even greater numbers of cases are settled 'informally' with settlement keyed to possible litigation outcome (discounted by risk, cost, delay).

The state of the law is of interest to the RP, though not to the OS defendants. Insofar as the law is favourable to the RP it is 'followed' closely in practice (subject to discount for RP's transaction costs). Transactions are built to fit the rules by creditors, police, draft boards and other RPs. Rules favoring OSs may be less readily applicable, since OSs do not ordinarily plan the underlying transaction, or less meticulously observed in practice, since OSs are unlikely to be as ready or able as RPs to invest in insuring their penetration to the field level.

Box III: OS vs. RP

All of these are rather infrequent types except for personal injury cases which are distinctive in that free entry to the arena is provided by the contingent fee. In auto injury claims, litigation is routinized and settlement is closely geared to possible litigation outcome. Outside the personal injury area, litigation in Box III is not routine. It usually represents the attempt of some OS to invoke outside help to create leverage on an organization with which he has been having dealings but is now at the point of divorce (for example, the discharged employee or the cancelled franchisee). The OS claimant generally has little interest in the state of the law; the RP defendant, however, is greatly interested.

Box IV: RP vs. RP

Let us consider the general case first and then several special cases. We might expect that there would be little litigation in Box IV, because to the extent that two RPs play with each other repeatedly, the expectation of continued mutually beneficial interaction would give rise to informal bilateral controls. This seems borne out by studies of dealings among businessmen[3] and in labor relations. Official agencies are invoked by unions trying to get established and by management trying to prevent them from getting established, more rarely in dealings between bargaining partners. Units with mutually beneficial relations do not adjust their differences in courts. Where they rely on third parties in dispute-resolution, it is likely to take a form (such as arbitration or a domestic tribunal) detached from official sanctions and applying domestic rather than official rules.

However, there are several special cases. First, there are those RPs who seek not furtherance of tangible interests, but vindication of fundamental cultural commitments. An example would be the organizations which sponsor much church–state litigation. Where RPs are contending about value differences (who is right) rather than interest conflicts (who gets what) there is less tendency to settle and less basis for developing a private system of dispute settlement.

Second, government is a special kind of RP. Informal controls depend upon the ultimate sanction of withdrawal and refusal to continue beneficial relations. To the extent that withdrawal of future association is not possible in dealing with government, the scope of informal controls is correspondingly limited. The development of informal relations between regulatory agencies and regulated firms is well known. And the regulated may have sanctions other than withdrawal which they can apply; for instance, they may threaten political opposition. But the more inclusive the unit of government, the less effective the withdrawal sanction and the greater the likelihood that a party will attempt to invoke outside allies by litigation even while sustaining the ongoing relationship. This applies also to monopolies, units which share the government's relative immunity to withdrawal sanctions. RPs in monopolistic relationships will occasionally invoke formal controls to show prowess, to give credibility to threats, and to provide satisfactions for other audiences. Thus we would expect litigation by and against government to be more frequent than in other RP vs. RP situations. There is a second reason for expecting more litigation when government is a party. That is, that the notion of 'gain' (policy as well as monetary) is often more contingent and problematic for governmental units than for other parties, such as businesses or organized interest groups. In some cases courts may, by proffering authoritative interpretations of public policy, redefine an agency's notion of gain. Hence government parties may be more willing to externalize decisions to the courts. And opponents may have more incentive to litigate against government in the hope of securing a shift in its goals.

A somewhat different kind of special case is present where plaintiff and defendant are both RPs but do not deal with each other repeatedly (two insurance companies, for example.) In the government / monopoly case, the parties were so inextricably bound together that the force of informal controls was limited; here they are not sufficiently bound to each other to give informal controls their bite; there is nothing to withdraw from! The large one-time deal that falls through, the marginal enterprise–these are staple sources of litigation.

Where there is litigation in the RP vs. RP situation, we might expect that there would be heavy expenditure on rule-development, many appeals, and rapid and elaborate development of the doctrinal law. Since the parties can invest to secure implementation of favorable rules, we would expect practice to be closely articulated to the resulting rules.

On the basis of these preliminary guesses, we can sketch a general profile of litigation and the factors associated with it. The great bulk of ligitation is found in Box II; much less in Box III. Most of the litigation in these Boxes is mass routine processing of disputes between parties who are strangers (not in mutually beneficial continuing relations) or divorced[4] – and between whom there is a disparity in size. One party is a bureaucratically organized 'professional' (in the sense of doing it for a living) who enjoys strategic advantages. Informal controls between the parties are tenuous or in-effective; their relationship is likely to be established and defined by official rules; in litigation, these rules are discounted by transaction costs and manipulated selectively to the advantage of the parties. On the other hand, in Boxes I and IV, we have more infrequent but more individualized litigation between parties of the same general magnitude, among whom there are or were continuing multi-stranded relationships with attendant informal controls. Litigation appears when the relationship loses its future value; when its 'monopolistic' character deprives informal controls of sufficient leverage and the parties invoke outside allies to modify it; and when the parties seek to vindicate conflicting values. . .

What happens when we introduce lawyers? Parties who have lawyers do better. Lawyers are themselves RPs. Does their presence equalize the parties, dispelling the advantage of the RP client? Or does the existence of lawyers amplify the advantage of the RP client? We might assume that RPs (tending to be larger units) who can buy legal services more steadily, in larger quantities, in bulk (by retainer) and at higher rates, would get services of better quality. They would have better information (especially where restrictions on information about legal services are present). Not only would the RP get more talent to begin with, but he would on the whole get greater continuity, better record-keeping, more anticipatory or preventive work, more experience and specialized skill in pertinent areas, and more control over counsel. . .

1. The discussion here focuses on litigation, but I believe an analagous analysis might be applied to the regulatory and rule-making phases of the legal process.
2. An offsetting advantage enjoyed by some OSs deserves mention. Since he does not anticipate continued dealings with his opponent, an OS can do his damnedest without fear of reprisal next time around or on other issues.
3. For example, cf. Macaulay's study below. – eds.
4. That is, the relationship may never have existed, it may have 'failed' in that it is no longer mutually beneficial, or the parties may be 'divorced'.

3. Doing Without Law
by Stewart Macaulay

From 'Non-Contractual Relations in Business: A Preliminary Study' American Sociological Review *(1963) vol. 28, pp. 55–67.*

What good is contract law? Who uses it? When and how? Complete answers would require an investigation of almost every type of transaction between individuals and organizations. In this report, research has been confined to exchanges between businesses, and primarily to manufacturers. Furthermore, this report will be limited to a presentation of the findings concerning when contract is and is not used and to a tentative explanation of these findings.

Tentative Findings

It is difficult to generalize about the use and nonuse of contract by manufacturing industry. However, a number of observations can be made with reasonable accuracy at this time. The use and nonuse of contract in creating exchange relations and in dispute settling will be taken up in turn.

The Creation of Exchange Relationships: In creating relationships, businessmen may plan to a greater or lesser degree in relation to several types of issues. . . [Our research shows] that (1) many business exchanges reflect a high degree of planning about four categories—description, contingencies, defective performances, and legal sanction—but (2) many, if not most, exchanges reflect no planning, or only a minimal amount of it, especially concerning legal sanctions and the effect of defective performances. As a result, the opportunity for good faith disputes during the life of the exchange relationship often is present.

The Adjustment of Exchange Relationships and the Settling of Disputes: While a significant amount of creating business exchanges is done on a fairly noncontractual basis, the creation of exchanges usually is far more contractual than the adjustment of such relationships and the settlement of disputes. Exchanges are adjusted when the obligations of one or both parties are modified by agreement during the life of the relationship. . . Disputes are frequently settled without reference to the contract, or potential or actual legal sanctions. There is a hesitancy to speak of legal rights or to threaten to sue in these negotiations. Even where the parties have a detailed and carefully planned agreement which indicates what is to happen if, say, the seller fails to deliver on time, often they will never refer to the agreement but will negotiate a solution when the problem arises, apparently as if there had never been any original contract. . . Law suits for breach of contract appear to be rare.

At times relatively contractual methods are used to make adjustments in ongoing transactions and to settle disputes. Demands of one side which are deemed unreasonable by the other occasionally are blocked by reference to the terms of the agreement between the parties. The legal position of the parties can influence negotiations even though legal rights of litigation are never mentioned in their discussions; it makes a difference if one is demanding what both concede to be a right or begging for a favor. Now and then a firm may threaten to turn matters over to its attorneys, threaten to sue, commence a suit, or even litigate and carry an appeal to the highest court which will hear the matter. Thus, legal sanctions, while not an everyday affair, are not unknown in business.

One can conclude that while detailed planning and legal sanctions play a significant role in some exchanges between businesses, in many business exchanges their role is small.

Tentative Explanations

Two questions need to be answered: (A) How can business successfully operate exchange relationships with relatively so little attention to detailed planning or to legal sanctions? and (B) Why does business ever use contract in light of its success without it?

Why are relatively noncontractual practices so common? In most situations contract is not needed.[1] Often its functions are served by other devices. Most problems are avoided without resort to detailed planning or legal sanctions because usually there is little room for honest misunderstandings or good faith differences of opinion about the nature and quality of a seller's performance. Although the parties fail to cover all foreseeable contingencies, they will exercise care to see that both understand the primary obligation on each side... Moreover, contract and contract law are often thought unnecessary because there are many effective non-legal sanctions. Two norms are widely accepted: (1) Commitments are to be honored in almost all situations; one does not welsh on a deal. (2) One ought to produce a good product and stand behind it. Then, too, business units are organized to perform commitments, and internal sanctions will induce performance.

The final type of nonlegal sanction is the most obvious. Both business units involved in the exchange desire to continue successfully in business and will avoid conduct which might interfere with attaining this goal. One is concerned with both the reaction of the other party in the particular exchange and with his own general business reputation. Not only do the particular business units in a given exchange want to deal with each other again, they also want to deal with other business units in the future. And the way one behaves in a particular transaction, or a series of transactions, will color his general business reputation. Blacklisting can be formal or informal... Thus often contract is not needed as there are alternatives.

Not only are contract and contract law not needed in many situations, their use may have, or may be thought to have, undesirable consequences. Detailed negotiated contracts can get in the way of creating good exchange relationships between business units.

Even where agreement can be reached at the negotiation stage, carefully planned arrangements may create undesirable exchange relationships between business units. Some businessmen object that in such a carefully worked out relationship one gets performance only to the letter of the contract. Such planning indicates a lack of trust and blunts the demands of friendship, turning a cooperative venture into an antagonistic horse trade. Yet the greater danger perceived by some businessmen is that one would have to perform his side of the bargain to its letter and thus lose what is called 'flexibility'. Businessmen may welcome a measure of vagueness in the obligations they assume so that they may negotiate matters in light of the actual circumstances.

Adjustment of exchange relationships and dispute settlement by litigation or the threat of it also has many costs. The gain anticipated from using this form of coercion often fails to outweigh these costs, which are both monetary and nonmonetary... Finally, the law of contract damages may not provide an adequate remedy even if the firm wins the suit; one may get vindication but not much money.

Why do relatively contractual practices ever exist? Although contract is not needed and actually may have negative consequences, businessmen do make some carefully planned contracts, negotiate settlements influenced by their legal rights and commence and defend some breach of contract law suits or arbitration proceedings. In view of the findings and explanation presented to this point, one may ask why. Exchanges are carefully planned when it is thought that planning and a potential legal sanction will have more advantages than disadvantages. Such a judgment may be reached when contract planning serves the internal needs of an organization involved in a business exchange. For example, a fairly detailed contract can serve as a communication device within a large corporation.

Also one tends to find a judgment that the gains of contract out-weigh the costs where there is a likelihood that significant problems will arise.[2] One factor leading to this conclusion is complexity of the agreed performance over a long period. Another factor is whether or not the degree of injury in case of default is thought to be potentially great... Similarly, one uses or threatens to use legal sanctions to settle disputes when other devices will not work and when the gains are thought to outweigh the costs. For example, perhaps the most common type of business contracts case fought all the way through to the appellate courts today is an action for an alleged wrongful termination of a dealer's franchise by a manufacturer. Since the franchise has been terminated, factors such as personal relationships and the desire for future business will have little effect; the cancel-lation of the franchise indicates they have already failed to maintain the relationship... Thus, often the dealer chooses to risk the cost of a lawyer's fee because of the chance that he may recover some compensation for his losses.

An 'irrational' factor may exert some influence on the decision to use legal sanctions. The man who controls a firm may feel that he or his organization has been made to appear foolish or has been the victim of fraud or bad faith. The law suit may be seen as a vehicle 'to get even' although the potential gains, as viewed by an objective observer, are outweighed by the potential costs.

The decision whether or not to use contract–whether the gain exceeds the costs–will be made by the person within the business unit with the power to make it, and it tends to make a difference who he is. People in a sales department oppose contract. Contractual nego-tiations are just one more hurdle in the way of a sale. Purchasing agents and their buyers are less hostile to contracts but regard attention devoted to such matters as a waste of time. In contrast, the financial control department–the treasurer, controller, or auditor–leans toward more contractual dealings. Contract is viewed by these people as an organizing tool to control operations in a large organization. It tends to define precisely and to minimize the risks to which the firm is exposed. Outside lawyers those with many clients may share this enthusiasm for a more contractual method of dealing. These lawyers are concerned with preventive law avoiding any possible legal difficulty. They see many unstable, and unsuccessful exchange transactions, and so they are aware of, and perhaps overly concerned with all of the things which can go wrong. Moreover, their job of settling disputes with legal sanctions is much easier if their client has not been overly casual about transaction planning. The inside lawyer, or house counsel, is harder to classify. He is likely to have some sympathy with a more contractual method of dealing. He shares the outside lawyer's 'craft urge' to see exchange transactions neat and tidy from a legal standpoint. Since he is more concerned with avoiding and settling disputes than selling goods, he is likely to be less willing to rely on a man's word as the sole sanction than is a salesman. Yet the house counsel is more a part of the organization and more aware of its goals and subject to its internal sanctions. If the potential risks are not too great, he may hesitate to suggest a more contractual procedure to the sales department. He must sell his services to the operating departments, and he must hoard what power he has, expending it on only what he sees as significant issues.

Obviously, there are other significant variables which influence the degree that contract is used. One is the relative bargaining power or skill of the two business units... Also, all of the factors discussed in this paper can be viewed as *components* of bargaining power–for example, the personal relationship between the presidents of the buyer and the seller firms may give a sales manager great power over a purchasing agent who has been instructed to give the seller 'every consideration'. Another variable relevant to the use of contract is the influence of third parties. The federal government, or a lender of money, may insist that a contract be made in a particular transaction or may influence the decision to assert one's legal rights under a contract.

Contract, then, often plays an important role in business, but other factors are significant. To understand the functions of contract the whole system of conducting exchanges must be explored fully. More types of business communities must be studied, contract litigation must be analyzed to see why the nonlegal sanctions fail to prevent the use of legal sanctions, and all of the variables suggested in this paper must be clarified more systematically.

1. The explanation that follows emphasizes a *considered* choice not to plan in detail for all contingencies. However, at times it is clear that businessmen fail to plan because of a lack of sophistication; they simply do not appreciate the risk they are running, or they merely follow patterns established in their firm years ago without re-examining these practices in light of current conditions.
2. Even where there is little chance the problems will arise, some businessmen insist that their lawyer review or draft an agreement as a delaying tactic. This gives the businessman time to think about making a commitment if he has doubts about the matter or to look elsewhere for a better deal while still keeping the particular negotiations alive.

4. Welfare Law and 'Needs'
by T. Prosser

From 'Poverty, Ideology and Legality: "Supplementary Benefits Appeals Tribunals and their Predecessors"' British Journal of Law and Society *(1977) vol. 4, pp. 39–60.*

During the last decade a new conception of poverty and its relief has developed, that of the welfare rights movement which has two basic characteristics. Firstly, 'welfare rights' is a rallying cry or polemical device based on a view of poverty not as misfortune requiring compassion and charity but as injustice requiring action to change the social system by which it is created and the administrative system by which it is relieved. Secondly, benefits to relieve poverty are conceived of as rights in a more fully legal sense, indeed as property rights to be protected by legal rules and judicial procedure rather than as largesse dependent on administrative discretion (as supplementary benefits still largely are). The most influential example of this view has been the work of Charles Reich in the USA.[1] Conflict is seen as inevitable in the enforcement of welfare rights, whereas in the [traditional British] model of tribunals (e.g. Supplementary Benefit Appeal Tribunals) [the] assertion of rights was often seen as a symptom of personal dishonesty or ingratitude.

There have been several effects of this movement on the tribunals. Firstly a much greater stress has been placed on the representation of appellants at hearings, and the published figures do show a much higher success rate for represented appellants than for those who attend on their own (though it should be noted that those represented by lawyers have been less successful than those represented by social workers or groups such as the Child Poverty Action Group or claimants' unions). However the proportion of appellants represented has remained low, as has the overall success rate of appeals.

The second effect of the welfare rights movement has been to boost the number of appeals lodged and heard. In 1975 68,795 were lodged and 32,759 were heard. However this still represents a rate of appeals heard of only about ½% of claims made. This low rate is due not to a lack of questionable decisions but rather to ignorance and fear by claimants. One study found that of a random sample of claimants almost 30% had grounds for appeal, and of those persuaded to do so almost 90% were successful.

The third effect of the movement has been to increase pressure for the judicalisation of the tribunals, i.e. the adoption of a more formal adjudicatory structure and hearing procedure. This pressure has not been confined to welfare rights groups but does represent a conception of the tribunals as deciding upon identifiable rights rather than administering a service over which there can be no real conflict. An example of such proposals have been those from the Child Poverty Action Group for the adoption of legally qualified chairmen, a system of precedent, further appeal to a body of experienced lawyers, etc. Sir Leslie Scarman has made similar suggestions, and the report of a research study funded by the Department of Health and Social Security itself has recommended *inter alia* legally qualified chairmen, a precedent system, further appeal to the National Insurance Commissioners and eventual integration into the National Insurance appeal system. The Lord Chancellor's Advisory Committee has recommended the extension of legal aid to the tribunals, and one group of writers (including the present Solicitor General) has gone so far as to recommend the replacement of the tribunals by 'Social Courts' at the level of the County Courts staffed by trained judges assisted by lay assessors.

Finally, for the first time applications have been made to the courts to quash tribunal decisions. The results of these have been somewhat mixed. The original application was successful and a policy of the Commission held unlawful[2] but the result was affected by legislation passed soon afterwards.[3] The following two cases were heard together by the Court of Appeal and revealed a marked reluctance by the court to intervene with a tribunal decision 'even though it may be said to be erroneous in point of law'.[4] The next two applications were successful.[5] In the most recent case the Queen's Bench Divisional Court refused to intervene in the exercise of one of the Commission's discretionary powers, holding it to be effectively unreviewable unless the tribunal were to go outside the conclusions to which a reasonable body might conceivably come.[6] Thus these attempts to involve the courts have been remarkably unsuccessful in contrast to developments in the USA. The effect seems to have been to leave considerable disillusionment not with legal techniques *per se* but with the willingness of the judges to enforce the rights of all.

Thus tribunals have developed from a situation of close control by the Unemployment Assistance Board in a period of intense political conflict over poverty and unemployment, to assume a greater degree of autonomy and a case-conference role with the decline of this conflict. They now present an uneasy mixture of this role with a more conflict-oriented one pressed on them by the welfare rights movement.[7]

The essential element distinguishing the supplementary benefit scheme from the other major means of income maintenance is the extent to which discretion plays an important part in the system. This is not to say that the various social security benefits do not contain elements of discretion but in supplementary benefits discretion has a role which is both central to the scheme and far-reaching.

This may appear surprising in view of the stress laid at the time of the introduction of the scheme on the concept of a 'right' or 'entitlement' to benefit. Indeed, at first the statutory provision appears to embody this approach:

> Every person in Great Britain of or over the age of 16 whose resources are insufficient to meet his requirements shall be entitled, subject to the provisions of this Act, to benefit . . .[8]

However, in the schedules one finds this major qualification:

> where there are exceptional circumstances . . . b) a supplementary allowance may be reduced below the amount so calculated (i.e. according to the previous provisions in the schedule) or may be withheld as may be appropriate to take account of those circumstances.[9]

This latter provision has been interpreted extremely widely. Under the 'Four-Week Rule' it was used to discontinue benefit after four weeks to a total of over 250,000 single, fit, unskilled men in areas where work was thought to be available. Thus a formal 'right' to benefit is given by the Act whilst at the same time care is taken that it does not necessarily extend to all groups of potential recipients. The disparity between apparent formal entitlement and the extent to which the Commission is able to exercise its powers emerges also in the recent cases involving students. In the last of these cases the fact that the claimant was a student was accepted as amounting to 'exceptional circumstances', and that therefore the Commission had an extremely wide discretion to award such benefit as it might think fit, and one in which the court would not intervene.[10] In addition areas of discretion based on 'need' are of considerable importance within the supplementary benefits scheme. Benefit may be increased in 'exceptional circumstances' and a single payment may be made to meet an 'exceptional need'.

One explanation for the extent of this discretion might be that at the time of the framing of the Act it was impossible to anticipate the eventualities that might arise and so the discretion represents an inevitable looseness in drawing up the Act or lack of subtlety in framing it which could now be remedied by clarification of the statute. Thus the supplementary benefit legislation could be seen as having a clear aim but as not being at a sufficient stage of refinement to meet this properly. Alternatively the discretion is often justified as a means of meeting varying individual needs. However the policies laid down by the Commission in their secret codes to guide the exercise of discretion have a strong tendency to coalesce into rigid rules, so that individual needs are not in fact met because these hidden rules do not allow it.

I suggest that the discretion is extensive because this is not an example of legislation designed to further a clear aim, which has certain deficiencies in meeting it, but it is an attempt to set up a scheme with varying and contradictory functions. The use of discretion guided by secret rules is a means of avoiding the open resolution of the political conflicts inherent in this. As Jordan has discussed, poor relief has never been designed purely to meet needs but has other functions which can be traced through from the first Poor Law and which have come to dominate the actual provision of benefits, for example maintaining the work ethic and enforcing low-paid work, enforcing family responsibility, and heading off the potential threat of the poor to the social order.[11] Similarly Piven and Cloward have documented in detail the role of the American relief system in forcing low-paid work and maintaining order.[12] This means that differing and contradictory considerations will come into play in deciding claims to benefit, and the structure of the Supplementary Benefits legislation with its large areas of discretion is an attempt to reconcile these contradictions:

> ... our social security (i.e. supplementary benefit) legislation tries to reconcile the development of a universalistic system to meet all needs with a traditional attitude to the poor which regards them as undeserving unless they can produce unambiguous evidence to the contrary, but really leaves it to the officials dealing with individual cases to effect the reconciliation.[13]

Thus the discretion can be seen as a means of providing different treatment for different types of claimant, as was the case with the 'four-week rule'. It will be noted that the provision for the reduction or withdrawal of benefit in exceptional circumstances applies only to supplementary allowances. The benefit of those over pensionable age cannot be reduced or withdrawn in this way. In their case the conflicts of function are much less prominent. Similarly, the system of providing discretionary extras based on 'need' and determined by internal, secret rules rather than open provision is a way of rationing benefits without the open resolution of the conflicts involved.

These conflicts in the provision of benefit are also an important element in actual tribunal hearings, emerging particularly strongly in the assessment of the moral character of the appellants. To understand the situation properly one must look at the nature of welfare relief in the economic system.

It is suggested that in more general terms the welfare State does not perform merely a philanthropic function. If one views society in terms of political and economic conflict it can be seen as having a role in preserving political order, in acting as a 'shock absorber' to prevent more serious attacks being made on the social order, or simply as an economic regulator to maintain demand. Thus poor relief may be seen as functional to the present economic system, or rather its actual existence is seen as functional. On the other hand, its ethical content is, in Thompson's words, 'a profoundly anti-capitalist' conception. This is echoed by Barratt Brown:

> Far from the increase in public spending having buttressed up the capitalist system ideologically as well as financially, what could be more totally destructive of the system's whole ethic than that people should deliberately choose leisure, should prefer not to work, should follow the hippies?[14]

A more recent and subtle account of this has been that of George and Wilding.[15] They explain the failure of the Welfare State to live up to expectations by the nature of the value system of capitalism, centred around the ethic of self-help, individualism, competition and achievement. Thus the welfare criterion of need is undermined by other values. An example is that the extensive advertising of benefits is of little avail when benefit recipients are strongly stigmatised.

The ideological contradictions are an essential element in the supplementary benefit scheme and emerge particularly strongly when the scheme is contrasted with those benefits based on the insurance principle rather than on 'need' where discretion is con-siderably more restricted. This is relevant to the tribunals in several ways. Firstly, the decision making cannot of course be a purely abstract process, particularly when it is 'based on need'. [Thus] an important element is the assessment of moral character which must largely be based on the contradictory ideological factors outlined. Secondly, because of the necessity of reconciling the conflicting con-siderations the area within which the tribunals work consists of very wide elements of discretion which are largely unstructured. The rules used to determine claims are secret and not available to the tribunals. The tribunals also have the role of legitimating decisions by their quasi-legal form and by reference to 'community values' which they are seen as bringing into decision making. In view of the reasons which I have suggested for the existence of the discretion attempts to structure it by developing clear standards and rules are likely to be more difficult in practice than has often been supposed. The concealment of the conflict of values involved has been an important element in enabling the smooth survival of the supplementary benefit system.

1. C. Reich, 'The New Property', *Yale Law Journal* (1964) vol. 73, p. 733 and 'Individual Rights and Social Welfare–The Emerging Legal issues', *Yale Law Journal* (1965) vol. 74, p. 1245.
2. *R. v. Greater Birmingham Appeal Tribunal, Ex. p. Simper* [1974] 1 Q.B. 543.
3. National Insurance and Supplementary Benefits Act 1973. See M. Partington, 'Some Thoughts on a Test-Case Strategy', *New Law Journal* (1974) vol. 124, pp. 236–8.
4. *R. v. Preston Supplementary Benefit Appeal Tribunal Ex p. Moore, R. v. Sheffield Supplementary Benefit Appeal Tribunal Ex p. Shine* [1975] 2 All E.R. 807. For comment see C. Smith, 'Judicial Attitudes to Social Security', *British Journal of Law and Society*, (1975) vol. 2, pp. 217–21.
5. *R. v. West London Supplementary Benefit Appeal Tribunal Ex p. Taylor* [1975] 2 All E.R. 790; *R. v. West London Supplementary Benefit Appeal Tribunal Ex p. Clarke* [1975] 3 All E.R. 513.
6. *R. v. Barnsley Supplementary Benefit Appeal Tribunal Ex p. Atkinson* [1976] 2 All E.R. 686. (Subsequent to drafting of above the Court of Appeal reversed this decision (The Times, 17 February 1977) but the decision is unlikely to have much practical effect.)
7. There have been further developments recently. On 18 January 1977, it was announced that the Department would gradually move towards the appointment of more legally qualified chairmen, that an appeal on point of law to the High Court will now be provided from the tribunals, that training for chairmen will be introduced, and a number of minor changes will be made. See *L. A. G. Bulletin*, February (1977).
8. Supplementary Benefit Act 1966, s. 6.
9. *Ibid.*, Sch. 2, para. 4(1).
10. *R. v. Barnsley Supplementary Benefit Appeal Tribunal Ex p. Atkinson, op. cit.,* esp. at 689.
11. B. Jordan, *Poor Parents* London, Routledge and Kegan Paul (1974).
12. F. F. Piven and R. Cloward, *Regulating the Poor* London, Tavistock (1972).
13. M. J. Hill, *The Sociology of Public Administration* London, Weidenfeld and Nicholson, (1972) p. 78.
14. M. Barratt Brown, 'The Welfare State in Britain' *Socialist Register* (1971) 185, p. 204.
15. V. George and P. Wilding, *Ideology and Social Welfare* London, Routledge and Kegan Paul (1976) pp. 106–29.

5. Legal Controls and Informal Order
by David Caplowitz

From The Poor Pay More, *New York, The Free Press (1967) pp. 20–5 and 29–30.*

We have reviewed the elements of the system of exchange that comprise the low-income market. For the consumer, these are the availability of merchandise, the 'easy' installments, and the reassurance of dealing with merchants who make them feel at home. In return, the merchant reserves for himself the right to sell low-quality merchandise at exorbitant prices.

But the high markup on goods does not insure that the business will be profitable. No matter what he charges, the merchant can remain in business only if customers actually pay. In this market, the customer's intention and ability to pay–the assumptions underlying any credit system–cannot be taken for granted. Techniques for insuring continuity of payments are a fundamental part of this distinctive economy.

Formal Controls

When the merchant uses an installment contract, he has recourse to legal controls over his customers. But as we shall see, legal controls are not sufficient to cope with the merchant's problem and they are seldom used.

Repossession – The merchant who offers credit can always repossess his merchandise should the customer default on payments. But repossession, according to the merchants, is rare. They claim that the merchandise receives such heavy use as to become practically worthless in a short time. And no doubt the shoddy merchandise will not stand much use, heavy or light. One merchant said that he will occasionally repossess an item, not to regain his equity, but to punish a customer he feels is trying to cheat him.

Liens Against Property and Wages – The merchant can, of course, sue the defaulting customer. By winning a court judgement, he can have the customer's property attached. Should this fail to satisfy the debt, he can take the further step of having the customer's salary garnisheed.[1] But these devices are not fully adequate for several reasons. Not all customers have property of value or regular jobs.

Furthermore, their employers will not hesitate to fire them rather than submit to the nuisance of a garnishment. But since the customer knows he may lose his job if he is garnisheed, the mere threat of garnishment is sometimes enough to insure regularity of payments.[2] The main limitation with legal controls, however, is that the merchant who uses them repeatedly runs the risk of forfeiting good will in the neighborhood.

Discounting Paper–The concern with good will places a limitation on the use of another legal practice open to merchants for minimizing their risk: the sale of their contracts to a credit agency at a discount. By selling his contracts to one of the licensed finance companies, the merchant can realize an immediate return on his investment. The problem with this technique is that the merchant loses control over his customer. As an impersonal, bureaucratic organization, the credit agency has recourse only to legal controls. Should the customer miss a payment, the credit agency will take the matter to court. But in the customer's mind, his contract exists with the merchant, not with the credit agency. Consequently, the legal actions taken against him reflect upon the merchant, and so good will is not preserved after all.

For this reason, the merchant is reluctant to 'sell his paper', particularly if he has reason to believe that the customer will miss some payments. When he does sell some of his contracts at a discount, his motive is not to reduce risk, but rather to obtain working capital. Since so much of his capital is tied up in credit transactions, he frequently finds it necessary to make such sales. Oddly enough, he is apt to sell his better 'paper', that is, the contracts of customers who pay regularly, for he wants to avoid incurring the ill will of customers. This practice also has its draw-backs for the merchant. Competitors can find out from the credit agencies which customers pay regularly and then try to lure them away from the original merchant. Some merchants reported that in order to retain control over their customers, they will buy back contracts from credit agencies they suspect are giving information to competitors.[3]

Credit Association Ratings – All credit merchants report their bad debtors to the credit association to which they belong. The merchants interviewed said that they always consult the 'skip lists' of their association before extending credit to a new customer. In this way they can avoid at least the customers known to be bad risks. This form of control tends to be effective in the long run because the customers find that they are unable to obtain credit until they have made good on their past debts. During the interviews with them, some consumers mentioned this need to restore their credit rating as the reason why they were paying off debts in spite of their belief that they had been cheated.

But these various formal techniques of control are not sufficient to cope with the merchant's problem of risk. He also depends heavily on informal and personal techniques of control.

Informal Controls

The merchant starts from the premise that most of his customers are honest people who intend to pay but have difficulty managing their money. Missed payments are seen as more often due to poor management and to emergencies than to dishonesty. The merchants anticipate that their customers will miss some payments and they rely on informal controls to insure that payments are eventually made.

All the merchants described their credit business as operating on a 'fifteen-month year', This means that they expect the customer to miss about one of every four payments and they compute the markup accordingly. Unlike the credit companies, which insist upon regular payments and add service charges for late payments, the neighborhood merchant is prepared to extend 'flexible' credit. Should the customer miss an occasional payment or should he be short on another, the merchant considers this a normal part of his business. To insure the close personal control necessary for this system of credit, the merchant frequently draws up a contract calling for weekly payments which the customer usually brings to the store. This serves several functions for the merchant. To begin with, the sum of money represented by a weekly payment is relatively small and so helps to create the illusion of 'easy credit'. Customers are apt to think more of the size of the payments than of the cost of the item or the length of the contract.

More importantly, the frequent contact of a weekly-payment system enables the merchant to get to know his customer. He learns when the customer receives his pay check, when his rent is due, who his friends are, when job layoffs, illnesses, and other emergencies occur–in short, all sorts of information which allow him to interpret the reason for a missed payment. Some merchants reported that when they know the customer has missed a payment for a legitimate reason such as illness or a job layoff, they will send a sympathetic note and offer the customer a gift (an inexpensive lamp or wall picture) when payments are resumed. This procedure, they say, frequently brings the customer back with his missed payments.

The short interval between payments also functions to give the merchant an early warning when something is amiss. His chances of locating the delinquent customer are that much greater. Furthermore, the merchant can keep tabs on a delinquent customer through his knowledge of the latter's friends, relatives, neighbors, and associates, who are also apt to be customers of his. In this way, still another informal device, the existing network of social relations, is utilized by the neighborhood merchant in conducting his business.[4]

The weekly-payment system also provides the merchant with the opportunity to sell other items to the customer. When the first purchase is almost paid for, the merchant will try to persuade the customer to make another. Having the customer in the store, where he can look at the merchandise, makes the next sale that much easier. This system of successive sales is, of course, an ideal arrangement – for the merchant. As a result, the customer remains continuously in debt to him. The pattern is somewhat reminiscent of the Southern sharecropper's relations to the company store. And since a number of customers grew up in more traditional environments with just such economies, they may find the arrangements acceptable. The practice of buying from peddlers, found to be common in these low-income areas, also involves the principle of continuous indebtedness. The urban low-income economy, then, is in some respects like the sharecropper system; it might almost be called an 'urban sharecropper system'.

The Customer Peddlers

Characteristic of the comparatively traditional and personal form of the low-income economy is the important role played in it by the door-to-door credit salesman, the customer peddler. The study of merchants found that these peddlers are not necessarily competitors of the store-owners. Almost all merchants make use of peddlers in the great competition for customers. The merchants tend to regard peddlers as necessary evils who add greatly to the final cost of purchases. But they need them because in their view, customers are too ignorant, frightened, or lazy to come to the stores themselves.

Thus, the merchants' apparent contempt for peddlers does not bar them from employing outdoor salesmen (or 'canvassers', as they describe the peddlers who work for one store or another). Even the merchants who are themselves reluctant to hire canvassers find they must do so in order to meet the competition. The peddler's main function for the merchant, then, is getting the customer to the store, and if he will not come, getting the store to the customer. But this is not his only function.

Much more than the storekeeper, the peddler operates on the basis of a personal relationship with the customer. By going to the customer's home, he gets to know the entire family; he sees the condition of the home and he comes to know the family's habits and wants. From this vantage point he is better able than the merchant to evaluate the customer as a credit risk. Since many of the merchant's potential customers lack the standard credentials of credit, such as having a permanent job, the merchant needs some other basis for discriminating between good and bad risks. If the peddler, who has come to know the family, is ready to vouch for the customer, the merchant will be ready to make the transaction. In short, the peddler acts as a fiduciary agent, a Dun and Bradstreet for the poor, telling the merchant which family is likely to meet its obligations and which is not.

Not all peddlers are employed by stores. Many are independent enterprisers (who may have started as canvassers for stores). A number of the independent peddlers have accumulated enough capital to supply their customers with major durables. These are the elite peddlers, known as 'dealers', who buy appliances and furniture from local merchants at a 'wholesale' price, and then sell them on credit to their customers. In these transactions, the peddler either takes the customer to the store or sends the customer to the store with his card on which he has written some such message as 'Please give Mr. Jones a TV set'. The merchant then sells the customer the TV set at a price much higher than he would ordinarily charge. The 'dealer' is generally given two months to pay the merchant the 'wholesale' price, and meanwhile he takes over the responsibility of collecting from his customer. Some 'dealers' are so successful that they employ canvassers in their own right. And some merchants do so much business with 'dealers' that they come to think of themselves as 'wholesalers' even though they are fully prepared to do their own retail business.

Independent peddlers without much capital also have economic relations with local merchants. They act as brokers, directing their customers to neighborhood stores that will extend them credit. And for this service they of course receive a commission. In these transactions, it is the merchant who accepts the risks and assumes the responsibility for collecting payments. The peddler who acts as a broker performs the same function as the merchant in the T.O. system. He knows which merchants will accept great risk and which will not, and directs his customers accordingly.

There are, then, three kinds of customer peddlers operating in these low-income neighborhoods who cooperate with local merchants: the canvassers who are employed directly by the stores; the small entrepreneurs who act as brokers; and the more successful entrepreneurs who operate as 'dealers'. A fourth type of peddler consists of salesmen representing large companies not necessarily located in the neighborhood. These men are, for the most part, canvassers for firms specializing in a particular commodity, e.g., encyclopedias, vacuum cleaners, or pots and pans. They differ from the other peddlers by specializing in what they sell and by depending more on contracts and legal controls. They are also less interested in developing continuous relationships with their customers.

Peddlers thus aid the local merchants by finding customers, evaluating them as credit risks, and helping in the collection of payments. And as the merchants themselves point out, these services add greatly to the cost of the goods. One storekeeper said that peddlers are apt to charge five and six times the amount the store charges for relatively inexpensive purchases. Pointing to a religious picture which he sells for $5, he maintained the peddlers sell it for as much as $30. And he estimated that the peddler adds 30 to 50 per cent to the final sales price of appliances and furniture.

Unethical and Illegal Practices

We uncovered some evidence that some local merchants engage in the illegal practice of selling reconditioned furniture and appliances as new. Of course, no merchant would admit that he did this himself, but five of them hinted that their competitors engaged in this practice. As we shall see, several of the consumers we interviewed were quite certain that they had been victimized in this way.

One unethical, if not illegal, activity widely practiced by stores is 'bait' advertising with its concomitant, the 'switch sale'. In the competition for customers, merchants depend heavily upon advertising displays in their windows which announce furniture or appliances at unusually low prices. The customer may enter the store assuming that the low offer in the window signifies a reasonably low price line. Under severe pressure, the storekeeper may even be prepared to sell the merchandise at the advertised price, for not to do so would be against the law. What most often happens, however, is that the unsuspecting customer is convinced by the salesman that he doesn't really want the goods advertised in the window and is then persuaded to buy a smaller amount of more expensive goods. Generally, not much persuasion is necessary. The most populat 'bait ad' is the announcement of three rooms of furniture for 'only $149' or 'only $199'. The customer who inquires about this bargain is shown a bedroom set consisting of two cheap and (sometimes deliberately) chipped bureaus and one bed frame. He learns that the spring and mattress are not included in the advertised price, but can be had for another $75 or $100. The living-room set in these 'specials' consists of a fragile-looking sofa and one unmatching chair. The frequent success of this kind of exploitation, known in the trade as the 'switch sale', is reflected in this comment by one merchant: 'I don't know how they do it. They advertise three rooms of furniture for $149 and the customers swarm in. *They end up buying a $400 bedroom set for $600 and none of us can believe how easily it is to make these sales.*'

In sum, a fairly intricate system of sales-and-credit has evolved in response to the distinctive situation of the low-income consumer and the local merchant. It is a system heavily slanted in the direction of a traditional economy in which informal, personal ties play a major part in the transaction. At the same time it is connected to impersonal bureaucratic agencies through the instrument of the installment contract. Should the informal system break down, credit companies, courts of law, and agencies of law enforcement come to play a part.

The system is not only different from the larger, more formal economy; in some respects it is a *deviant* system in which practices that violate prevailing moral standards are commonplace. As Merton has pointed out in his analysis of the political machine, the persistence of deviant social structures can only be understood when their social functions (as well as dysfunctions) are taken into account.[5] The basic function of the low-income marketing system is to provide consumer goods to people who fail to meet the requirements of the more legitimate, bureaucratic market, or who choose to exclude themselves from the larger market because they do not feel comfortable in it. As we have seen, the system is extraordinarily flexible. Almost no one – however great a risk – is turned away. Various mechanisms sift and sort customers according to their credit risk and match them with merchants ready to sell them the goods they want. Even the family on welfare is permitted to maintain its self-respect by consuming in much the same way as do its social peers who happen not to be on welfare.

1. It is of some interest that the low-income families we interviewed were all familiar with the word 'garnishees'. This may well be one word in the language that the poorly educated are more likely to know than the better educated.
2. Welfare families cannot, of course, be garnisheed, and more than half of the merchants reported that they sell to them. But the merchants can threaten to disclose the credit purchase to the welfare authorities. Since recipients of welfare funds are not supposed to buy on credit, this threat exerts powerful pressure on the family.
3. Not all merchants are particularly concerned with good will. A few specialize in extending credit to the worst risks, customers turned away by most other merchants. These men will try to collect as much as they can on their accounts during the year and then will sell all their outstanding accounts to a finance company. As a result, the most inadequate consumers are apt to meet with the bureaucratic controls employed by the finance company. For a description of how bill collectors operate, see Hillel Black, *Buy Now, Pay Later*, New York, William Morrow and Co. (1961) ch. 4.
4. The merchant's access to these networks of social relations is not entirely independent of economic considerations. Just as merchants who refer customers receive commissions, so customers who recommend others are often given commissions. Frequently, this is why a customer will urge his friends to deal with a particular merchant.
5. Robert K. Merton, *Social Theory and Social Structure*, rev. ed., New York, The Free Press of Glencoe (1957) pp. 71–82.

6. Order Maintaining Ceremonies
by Harold Garfinkel

From 'Conditions of Successful Degradation Ceremonies', The American Journal of Sociology (*1956*) *vol. 61, pp. 420–4.*

Any communicative work between persons, whereby the public identity of an actor is transformed into something looked on as lower in the local scheme of social types, will be called a 'status degradation ceremony'. Some restrictions on this definition may increase its usefulness. The identities referred to must be 'total' identities. That is, these identities must refer to persons as 'motivational' types rather than as 'behavioral' types, not to what a person may be expected to have done or to do, but to what the group holds to be the ultimate 'grounds' or 'reasons' for his performance.

The grounds on which a participant achieves what for him is adequate understanding of why he or another acted as he did are not treated by him in a utilitarian manner. Rather, the correctness of an imputation is decided by the participant in accordance with socially valid and institutionally recommended standards of 'preference'. With reference to these standards, he makes the crucial distinctions between appearances and reality, truth and falsity, triviality and importance, accident and essence, coincidence and cause. Taken together, the grounds, as well as the behavior that the grounds make explicable as the other person's conduct, constitute a person's identity. Together, they constitute the other as a social object. Persons identified by means of the ultimate 'reasons' for their socially categorized and socially understood behavior will be said to be 'totally' identified. The degradation ceremonies here discussed are those that are concerned with the alteration of total identities.

It is proposed that only in societies that are completely demoralized, will an observer be unable to find such ceremonies, since only in total anomie are the conditions of degradation ceremonies lacking. Max Scheler argued that there is no society that does not provide in the very features of its organization the conditions sufficient for inducing shame. It will be treated here as axiomatic that there is no society whose social structure does not provide, in its routine features, the conditions of identity degradation. Just as the structural conditions of shame are universal to all societies by the very fact of their being organized, so the structural conditions of status degradation are universal to all societies. In this framework the critical question is not whether status degradation occurs or can occur within any given society. Instead, the question is: starting from any state of a society's organization, what program of communicative tactics will get the work of status degradation done?

First of all, two questions will have to be decided, at least tentatively: *What are we referring to behaviorially when we propose the product of successful degradation work to be a changed total identity?* And *what are we to conceive the work of status degradation to have itself accomplished or to have assumed as the conditions of its success?*

Degradation ceremonies fall within the scope of the sociology of moral indignation. Moral indignation is a social effect. Roughly speaking, it is an instance of a class of feelings particular to the more or less organized ways that human beings develop as they live out their lives in one another's company. Shame, guilt, and boredom are further important instances of such affects.

Any affect has its behavioral paradigm. That of shame is found in the withdrawal and covering of the portion of the body that socially defines one's public appearance – prominently, in our society, the eyes and face. The paradigm of shame is found in the phrases that denote removal of the self from public view, i.e., removal from the regard of the publicly identified other: 'I could have sunk through the floor; I wanted to run away and hide; I wanted the earth to open up and swallow me.' The feeling of guilt finds its paradigm in the behavior of self-abnegation – disgust, the rejection of further contact with or withdrawal from, and the bodily and symbolic expulsion of the foreign body, as when we cough, blow, gag, vomit, spit, etc.

The paradigm of moral indignation is *public* denunciation. We publicly deliver the curse: 'I call upon all men to bear witness that he is not as he appears but is otherwise and *in essence* of a lower species.'

The social affects serve various functions both for the person as well as for the collectivity. A prominent function of shame for the person is that of preserving the ego from further onslaughts by withdrawing entirely its contact with the outside. For the collectivity shame is an 'individuator'. One experiences shame in his own time.

Moral indignation serves to effect the ritual destruction of the person denounced. Unlike shame, which does not bind persons together, moral indignation may reinforce group solidarity. In the market and in politics, a degradation ceremony must be counted as a secular form of communion. Structurally, a degradation ceremony bears close resemblance to ceremonies of investiture and elevation. How such a ceremony may bind persons to the collectivity we shall see when we take up the conditions of a successful denunciation. Our immediate question concerns the meaning of ritual destruction.

In the statement that moral indignation brings about the ritual destruction of the person being denounced, destruction is intended literally. The transformation of identities is the destruction of one social object and the constitution of another. The transformation does not involve the substitution of one identity for another, with the terms of the old one loitering about like the overlooked parts of a fresh assembly, any more than the woman we see in the department-store window that turns out to be a dummy carries with it the possibilities of a woman. It is not that the old object has been overhauled; rather it is replaced by another. One declares, '*Now*, it was otherwise in the first place.'

The work of the denunciation effects the recasting of the objective character of the perceived other: The other person becomes in the eyes of his condemners literally a different *new* person. It is not that the new attributes are added to the old 'nucleus'. He is not changed, he is reconstituted. The former identity, at best, receives the accent of mere appearance. In the social calculus of reality representations and test, the former identity stands as accidental; the new identity is the 'basic reality'. What he is now is what, 'after all', he was all along.

The public denunciation effects such a transformation of essence by substituting another socially validated motivational scheme for that previously used to name and order the performances of the denounced. It is with reference to this substituted, socially validated motivational scheme as the essential grounds, i.e., the *first principles*, that his performances, past, present, and prospective, according to the witnesses, are to be properly and necessarily understood. Through the interpretive work that respects this rule, the denounced person becomes in the eyes of the witnesses a different person.

How can one make a good denunciation?
To be successful, the denunciation must redefine the situations of those that are witnesses to the denunciation work. The denouncer, the party to be denounced (let us call him the 'perpetrator'), and the thing that is being blamed on the perpetrator (let us call it the 'event') must be transformed as follows:
   1. Both event and perpetrator must be removed from the realm of

their everyday character and be made to stand as 'out of the ordinary'.

2. Both event and perpetrator must be placed within a scheme of preferences that shows the following properties:

A. The preferences must not be for event A over event B, but for event of *type* A over event of *type* B. The same typing must be accomplished for the perpetrator. Event and perpetrator must be defined as instances of a uniformity and must be treated as a uniformity throughout the work of the denunciation. The unique, never recurring character of the event or perpetrator should be lost. Similarly, any sense of accident, coincidence, indeterminism, chance, or momentary occurrence must not merely be minimized. Ideally, such measures should be inconceivable; at least they should be made false.

B. The witnesses must appreciate the characteristics of the typed person and event by referring the type to a dialectical counterpart. Ideally, the witnesses should not be able to contemplate the features of the denounced person without reference to the counterconception, as the profanity of an occurrence or a desire or a character trait, for example, is clarified by the references it bears to its opposite, the sacred. The features of the mad-dog murderer reverse the features of the peaceful citizen. The confessions of the Red can be read to teach the meanings of patriotism. There are many contrasts available and any aggregate of witnesses this side of a complete war of each against all will have a plethora of such schemata for effecting a 'familiar', 'natural', 'proper', ordering of motives, qualities, and other events.

From such contrasts, the following is to be learned. If the denunciation is to take effect, the scheme must not be one in which the witness is allowed to elect the preferred. Rather, the alternatives must be such that the preferred is morally required. Matters must be so arranged that the validity of his choice, its justification, is maintained by the fact that he makes it. The scheme of alternatives must be such as to place constraints upon his making a selection 'for a purpose'. Nor will the denunciation succeed if the witness is free to look beyond the fact that he makes the selection for evidence that the correct alternative has been chosen, as, for example, by the test of empirical consequences of the choice. The alternatives must be such that, in 'choosing', he takes it for granted and beyond any motive for doubt that not choosing can mean only preference for its opposite.

3. The denouncer must so identify himself to the witnesses that during the denunciation they regard him not as a private but as a

publicly known person. He must not portray himself as acting according to his personal, unique experiences. He must rather be regarded as acting in his capacity as a public figure, drawing upon communally entertained and verified experience. He must act as a bona fide participant in the tribal relationships to which the witnesses subscribe. What he says must not be regarded as true for him alone, not even in the sense that it can be regarded by denouncer and witnesses as matters upon which they can become agreed. In no case, except in a most ironical sense, can the convention of true-for-reasonable-men be invoked. What the denouncer says must be regarded by the witnesses as true on the grounds of a socially employed metaphysics whereby witnesses assume that witnesses and denouncer are alike in essence.

4. The denouncer must make the dignity of the supra-personal values of the tribe salient and accessible to view, and his denunciation must be delivered in their name.

5. The denouncer must arrange to be invested with the right to speak in the name of these ultimate values. The success of the denunciation will be undermined if, for his authority to denounce, the denouncer invokes the personal interest that he may have acquired by virtue of the wrong done to him or someone else. He must rather use the wrong he has suffered as a tribal member to invoke the authority to speak in the name of these ultimate values.

6. The denouncer must get himself so defined by the witnesses that they locate him as a supporter of these values.

7. Not only must the denouncer fix his distance from the person being denounced, but the witnesses must be made to experience their distance from him also.

8. Finally, the denounced person must be ritually separated from a place in the legitimate order, i.e., he must be defined as standing at a place opposed to it. He must be placed 'outside', he must be made 'strange'.

These are the conditions that must be fulfilled for a successful denunciation. If they are absent, the denunciation will fail. Regardless of the situation when the denouncer enters, if he is to succeed in degrading the other man, it is necessary to introduce these features.

Not all degradation ceremonies are carried on in accordance with publicly prescribed and publicly validated measures. Quarrels which seek the humiliation of the opponent through personal invective may achieve degrading on a limited scale. Comparatively few persons at a time enter into this form of communion, few benefit from it, and the fact of participation does not give the witness a definition of the other that is standardized beyond the particular group or scene of its occurrence.

The devices for effecting degradation vary in the feature and effectiveness according to the organization and operation of the system of action in which they occur. In our society the arena of degradation whose produce, the redefined person, enjoys the widest transferability between groups has been rationalized, at least as to the institutional measures for carrying it out. The court and its officers have something like a fair monopoly over such ceremonies, and there they have become an occupational routine. This is to be contrasted with degradation undertaken as an immediate kinship and tribal obligation and carried out by those who, unlike our professional degraders in the law courts, acquire both right and obligation to engage in it through being themselves the injured parties or kin to the injured parties.

Factors conditioning the effectiveness of degradation tactics are provided in the organization and operation of the system of action within which the degradation occurs. For example, timing rules that provide for serial or reciprocal 'conversations' would have much to do with the kinds of tactics that one might be best advised to use. The tactics advisable for an accused who can answer the charge as soon as it is made are in contrast with those recommended for one who has to wait out the denunciation before replying. Face-to-face contact is a different situation from that wherein the denunciation and reply are conducted by radio and newspaper. Whether the denunciation must be accomplished on a single occasion or is to be carried out over a sequence of 'tries', factors like the territorial arrangements and movements of persons at the scene of the denunciation, the numbers of persons involved as accused, degraders, and witnesses, status claims of the contenders, prestige and power allocations among participants, all should influence the outcome.

In short, the factors that condition the success of the work of degradation are those that we point to when we conceive the actions of a number of persons as group-governed. Only some of the more obvious structural variables that may be expected to serve as predictors of the characteristics of denunciatory communicative tactics have been mentioned. They tell us not only how to construct an effective denunciation but also how to render denunciation useless.

IV Law and Legal Control

1. Introduction

The very fact that law exists in society suggests that there is behaviour which it is desired to control. However the existence of other rules and norms in society similarly suggests control. One problem for a sociology of law is therefore to distinguish legal from non-legal means of control, and to understand how they are related to one another.

Law itself uses many different forms of control. Sometimes it creates formal institutions to exercise its control and to search out deviants. These may take many forms ranging from police to inspectorates. Frequently law creates no specific institutions, but relies instead upon litigants to activate its controlling powers through the regular courts. Why different types of control are used for different types of law, and differentially activated, needs sociological explanation. Ultimately law claims absolute power to control. Many writers, from Weber to Lenin, have suggested that a defining characteristic of law is that it claims a monopoly over the use of force within a given territory. Yet even at this margin we have to determine what distinguishes the 'legal' from the 'illegal' use of force . . . and what explains the shift from one to the other.

This, however, does not exhaust the sociological questions we should ask about law and control. Even where law creates a mechanism for control, we still need to discover how that mechanism is actually used and works in reality. Police and courts may exist, but how do they achieve control, how are their methods related to legality and what is the explanation of the way they behave? Where law does not create a control institution we need to explain why private institutions (such as debt collectors or security companies) develop and what logic controls their actions. How do institutions, occupations and professions which are ostensibly not about implementing legal control contribute in areas within their purview to maintaining the control that is required by law? Finally, how are law and its functionaries themselves controlled, and how is this explained?

The writings that follow reveal some of the important dimensions of formal and informal control and their relationships to legal sanctions. Some answers to the questions we have raised are suggested.

2. The Collection Routine
by Paul Rock

From Making People Pay, *London, Routledge and Kegan Paul (1973) pp. 51–6.*

When a successful applicant passes the stage of credit sanctioning, he may take any one of a number of prepared routes before he becomes of no further interest to his creditor. From a creditor's point of view, the ideal route is a strict adherence to the norms established in the contract. A debtor who commits himself to paying eighteen monthly instalments will pay those instalments in eighteen months without any intervention from the creditor. The most common path, however, combines eventual repayment with minor forays into an enforcement career. Every time a person receives a notice from a gas board, a rating authority or a commercial concern, he enters a carefully contrived system of social control. Most creditors expect that the majority of their agreements will go into default on at least one occasion and, at any single time, their enforcement will be directed at some 10 per cent of their customers.

The organized response to default is superficially simple but analytically complex. It maps out alternative sequences of action which can be applied to different 'types' of default. The sequences are all variants of one basic model: a stream of ever more threatening letters; a personal confrontation between debtor and creditor; and, finally, enforcement prosecuted by debt-collectors or the courts.

This process conforms to Roth's definition of the career as 'a series of related and definable stages or phases of a given sphere of activity that a person goes through on the way to a more or less definite and recognizable end-point or goal (or series of goals)'.[1] Any career can be described in terms of its key structural characteristics; its complexity, duration, intensity of experience, direction, goal, spacing, pacing, tempo and prevailing rational and sentimental order.[2] These features are all interrelated and their interaction becomes especially complicated when a career is as protracted as an enforcement sequence.

Any deliberately constructed career is shaped primarily by the purposes which it is supposed to serve. Enforcement has no single purpose. It is not only aimed at the rapid recovery of debts, it also performs ancillary functions and is subordinated to other institutional goals. It is evident that creditors are chiefly concerned with finance, and financial criteria dominate their handling of default. Enforcement cannot be conducted in a way which conflicts with a creditor's companion demand for economy. Creditors will be reluctant enforcers if the collection of debts costs more than the amounts which they can recover. They may even resort to a token display of vigilance and abandon any pretence of serious action:

> It usually takes about three months before they get a final letter from us saying we're going to do this, that and the other. In actual fact, we do *nothing*. I don't even take them to court because it's not worth it. [Creditor 3.]

Most firms establish an arbitrary 'write-off' figure which represents the minimum debt they are prepared actively to collect. The margin is based on the cost of enforcement and the extent to which a creditor imagines himself to be vulnerable to the predatory professional debtor. Present losses may be countenanced if they avert a larger future default:

> If the sum of money's smallish, we decide whether it's *worth* spending money to get less than we spend. Alternatively, we may take the option that things have been too lax and lenient. You're getting a reputation for an easy mark. Even if it costs you a few bob or a few pound, to go ahead with a half dozen people who are obviously nasty cases and, even if you lose money, deal with them in the court. [Creditor 16.]

Above all, the margin reflects the autonomy of a creditor's enforcement department. External institutions may impose an unwelcome 'write-off' figure. Solicitors and debt-collectors may simply refuse to take action about certain sums. Relations within a creditor's organization may also bring about particular decisions which run counter to the department's conception of a suitable margin. A relatively powerless department may have to harass debtors for trifling sums:

> It's not worthwhile pursuing them but it's just as difficult for us to get thirteen bob written off on a month's schedule as it is for us to issue a summons. [Creditor 10, a gas board.]

Creditors must structure the whole enforcement system so that it is not unduly expensive. Although all enforcement agencies are troubled by economic restraints, debt-collecting institutions are uniquely restrained. Murder, drug addiction and other forms of deviance cannot be neatly measured in monetary terms and their prosecution is impelled by 'moral' pressures which resist such measurement. Collection, however, is peculiarly susceptible to costing. The ostensible aim of enforcement is the reduction of economic loss, and collection is governed by considerations of how cheaply an efficient system can be administered and how financially advantageous each step is likely to be. A creditor who is owed large individual sums will therefore tend to be more strenuous than a firm whose debts average a few pounds.

Enforcement is strongly influenced by economy because it almost always involves a creditor in loss. The Inland Revenue permits certain companies to claim allowances in taxation for bad debt and the expenses incurred in enforcement.[3] Such allowances are assessed at Corporation Tax Rate which, at present [1969], is 42½ per cent. Hence, for every £100 lost by a firm, £42.50 can be deducted from its taxable profits. A fortunate creditor might regain his county court costs in full but he cannot totally recover what he spent on debt-collectors, solicitors and his own enforcement machinery. In consequence, he will lose money even when his debtor repays the debt. When the debt has to be written off altogether, less than half can be recouped. The growth of consumer credit has transformed collection into an enterprise which deals with millions of pounds each year and the management of careers has therefore become extremely expensive.

There is no certainty that enforcement costs will be recovered from a recalcitrant debtor. Some debts are discharged by people who do not pay the costs of an action, whilst others are abandoned as irretrievable. Any large creditor stands to lose a substantial sum each year because he may have to pursue several thousand accounts. Enforcement leads to an inevitable diminution of profits and creditors try to make this loss as small as possible. Their search for in-expensive remedies affects all collection policies ...

Straightforward enforcement may be upset by a perceived need to deter potential defaulters. In some cases, debt collection may simply become a gigantic exercise in deterrence. Most creditors budget for bad debt and they can claim allowances for it in taxation. They can also adjust their prices by gearing them to their expectation of default. Their main concern is to keep their losses within 'manageable' proportions and their chief fear is an increase in the numbers of their 'bad' accounts. Their losses may grow to a bank-rupting size if they do not conspicuously collect debts. The money they lose is an inevitable consequence of their acceptance of marginal applicants, the duplicity of professional debtors and the poor luck of the unfortunate debtors. No creditors can avoid loss and some firms welcome it as a sign of their exhaustive exploitation of the consumer market:

> If we get caught, we get caught quite often by professional tricksters and by people who are just not too keen on paying. We collect and, to be quite frank ... we write off this bad debt. Our only interest in collecting bad debt, or attempting to collect it, is *pour discourager* (sic) *les autres*. We just don't want it to escalate. It's not worth our while to chase it up. If I had my way, I'd say 'scrub the whole damn lot and write it off because it's far more trouble than it's worth'. [Creditor 5.]

Successful deterrence hinges on forcing harassed debtors to play a role in a drama enacted for an audience of professional and feckless defaulters. Enforcement must be visible, frightening and seemingly unavoidable. A creditor who stresses a deterrent function of collection commits himself to a special presentation of the institution he serves:

> We're very keen on publicity. If we prosecute a hirer, we're very keen that we should get publicity about it. We try and get it as much as we can, to get it as a deterrent. [Creditor 24.]

This search for publicity can pose an acute problem for an enforcer. A creditor plays a number of roles and these place disparate demands on the organization of his public face. The role of enforcement is what Hughes[4] calls 'dirty work'; it is squalid, and does not confer prestige. It also conflicts with another image which a creditor hopes to promote. Firms usually want to represent themselves as the attractive and co-operative suppliers of a desired service:

> Let me put it this way. No person who has been a client of this company has ever gone to prison for debt. Our whole business is built up, and you'll find all moneylenders'll tell you the same, their business is really built upon a friendly atmosphere between lender and borrower. And, if you don't have that friendly atmosphere, you might as well get out of business altogether. [Creditor 30.]

The dirty work of collection cannot easily be disentangled from the other work of the creditor. He may achieve something of a solution by delegating the damaging part of enforcement to an outside agency with another name. One bank, for example, experimented with a debt-collector: its collection manager observed, 'I think some of their methods are a great deal more ruthless than the bank's, and one of the things that's exercising our minds is how closely the bank's name will be linked with whatever methods are being adopted.' (Creditor 1.) An enforcement career will be strongly influenced by the choice taken by a firm. A creditor who want to impress his respectable aspect on the outside world may well curtail all collection that tarnishes it. Bad publicity may stem from a creditor's mistakes and the selection of inappropriate targets for tough enforcement will lead to sympathy for the debtors and criticism of the creditor. There are deficiencies in the creditor's system of acquiring information about defaulters and the task of differentiating between types of debtor is expensive and of limited utility. As a result, a creditor may be unable to avoid selecting debtors whose pursuit will harm him. In many cases, therefore, a creditor does not extend his information-acquiring mechanisms but restricts all vulnerable modes of enforcement:

> On the whole, the bank finds this [execution on goods] very, very unsavoury. It always attracts publicity. I mean, the average county court judgment and court order attract no publicity at all. But the bailiff going knocking on the door and working on investigating what's available for creditors, *always* attracts publicity and the last thing we want is publicity. And therefore in ——— Bank, anyway, and particularly bearing in mind too – this has some effect on the position – the majority of our branches are in the North West in some of the smaller communities where it'd

get even more publicity than in London. You see, London is a bit different. I mean, local influences are just about nil. You can probably get away with all sorts of things in London, doing things to people and threatening them, which people would never raise an eyebrow. [Creditor 12.]

The goals of deterrence and the avoidance of publicity may prove irreconcilable and one may have to give way to the other. Creditors who define both as desirable will have to tailor enforcement so that it permits the use of sanctions innocuous to them, the elaboration of their methods of differentiating between cases, and attack on unquestionably deviant debors. These demands may impose economic and organizational stresses which can be resolved only by emasculating the potency of their collection system. Discreet enforcement is unlikely to be the most effective enforcement. Moreover, it is interesting that 'bad publicity' can be doubly bad for the creditor. Not only might such publicity deter potential customers, it can also justify the selection of the creditor as a victim by defaulters. The moral status of a vengeful creditor is even lower than that of a benign one. Impersonal organizations tend to be regarded a legitimate targets for predatory activity; the discredited organization becomes an even more vulnerable victim.

1. J. Roth, *Timetables*, Indianapolis, Bobbs Merrill (1963) p. xviii.
2. B. Glaser and A. Strauss, *Status Passage*, London, Routledge and Kegan Paul (1971).
3. cf. B. Pinson, *Revenue Law*, London, Sweet and Maxwell (1968) pp. 49–50.
4. E. Hughes, *Men and Their Work* New York, Free Press (1958) pp. 52–4.

3. Police Work
by Jerome H. Skolnick

From Justice without Trial, *New York, John Wiley (1966) pp. 112–37.*

This research concentrates upon the social foundations of legal procedures designed to protect democratic society, where the highest stated commitment is to the ideal of legality, a focal point of tension exists between the substance of order and the procedures for its accomplishment. 'The basic and anguishing dilemma of form and substance in law can be alleviated, but never resolved, for the structure of legal domination retains its distinguishing features only as long as this dilemma is perpetuated.'[1] This dilemma is most clearly manifested in law enforcement organizations, where both sets of demands make forceful normative claims upon police conduct.

First we suggest that the dilemma of the police in democratic society arises out of the conflict between the extent of initiative contemplated by nontotalitarian norms of work and restraints upon police demanded by the rule of law. Second, we consider the meaning of police professionalization, pointing out its limitations according to the idea of managerial efficiency. Finally, we discuss how the policeman's conception of himself as a craftsman is rooted in community expectations, and how the ideology of police professionalization is linked to these expectations. Thus, we focus upon the relation between the policeman's conception of his work and his capacity to contribute to the development of a society based upon the rule of law as its master ideal.

Occupational Environment and the Rule of Law
Five features of the policeman's occupational environment weaken the conception of the rule of law as a primary objective of police conduct. One is the social psychology of police work, that is, the relation between occupational environment, working personality, and the rule of law. Second is the policeman's stake in maintaining his position of authority, especially his interest in bolstering accepted patterns of enforcement. Third is police socialization, especially as it influences the policeman's administrative bias. A related factor is the pressure put upon individual policemen to 'produce' – to be efficient rather than legal when the two norms are in conflict. Finally, there is the policeman's opportunity to behave inconsistently with the rule of law as a result of the low visibility of much of his conduct.

Although it is difficult to weigh the relative import of these factors, they all seem analytically to be joined to the conception of policeman as *craftsman* rather than as *legal actor*, as a skilled worker rather than as a civil servant obliged to subscribe to the rule of law. The significance of the conception of the policeman as a craftsman derives from the differences in ideology of work and authority in totalitarian and nontotalitarian societies. Reinhard Bendix has contended that the most important difference between totalitarian and nontotalitarian forms of subordination is to be found in the managerial handling of problems of authority and subordination. . . .[2] In brief, the managerial ideology of nontotalitarian society maximizes the exercise of discretion by subordinates, while totalitarian society minimizes innovation by working officials.[3]

This dilemma of democratic theory manifests itself in every aspect of the policeman's work, as evidenced by the findings of this study. In explaining the development of the policeman's 'working personality', the dangerous and authoritative elements of police work were emphasized. The combination of these elements undermines attachment to the rule of law in the context of a 'constant' pressure to produce. Under such pressure, the variables of danger and authority tend to alienate the policeman from the general public, and at the same time to heighten his perception of symbols portending danger to him and to the community. Under the same pressure to produce, the policeman not only perceives possible criminality according to the symbolic status of the suspect; he also develops a stake in organized patterns of enforcement. Internal controls over policeman reinforce the importance of administrative and craft values over civil libertarian values. These controls are more likely to emphasize efficiency as a goal rather than legality, or, more precisely, legality as a means to the end of efficiency.

The dilemma of democratic society requiring the police to maintain order and at the same time to be accountable to the rule of law is thus further complicated. Not only is the rule of law often incompatible with the maintenance of order but the principles by which police are governed by the rule of law in a democratic society may be antagonistic to the ideology of worker initiative associated with a nontotalitarian philosophy of work. In the same society, the ideal of legality rejects discretionary innovation by police, while the ideal of worker freedom and autonomy encourages such initiative. Bureaucratic rules are seen in a democracy as 'enabling' regulations, while the regulations deriving from the rule of law are intended to constrain the conduct of officials.

Professionalism and Police Conduct

The idea of professionalism is often invoked as the solution to the conflict between the policeman's task of maintaining order and his accountability to the rule of law. There are, however, costs in developing a professional code based upon the model of administrative efficiency. Such a conception of professionalism not only fails to bridge the gap between the maintenance of order and the rule of law; in addition it comes to serve as an ideology undermining the capacity of police to be accountable to the rule of law ... As a system of organization, bureaucracy can hope to achieve efficiency only by allowing officials to initiate their own means for solving specific problems that interfere with their capacity to achieve productive results ... [While] it is certainly true, as Bendix asserts, that 'a belief in legality means first and foremost that certain formal procedures must be obeyed if the enactment or execution of a law is to be considered legal.'[4] At the same time, while legality may be seen as comprising a set of unchanging ideals, it may also be seen as a working normative system which develops in response to official conduct. The structure of authoritative regulations is such that legal superiors are not part of the same organization as officials and are expected to be 'insensitive' to 'productive capacity' as contrasted with legality. Thus, for example, a body of case law has been emerging that attempts to define the conditions and limits of the use of informants. Legality, therefore, develops as the other side of the coin of official innovation. To the extent that police organizations operate mainly on grounds of administrative efficiency, the development of the rule of law is frustrated. Therefore, a conception of professionalism based mainly on satisfying the demands of administrative efficiency also hampers the capacity of the rule of law to develop.

[If this is to change] what must occur is a significant alteration in the ideology of police, so that police 'professionalization' rests on the values of a democratic legal order, rather than on technological proficiency. No thoughtful person can believe that such a transformation is easily achieved. The argument is always essentially the same: that the efficient administration of criminal law will be hampered by the adoption of procedures designed to protect individual liberties. The police adminstrators on the whole are correct. They have been given wide and direct responsibility for the existence of crime in the community, and it is intrinsically difficult for them to accustom themselves to the basic idea of the rule of law: that the main purpose of law is, in fact, to make their task more difficult.

The Community and Police Conduct

If the police are ever to develop a conception of *legal* as opposed to *managerial* professionalism, they will do so only if the surrounding community demands compliance with the rule of law by rewarding police for such compliance, instead of looking to the police as an institution solely responsible for controlling criminality. In practice, however, the reverse has been true. The police function in a milieu tending to support, normatively and substantively, the idea of administrative efficiency that has become the hallmark of police professionalism. Legality, as expressed by both the criminal courts community with which the police have direct contact, and the political community responsible for the working conditions and prerogatives of police, is a weak ideal.

An 'order' perspective based upon managerial efficiency also tends to be supported by the civic community. The so-called power structure of the community, for example, often stresses to the police the importance of 'keeping the streets clear of crime ...' The emphasis on the maintenance of order is also typically expressed by the political community controlling the significant rewards for the police – money, promotions, etc.

In contrast to that of political authority, the power of appellate courts over the police is limited. In practice, the greatest authority of judges is to deny the merit of the prosecution. Thus, by comparison to the direct sanctions held by political authority, the judiciary has highly restricted *power* to modify the police behavior. Not only do appellate courts lack direct sanctions over the police but there are also powerful political forces that, by their open opposition to the judiciary, suggest an alternative frame of reference to the police. By this time, however, the police have themselves become so much a part of this same frame of reference that it is often difficult to determine whether it is the political figure who urges 'stricter law enforcement' on the policeman, or the law enforcement spokesman who urges the press and the politician to support his demands against laws 'coddling criminals'.

1. Reinhard Bendix, *Nation-Building and Citizenship* New York, John Wiley (1964),
   p. 112.
2. See his *Work and Authority in Industry* New York, Harper Torchbook, (1963); and
   Nation-Building and Citizenship New York, John Wiley, (1964).
3. There is, perhaps, some ambiguity in this posing of the situation of the worker in
   totalitarian society. Police in a totalitarian society may have the opportunity to
   exercise a great deal of 'initiative'. See Simon Wolin and Robert M. Slusser (eds.),
   The Soviet Secret Police, New York, Praeger (1957), *passim*; and Jacques Delarue,
   The Gestapo (trans. Mervyn Sevill) New York, William Morrow and Company
   (1964), *passim*.
4. Bendix, *Nation-Building, op. cit.*, p. 112.

4. The Army and Control
by S. E. Finer and F. Kitson

*From (i) S. E. Finer, The Man on Horseback: The Role of the Military in
Politics, London, Pall Mall Press (1969) p. 6 and pp. 14–22; (ii) F. Kitson, Low
Intensity Operations, London, Faber and Faber (1971) pp. 68–70.*

(i)

The armed forces have three massive political advantages over
civilian organizations: a marked superiority in organization, a
highly emotionalized symbolic status, and a monopoly of arms.
They form a prestigious corporation or Order, enjoying over-
whelming superiority in the means of applying force. The wonder,
therefore, is not why this rebels against its civilian masters, but why it
ever obeys them.

Politically the armed forces suffer from two crippling weaknesses.
These preclude them, save in exceptional cases and for brief periods
of time, from ruling without civilian collaboration and openly in
their own name. Soldiers must either rule through civilian cabinets
or else pretend to be something other than they are.

One weakness is the armed forces' technical inability to administer
any but the most primitive community. The second is their lack of
legitimacy: that is to say, their lack of a moral title to rule.

The technical inadequacy of the armed forces: As an economy
advances, as the division of labour becomes more and more

extensive, as the secondary and then the tertiary services expand, and as the society requires the existence of a trained professional bureaucracy, of technicians, labour organizations, and the like – so the army ceases to be able to rule by its own resources alone. Its aim must be to cajole or to coerce the civilians and their organizations into collaboration. And to the extent that it has to depend on them, so to that extent is it weakened.

The right to govern: Now in an advanced society, i.e. just where the military's technical inability to rule is at its greatest, its moral inadequacy hampers it still further, by denying it the civilian collaboration it must secure. For the second and cardinal weakness of the military as a political force is its lack of title to govern.

Rule by force alone, or the threat of such force, is inadequate: in addition, government must possess *authority*. It must be widely recognized not only as the government but as the lawful, the rightful government. A government that based its rule on the fact that it was materially stronger than any other force or forces in society would prove both shortlived and ineffective.

This is not 'moralizing'. It is a generlization based on experience, and is capable of simple explanation. First of all, such government would be impermanent. The reason is simply that the claim to rule by virtue of superior force invites challenge; indeed it is itself a tacit challenge, to any contender who thinks he is strong enough to chance his arm. 'If force creates right,' wrote Rousseau, 'the effect changes with the cause. Every force that is greater than the first succeeds to its right. As soon as it is possible to disobey with impunity disobedience is legitimate; and the strongest being always in the right, the only thing that matters is to act so as to become the strongest.'[1] It is indeed! And this succinctly explains one of the most usual consequences of a military coup, namely a succession of further coups by which new contenders aim to displace the first-comers ... Thus governments that have achieved power by force have to defend it against one challenge after another. Such governments, therefore, either fall to further coups or hasten to convert themselves into something else: that is to say, to ground their claim to govern on something other than their successful seizure of power. They seek, in short, to exercise a *right* to govern; or, as the expression goes, to *legitimize* themselves ... A military junta legitimizes itself in order to slam the door of morality in its challengers' face. Until it has done so, it bears the mark of Cain. It is outlaw. Let it once be legitimized, and it is entitled to hunt down the new contenders for power as rebels or mutineers. . . .

The moral inadequacy of military intervention: when the military breaches the existing political order, it will be forced to claim a moral authority for its actions. Now in certain societies the public are most unlikely to recognize any such claim; and will indeed resist it.

Whether and how far a people will recognize or resist it, depends on the *political formula* current among them. This political formula is that widespread sentiment or belief on which the title to govern is grounded. Such are, or have been, the 'will of the people', 'the divine right of the monarch', the consciousness of forming a distinct nation, fidelity to a dynasty and so forth. Where public attachment to civilian institutions is strong, military intervention in politics will be weak. It will take the form, if it occurs at all, of working upon or from behind these institutions – be they throne or parliament – according to the political formula current. By the same token, where public attachment to civilian institutions is weak or non-existent, military intervention in politics will find wide scope – both in manner and in substance.

We can therefore think of societies as being at different levels of political culture according to their observed degree of attachment to civil institutions. At the highest political culture levels will be countries like Britain or the United States, where attachment to civilian institutions is very strong. At the lowest level will be those countries like, perhaps Haiti or the Congo today, or Argentina, Mexico and Venezuela a hundred years ago, where a conscious attachment to civilian institutions does not exist at all. Now it is a striking fact that people may have a high level of artistic or material culture but a very low level of political culture. 'Many people have had periods of material and intellectual splendour and yet, as it were by a sort of fatal curse, have never been able to rid themselves of certain types of political organization that seem to be utterly unsuited to ensuring any real progress in the morality of their governing classes.'[2]

In lands of a low political culture the need for legitimacy will not, and indeed has not proved a serious handicap to the military. But in countries of mature or advanced political culture it will prove crippling. In such countries, countries where attachment to civilian institutions is strong and pervasive, the attempts of the military to coerce the lawful government, let alone supplant it, would be universally regarded as usurption. This, the moral barrier, is what has prevented the military, for all its organization, prestige and power, from establishing its rule throughout the globe.

1. J. J. Rousseau, *The Social Contract*, Book 1, Chapter 3.
2. G. Mosca (ed. A. Livingston), *The Ruling Class*, p. 133.

[*Editors' note*: Such an appreciation of the limitations on the military, as suggested by Professor Finer, is however put in a rather different light by Brigadier Frank Kitson.]

(ii)

Although action against those involved in subversion may not be possible, preparations for dealing with the situation can, and should be made, and in this context the army should become involved as soon as a threat is detected, in an advisory capacity . . . It is the job of soldiers to know how to use civil as well as military methods for fighting subversion, because fighting is a military occupation and members of the civil administrations are not taught how to do it. This is as true at the national level as it is at the provincial or district level, and representatives of the armed forces should be brought into the business from the very beginning. There is no danger of political repercussions to this course of action, because consultation can be carried out in strictest secrecy. The danger of not doing it is that the situation will be looked at only by those personally concerned with governing or administering the country affected, and such people will not as a rule be qualified to interpret what they discover in the light of study and of experience gained over the years in different parts of the world. It is extremely difficult for people who have not studied subversion in detail to interpret the threat accurately during the all important early stages, because only a small proportion of the enemy's activities are likely to come to light at that time . . .

Perhaps the first bit of advice which the armed forces should give to the government is to set up machinery at the top into which further advice can be fed because unless a supreme council for dealing with the trouble is formed . . . it is unlikely that sound advice will get to the right quarters or be acted upon resolutely. If command machinery can be set up at the lower levels so much the better, but for political reasons it may not be possible in the early stages. In any case it is a mistake for machinery to be set up at a lower level unless there is a supreme council above it, because if this happens, the members of the subordinate group will get instructions from their various superiors at the national level which may be contradictory and will at best be unco-ordinated.

Having got the machinery established, the next task for the military leadership is to present to the supreme council a number of issues of a joint military civilian nature on which firm policy rulings should be taken before operations against those practising subversion can start. An excellent example concerns the way in which the Law should work. Broadly speaking there are two possible alternatives, the first one being that the Law should be used as just another weapon in the government's arsenal, and in this case it becomes little more than a propaganda cover for the disposal of unwanted members of the public. For this to happen efficiently, the activities of the legal services have to be tied into the war effort in as discreet a way as possible which, in effect, means that the member of the government responsible for law, either sits on the supreme council or takes his orders from the head of the administration. The other alternative is that the Law should remain impartial and administer the laws of the country without any direction from the government. Naturally the government can introduce new legislation to deal with the subversion which can be very tough if necessary, and once this becomes law the legal services will administer justice based on it. But the resulting situation is very different from that described in the first alternative because in the second case the officers of the law will recognize no difference between the forces of government, the enemy, or the uncommitted part of the population. Anyone violating the law will be treated in the same way, and the full legal procedure, complete with its safeguards for the individual, will operate on behalf of friend and foe alike. As a rule the second alternative is not only morally right but also expedient because it is more compatible with the government's aim of maintaining the allegiance of the population. But operating in this way can result in delays which might be impossible to accept if, for example, it looked as if subversion was going to be used in conjunction with an orthodox invasion or with the threat of one. The system might also prove unworkable if it were found to be politically impossible to get sufficiently severe emergency regulations on to the statute book. The point of raising this matter here is not to discuss it for its own sake, which out of the context of a particular situation would be pointless, but to describe the sort of issue which ought to be put to the supreme political body by the military authorities after consultation with the other government departments concerned together with all the operational implications both civil and military before the start of operations. Unless this is done, policy on matters important to the outcome of the struggle will just grow up as opposed to being decided on consciously in the light of all the relevant factors.

A further example of an issue of this sort concerns the extent to which force should be used, either by the police or by the army. In this case the politicians will rightly want to avoid the use of force as far as possible, and for as long as possible, because of the adverse effect it is bound to have on public opinion in the world at large and at home. At the same time there are military difficulties about using too little force and about delaying its application for too long, and these difficulties. . . . must be presented to the political leadership by the military authorities after consultation with the other parties concerned, particularly the police.

5. Control in a Magistrates' Court
by Pat Carlen

From Magistrates' Justice, *London, Martin Robertson (1976) pp. 98–127.*

The contradictions which defendants in magistrates' courts experience as absurd are the inevitable attributes of an implausible social institution. For a magistrates' court is an institution rhetorically functioning to perpetuate the notion of possible justice in a society whose total organisation is directed at the maintenance of the capitalist exploitation of labour, production and control ...

Throughout I am engaged in a two-fold task of argument and analyses.

The arguments are:

1. That whenever the legitimacy of legal and judicial processes is threatened, routine devices (hereafter called remedial routines) are employed to remedy the situation.
2. That these remedial routines reassert an appearance of legal absolutism.
3. That it is only through a specialised and selective treatment of some extra-legal (regulative) rules as absolute for all practical purposes that the contours of an absolutely *legal* morality can by systematically and consequentially reasserted within the courts.
4. That attempts by defendants to explicate the situational rules operative in *particular* cases are suppressed so that their absurd relationships to abstract legal rules do not become apparent.

The analyses suggest that the formal dimensions of this absolute morality as it is portrayed in the courts are six-fold:

1. Legal rules are portrayed as being homogeneous; as stemming from, and denoting, a consensual morality whose connotations are internally consistent.
2. Legal rules are portrayed as being unproblematic; as governing practices whose situational attributes are antecedently known and accounted for.
3. Legal rules are portrayed as being external; the mode and substance of their applications are presented as being beyond the discretion of their human agents.
4. Legal rules are presented as being inevitable; as being, by their nature, not open to question.
5. Legal rules are presented as being essential; as being necessary to an underlying reality existing independently of what human beings make of it.
6. Legal rules are presented as being eternal; an aura of timelessness (and universality) surrounds their ritual production.[1]

Such transformation and translation of situational contingencies into historical realities are not peculiar to law-making and law-enforcement. In hierarchical societies where people increasingly share a partial knowledge of the constellation and simultaneity of contradictory symbolic performances, the *negotiation* of a common-sensical conception of legal absolutism is conducive to an appearance of social justice.

Social Rules and Judicial Order
Judicial settings are directed towards defence of rhetorical forms
which deny the strategic and material principles of social structure
and human consciousness. Preventive measures taken to arrest
innovative strategies, incursions on hierarchy and privileges of
interpretation also prevent erosion of the acceptable mediations of
morality.

In magistrates' courts legal and extra-legal rules are not only
instrumental in the management of the judicial process, they also
serve to maintain and partially legitimate a symbol – law – whose
absolutely proper relationship to its historical referents has to be
continuously reasserted. Because of the incongruity between the
law's imputed abstract meanings and its realised situational
meanings, the management of the judicial process is problematical.
Situationally, it is the magistrate's definitions of legal and social
order which appear to prevail, but such definitions are bounded by
the pre-existent constitutive elements of a legal-judicial order (the
explicit, legal rules) and by the pre-existent regulative elements of a
capitalist social formation (the tacit, taken-for-granted rules). The
appearance of a personalised and individualised resolution of
conflict is only possible because of a professional acquiescence in the
presentation of judicial procedures and decisions as emanations
from absolute rules which transcend situational contingencies. The
paradoxical geneses of the symbolic legal order are revealed in the
management of the judicial process.

The Magistrate's Mandate and the Defendant's Dilemma
In hierarchical societies, implicit and explicit rules of social interaction seldom articulate fully to legitimate the judical process. The
main point here, however, is that although, in the lower courts, it is
the magistrate who decides the final mix, each magistrate is himself
constrained at least by:

1. written rules which affect (even if only symbolically) the court's
   administration and powers;
2. the pervasive but hierarchically contrived 'natural attitude', which
   enables people to feel that they 'know the score' in this setting
   because of the 'commonsense' assumption of shared meanings;
3. the socially immanent and symbolically constrained conceptions
   of law; and of the contradictory nature of the temporal and
   material reality underlying it.

The diffuse nature of these rules is situationally contained by the magistrate's recognition of a twin imperative. He strives not only to pass the 'appropriate' sentence (the overt symbolic act) but also to ensure that the 'appropriate' sentence is seen as such (the covert symbolic act). . . .

The Formal Imposition of a Classificatory Frame of Legal Relevancies

The major substantive concept of a magistrates' court during the hearing of criminal cases is control. The formal rules provide a frame which predetermines the *sequence* of questioning, the *timing* of transmission of new items of information and the *placing* of substantive knowledge within a system of pre-existent relevancies. Thus, to amplify a statement of Bernstein's: 'Because of the hierarchical ordering of the knowledge in *time (and in place)* certain questions may not enter into a particular frame.'[2] The obvious example of this in a law court are the formal rules of evidence. What I am more interested in delineating are the ways in which all kinds of formal and explicit rules can be articulated with informal or even tacit rules so that challenges to the existent hierarchy of relevancies are legally portrayed as being absurd.[3]

The Formal Imposition of a Classificatory Frame for Distinguishing between Order and Absurdity

Consequent upon the magistrates' and lawyers' more extensive competence in using the variety of rules which can be invoked to account for the application of a legal rule, an outstanding feature of their courtroom performances is their success at imposing shifting, and often opposed, classificatory frames of relevancies. As is suggested in the analyses of the remedial routines, official rule-usage is no more and no less absurd than the defendants' strategies for opposing it, but officials can successfully superimpose absurdity upon absurdity because of their control of the formal and substantive symbolic boundaries of courtroom interaction. This control allows them to put an absolutely transcendental legal gloss upon situationally contrived meanings. Too often, however, the defendant, by contrast, has to rely solely upon the taken-for-granted meanings of justice, law, respectability and honesty without being allowed to employ competently a legal rhetoric to account for such meanings. Once *he* challenges the absolutism of legal rules on the grounds of an overt appeal to commonsense, the defendant's challenge can be portrayed as being either out of place, out of time, out of mind or out of order.

Judicial presentations of legal rules present them as being:	Routine strategies by defendants imply that legal rules are:	Remedial routines portray the routine strategies as:
HOMOGENEOUS	PLURALISTIC	
UNPROBLEMATIC	PROBLEMATIC	out of place
EXTERNAL	INTENTIONAL	out of time
INEVITABLE	CONTINGENT	out of mind
ESSENTIAL	PHENOMENAL	out of order
ETERNAL	TEMPORAL	

Analysis of the Remedial Routines
Reading and re-reading the verbal and non-verbal interchanges which I wrote down during court sessions suggested patterned responses to situations which appeared to have similarities of form or substance. Their main similarity was that they had all evolved at times when either the ritual, administration or legitimacy of the law had seemed threatened. This is why I have called them remedial routines. Most of the sequences of interaction produced here can be observed daily in the Metropolitan Magistrates' Courts. . . .

[*Editors' note*: One of the ways in which order and control are exercised in the magistrates' court is discussed below: it should be regarded as an example of the overall strategy involved.]

Continuous Redefinition of the Social Meanings of the Law

Even if a majority of the population agrees (privately) with the challenge – or rejection – of the absolute morality, it will normally be impossible for an individual to show this to be the case, since anyone who (publicly) challenges the absolute morality will be subject to the same stigmatization. It is for this reason we get the public obeisance to and celebration of the absolute morality.[4]

Reaffirmation of the multidimensional and immaculate conception of law is the final symbolic triumph as the magistrate presents his reasons for disposing of a case in a particular fashion. Before he passes sentence the magistrate says, 'What have you to say to me about this?', or 'Have you anything to say to me?' Laurie Taylor, commenting on the range of responses to motivational questions, has written: 'The deviant who is questioned will often produce an account which is found to be utterly incredible. Alternatively, he may remain silent.'[5] Many defendants do remain silent. They recognise that any response whatever will be perceived as inadequate, for from experience in the courts they know that defendants' definitions of situations are not allowed to go unchallenged. These defendants tend to respond with: 'Nothing I can say, really', or: 'What *can* I say?' A third response is to show repentance, a fourth is to offer a self-justification. None of these responses is sufficient to maintain the immaculate and symbolic conception of the law as absolute. The absurdity of any one of these accounts has to be explicated. Consequently, and depending upon the defendant's implied interpretation of the law and his relation to it, the magistrate has to reply differentially by fusing the defendant's interpretation of law with the interpretation of law operative in this particular case. Magistrates vindicate the law by effecting a symbolic union between commercial interests and ethics. In analysing the magisterial theorising in the lower courts it is very difficult to separate the two.

Even at the end of the trial the notion of equality under the law has to be perpetuated. Defendants are not allowed to 'pass' unchallenged. If they attempt to the magistrate says, 'So you've nothing to say to me, eh? Why is that?', or, 'I'm still not satisfied as to what prompted you to do it.' If the defendant remains adamant the magistrate, despairing of talk, shakes his head and sighs, thereby indicating that the defendant is abrogating his responsibility to appear as an equal among adversaries in search of justice. Many defendants, however, are prepared to show repentance: some offer a justification. Unchallenged, either the repentant (moral) stance or the justificatory (economic/ethical) stance would weaken the symbolic power of the law to coerce.

For the small group of defendants who deny the law's right to judge them, magistrates tend to 'play down' the symbolic and ethical attributes of law and euphemistically reinterpret its coercive elements. Trace this process in the following dialogue:

Warrant officer: Charge one, Sir. [*to defendant*] Take your hands out of your pockets, please.

[*The charge of drunkenness is read and the defendant pleads guilty.*]
Magistrate: Is there anything you wish to say to me?
Defendant: Would you listen if I did?
Magistrate: Yes.
Defendant: Why do you object to people being drunk . . . and then make them pay?
Magistrate: Someone has to pay – for the police to take you in and put you up for the night. It all costs money . . . this kind of thing. Does that make it clear?
Defendant: I don't think you want an explanation.
Magistrate: It's not a question of whether *I* want you to say anything or not. The question is, whether *you* want to. You can say anything you want.
Defendant: I don't think I've anything to say that you would want to hear.
Magistrate: Very well, then. Pay one pound.

Not many defendants see 'any point' in challenging the law, but more are willing to attempt mitigation of their offence. Yet even those who express repentance pose problems for the magistrate. . . .

Defendants' expressions of repentance pose problems at the sentencing stage. Magistrates also have to step carefully when justifying their sentences for 'marginal' crimes. Even greater problems, however, appear to be posed by defendants who try to influence the sentence by justifying their actions.

Verbal ploys designed to influence the magistrate are substantially of two types; but the defendant's reading of the law and its relationship to society is usually one-sided. Either he implies that existent society is such that his action should be excused; or he makes reference to some possible moral order with which he will realign his future actions. Wherever the defendant locates his action in relation to law and society, the magistrate, speaking last, justifies his sentence by a rendering of the alternative relationship, the one which, in this particular case, is strategic in showing that the defendant, although invited to share in defining the situation, is ultimately not fit to judge. Once the defendant, already found to be socially incompetent, can be established as *legally* incompetent, the law as final arbiter can appear to be legitimated.

In the following dialogue a ticket-collector, who has entered a plea of guilty to the charge of stealing from the London Transport Authority (pocketing fares at the barrier), offers a reading of societal practices whose acceptance would completely undermine the ethical undertakings of the law.

> Magistrate: What do you want to say?
> Defendant: Well, it's something that can happen any time. Everybody does it. I didn't mean to do it.
> Magistrate: Mr Grant! You have pleaded guilty to four charges under the Theft Act which all involve intention. Do you wish to change your plea? Which is what you should do, if you now say that you had not intention.
> Defendant: No, Sir.
> Magistrate: This is sad, very sad. So tragic. Your whole character and job gone for this miserable little amount. One doesn't like to moralise, but there is this attitude of anything goes.

Refutation of the assertion that 'everybody does it' is not attempted; instead the magistrate concentrates on an explication of the legal position and the legal definition of moral responsibility.

Mr Grant denied moral responsibility for his action and was firmly reminded that the court would not accept as an excuse the notion that 'anything goes'. Yet sometimes, as in this final dialogue, a magistrate has to point out that economic constraints are inimical to good intentions. A woman has pleaded guilty to keeping a brothel:

> Magistrate: What have you to say about this?
> Defendant: Well, Sir, I have four children in care and I have been trying to get custody. I have been told that I can have them when I can provide a home for them, and that's why I was doing this.
> Magistrate: What are you going to do now?
> Defendant: Well, I suppose I'll have to get a decent job.
> Magistrate: Have you any qualifications?
> Defendant: No, Sir.
> Magistrate: No qualifications! Well then, you see it is very difficult. I can't see how you would earn enough; and if you went back to these kind of practices you would lose custody again if it could be said that by living with you the children were in moral danger.
> I think you must see a probation officer and let's see what your chances are.

In the case of the ex-ticket-collector the magistrate invoked the legalistic notion of *mens rea* as the decisive legal rule for interpreting action, yet in the above case the magistrate, though not questioning the woman's intention to reform, questions the efficacy of intention against the potency of the coercive commonsense definition of the absoluteness of economic reality.

Defendants, when considering the possible efficacy of various strategies which might influence the outcome of their trials, often reject each one with the words, 'No, you can't win in the courts, can you?' These two final extracts have been presented as demonstrations of the master technique for ensuring that defendants don't win: they demonstrate how magistrates impose contradictory classificatory frames for distinguishing between order and absurdity.

1. This analysis is clearly derivative of Douglas's work. See pp. 153–158 of the present volume [eds].
2. Basil Bernstein, *Class, Codes and Control*, London, Routledge and Kegan Paul (1971).
3. For a good discussion of what can happen when the rules of place are broken see Erving Goffman, *Relations in Public*, London, Allen Lane (1971).
4. Jack D. Douglas, *Deviance and Respectability*, New York, Basic Books (1970).
5. Laurie Taylor, 'The significance and interpretation of replies to motivational questions: the case of sex offenders', *Sociology*, vol. 6, no. 1, 1972.

6. Professional Control
by *Terence J. Johnson*

From Professions and Power, *London, Macmillan (1972) pp. 41–84.*

In identifying the nature of occupational activities we must first look at the general consequences of the social division of labour. In all differentiated societies, the emergence of specialised occupational skills, whether productive of goods or services, creates relationships of *social and economic dependence* and, paradoxically, relationships of *social distance*. Dependence upon the skills of others has the effect of reducing the common area of shared experience and knowledge and increases social distance; for the inescapable consequence of specialisation in the production of goods and services is *un*specialisation in consumption. This consequence flows from the crystallisation and development of all specialised occupations. While specialisation creates systematic relationships of interdependence, it also introduces potentialities for autonomy. It is social distance as a product of the division of labour which creates this potentiality for autonomy, but it is not to be identified with it. Rather, social distance creates a structure of uncertainty, or what has been referred to as indeterminacy, in the relationship which must be resolved. There is an *irreducible but variable* minimum of uncertainty in any consumer–producer relationship, and, depending on the degree of this indeterminacy and the social structural context, various institutions will arise to reduce the uncertainty. Power relationships will determine whether uncertainty is reduced at the expense of producer or consumer. Those occupations which are associated with peculiarly acute tensions, as described above, have given rise to a number of institutionalised forms of control, 'professionalism' being one. Professionalism, then, becomes redefined as a peculiar type of occupational control rather than an expression of the inherent nature of particular occupations. A profession is not, then, an occupation, but a means of controlling an occupation. Likewise, professionalisation is a historically specific process which some occupations have undergone at a particular time, rather than a process which certain occupations may always be expected to undergo because of their 'essential' qualities. In order to place this peculiar form of occupational control in context, a typology of institutionalised orders of control will be suggested. In drawing up a typology it has been found useful to focus on the core of uncertainty – the producer–consumer relationship. There are three broad resolutions of the tension existing in the producer–consumer relationship which are historically identifiable:

1. In which the producer defines the needs of the consumer and the manner in which these needs are catered for. This type will be referred to as *collegiate* control and is exemplified by the emergence of autonomous occupational associations. Identifiable sub-types of *collegiate* control are *professionalism*, which in its most fully developed form was the product of social conditions present in nineteenth-century Britain, and *guild* control which emerged as one of the phenomena associated with urbanisation in late medieval Europe. The following discussion will be restricted to professionalism, which followed the rise to power of an urban middle class and attained its most extreme expression in the organisation of law practice in England.

2. In which the consumer defines his own needs and the manner in which they are to be met. This type includes both oligarchic and corporate forms of *patronage* as well as various forms of *communal* control. *Oligarchic patronage* has arisen in those traditional societies where an aristocratic patron or oligarchy was the major consumer of various types of services and goods – where the artist and craftsman, architect and physician, were tied to the great houses. Corporate patronage refers to the condition in which a major part of the demand for an occupation's services comes from large corporate organisations. Communal control refers to a situation where a community as a whole or a community organisation imposes upon producers communal definitions of needs and practice.

3. In which a third party mediates in the relationship between producer and consumer, defining both the needs and the manner in which the needs are met. There are various institutional forms of this *mediative* type also, perhaps the most conspicuous example being *capitalism*, in which the capitalist entrepreneur intervenes in the direct relationship between the producer and consumer in order to rationalise production and regulate markets. No less significant, however, is *state mediation*, which will be the example discussed below, in which a powerful centralised state intervenes in the relationship between producer and consumer, initially to define what the needs are, as with the growth in Britain of state welfare policies.

Professionalism arises where the tensions inherent in the producer–consumer relationship are controlled by means of an institutional framework based upon occupational authority. This form of control occurs only where certain conditions exist, giving rise to common characteristics in organisation and practice. For example, only where there exists an effective demand for the occupational skills from a large and relatively heterogeneous consumer group can the institution of professionalism fully emerge. Consumers will normally have diverse interests; they are unorganised, dependent and exploitable. Dependence arises out of the creation of needs which may themselves be differentially distributed according to socio-economic status. In Britain, for example, the incidence of problems defined as legal is higher in the middle class than in the working class, and as compared with medical services the elasticity of demand for legal services is greater.

Where the consumers are a large and heterogeneous group, any attempt by the occupation to extend technically-based authority to a broad social control of practice is likely to be more successful than in contexts where there is a single client or a small group of powerful clients. The social extension of an occupation's authority may be gauged by the degree to which its collective pronouncements on a wide variety of issues – perhaps only tenuously related to the field of practice – are regarded as authoritative contributions. While the legal and medical associations have been listened to with respect in England on such diverse issues as the economy, juvenile delinquency, drug use and the organisation of social welfare, the collective voice of architecture is muted even in areas directly associated with building policy.

The conditions for professionalism developed in Britain in the second half of the nineteenth century in association with the rise to power of an urban middle class, which provided an expanding market for various services based largely on individual needs, whether private or entrepreneurial. The Industrial Revolution opened the floodgates of professionalisation. Scientific and technological developments crystallised into new techniques, providing a basis for emergent occupations. Needs which had been restricted to the upper stratum of society filtered down and outwards so that medicine, law and architecture, for example, were no longer small, socially prescribed cliques, but large associations servicing competing status groups of near equals. The potentiality for the creation of colleague-controlled institutions of practice also related to the practitioners' membership of, or association with, an existing or emergent powerful social grouping. The emerging urban middle class of nineteenth-century Britain not only created an expanding demand for professional services, but also provided recruits for the growing ranks of professionals. Middle-class power provided the basis from which the expanding 'professions' created their own autonomous organisations.

Under professionalism, the producer–consumer relationship will normally be a fiduciary, one-to-one relationship initiated by the client and terminated by the professional. Consumer choice, a major element in consumer control, is weakened under such conditions and made ineffective by virtue of the consumers' heterogeneity and individualisation. The one-to-one relationship under professionalism refers to the fact that solo practice is the norm, although various forms of partnership are possible. The fee is the all-important mechanism of defining client needs, and the client's only appeal is to a body made up of the relevant practitioners.

Professionalism is associated with a homogeneous occupational community. Homogeneity of outlook and interest is associated with a relatively low degree of specialisation within the occupation and by recruitment from similar social backgrounds. Where the norm of 'general practice' has given way to the proliferation of highly specialised sub-groupings, the community identity of the occupation is threatened by divergent interests and 'missions'. It is likely then that a fully developed system of professionalism can emerge only where specialisation is relatively low.

The major collegiate functions of the occupational group are carried out by a practitioner association or guild which bestows status and identity and attempts to sustain uniform interests among the members and promote uniform policies by imposing a monopoly on practice in the field and regulating entry to it. It is important to point out that the mere existence of an association or union is not in itself an indication of professionalism. For example, registration of practitioners which entails a monopoly of practice may be in the hands of the occupation, such as is the case with lawyers in England, or admittance to practice in a particular field may be controlled by a government department, as is the case with the auditing of public companies. In the latter case bureaucratic control is a severe limitation upon the development of professionalism. In the case of professionalism the occupational association is the registering body, and it develops effective sanction mechanisms for controlling not only occupational behaviour but also non-occupational behaviour. The association will also attempt to impose a uni-portal system of entry to the occupation in order to ensure that shared identity is reinforced by the creation of similar experiences of entry and socialisation. It is important to note here that the development of educational institutions providing 'recognised' courses for entry to such occupations, far from being an indication of the process of professionalisation, as is often argued in relation to the growth of vocational university courses, may in fact be symptomatic of de-professionalisation, by imposing on an occupation a multi-portal system of entry.

Under professionalism, a continuous and terminal status is shared by all members. Equal status and the continuous occupational career are important mechanisms for maintaining a sense of identity, colleague-loyalty and shared values. Also, the myth of a community of equal competence is effective in generating public trust in a system in which members of the community judge the competence of one another.

Occupational norms are inculcated during lengthy periods of training. The assimilating institutions are characterised by close supervision within an apprenticeship system and peer-solidarity through the creation of vocational schools which are directly or effectively controlled by practitioners. Associational forms of organisation, a developed network of communication and a high level of interaction all help to maintain the subculture and *mores* of the occupation.

Finally, community-generated role-definitions and standards are maintained by a code of ethics and autonomous disciplinary procedures. This elaborate and formalised system of norms regularises such behaviours as securing appointments, conducting referrals, handling consultations, acquiring and receiving clients, re-compensing a sponsor and relating to peers, superiors and subordinates.

Under professionalism occupational ideologies lay great stress on the essential worth of practice. Justice, health and technological progress are variously regarded as the central values of social existence by the practitioners of each associated expertise. The occupational community regards itself as the repository of specialised knowledge, guaranteeing, for example, the autonomy of law. Prestige within the occupation is dependent upon colleague evaluation and, as a result, technical competence is a significant criterion of individual worth. Also, innovations in the application of basic research are prestigeful where they do not threaten the existing power position of the occupation in the society or dominant groups within the occupation. In all service-related matters the occupational community is believed to be wiser than the layman. From such beliefs the occupational community derives an ethical sense of full responsibility. No group is more morally outraged when laymen put forward opinions on occupationally related matters. Attempts to extend occupational authority to wider areas of social life are at times pursued with missionary zeal and take on broad political significance. This is particularly true of law, for example, where social dissensus over conceptions of justice attracts lawyers into the political arena.

We are, in part, engaged here in an analysis of professionalism as an ideology. Elements of the ideology are most forcibly and clearly expressed by those occupational groups 'making claims for professional status' and engaged in an ideological struggle. Such occupations lay great stress on the need for occupational and individual independence as a precondition of fulfilling obligations to consumers. Among a number of service occupations this claim is associated with the emphasis laid upon the diagnostic relationship. The diagnostic relationship is given pre-eminence by those practitioners who personally confront laymen as an essential part of their work task and consequently need to have their expertise taken for granted. The direct pressure of consumer scepticism upon individual practitioners is professionally controlled where equal competence in diagnosis is legitimated, and where external evaluations of diagnosis are effectively eliminated.

The ideology of professionalism claims a direct relationship between length of training and status – that high economic and social rewards are justified by the length of training necessary to acquire certain skills. In fact, the highest status has generally been achieved by those occupations where the technical content of the role is relatively low. Those professions which are 'client-based' and diagnostically oriented provide services in which the element of non-technical interpersonal skills is most important. This is the case with the lawyer, who is constantly involved in client problems which do not demand a high level of expertise in law, but general personal skills in human relations. Also, in England, where the law profession is divided between solicitors and barristers, the barristers, who are the 'specialists', receive a less impressive professional training than do solicitors, who operate as generalists to a much greater extent. Whilst within any given occupation the level of rewards is not invariably related to length of training through specialisation, it is an important fact that occupational groups use this belief as a major lever in their struggles for status.

No occupation which is characterised by professionalism as a form of control is static and unchanging. There are major tensions existing within such a system which are constantly threatening its stability. A major tension at the core of professionalism is the conflicting pressure stemming from the relationship between occupational authority on the one hand and consumer choice on the other. Where the heterogeneity of the consumers is most significantly expressed in class or ethnic divisions, a systematic pressure towards differentiation within the occupation exists. Where law practices offer their services exclusively to one ethnic or class group, there will arise competing conceptions of the role of law and conceptions of justice within the profession itself. The occupational fission which results from these conditions is a consequence of 'client' specialisation rather than deriving from specialist techniques which, as has already been argued, are themselves a source of diversity. The strains which create instability in *professionalism* as a form of occupational control also suggest the possibility of new controlling institutions emerging as a result of consumer power, where such power acts as a systematic source of pressure upon practitioners. Various forms of consumer control occur, and their institutionalisation gives rise to forms of occupational organisation, practices and culture which differ from *professionalism*. Discussion will be restricted to one form of control; corporate patronage, in so far as it affects occupations which otherwise have a high potentiality for autonomy [such as law].

Fully developed institutions of patronage arise where consumers have the capacity to define their own needs and the manner in which those needs are catered for. In such cases the members of occupations applying esoteric knowledge are themselves 'clients', having neither exclusive nor final responsibility for their services; ultimate authority in the assessment of process and product lies with the patron or patrons. Patronage arises where the dominant effective demand for occupational services comes from a small, powerful, unitary clientele. This can occur where an aristocratic elite, sharing common interests, monopolises services. Similarly, a patronage system can develop where a few large-scale corporations are the major consumers of 'expert' services.

Various forms of mediative control of occupational activities are possible, but for present purposes we shall concentrate upon the conditions and characteristics of state control; that is, where the state intervenes in the relationship between practitioner and client in order to define needs and/or the manner in which such needs are catered for. Mediation arises where the state attempts to remove from the producer or the consumer the authority to determine the content and subjects of practice. It may do so with a minimum of encroachment upon an existing system of *professionalism*, through grants-in-aid to needy members of the public – grants which may be administered by the occupation itself. Where this is the case, the effect of intervention may be to support for a time at least existing institutions of *professionalism*. Legal aid, in many instances, operates in this way, by supporting underemployed practitioners who might otherwise be a source of dissension within the occupation, and a threat to the maintenance of the 'community'. At the other extreme, the state may attempt to ensure a desired distribution of occupational services through the medium of a state agency which is the effective employer of all practitioners who have a statutory obligation to provide a given service. This is the case with local government social services such as child welfare, health visiting, etc. The attempt to define who is to receive the service through the creation of a government agency will also give rise to supervision of the manner in which the service is provided – in Britain through such formal agencies as local government welfare committees or the school inspectorate. The influence of the state in Britain today may be gauged not only in terms of the state provision of various services, but also in the degree to which there exist legislative definitions of who may practise and under what conditions they may command the acquiescence of consumers.

The effect of state mediation has been to extend services to consumers who are defined on the basis of 'citizenship' rather than social origin or ability to pay fees. As a result there is an even greater diversity in the status characteristics of the consumers than is the case under *professionalism* and certainly under systems of *patronage*. However, the major significance of this form of control lies not in the social composition of the consumers but in the creation of a guaranteed 'clientele'. While it is generally agreed that state mediation in the provision of services associated with personal and social welfare operates to guarantee a service to everyone, its significance for the organisation and practice of an occupation rests largely in guaranteeing consumers. Aspects of uncertainty in the producer–consumer relationship are 'managed' by reducing possibilities of exploitation in both directions. The guarantee operates not only to increase the level of consumer demand, but also reduces the practitioner's dependence upon 'clients' by limiting the consequences of consumer choice. The social character of the consumers is perhaps less important than their unique availability.

State mediation will also tend to undermine existing social bases of recruitment. The control of recruitment to an occupation is an important means open to the state of ensuring that a universal service is provided, and it can achieve this end by expanding academic channels into the occupation. As a result, various forms of sponsorship and mechanisms of exclusiveness, such as the payment of fees to enter articles, are undermined. While under *professionalism* entry to an occupation is regulated by professionally controlled schools and examinations, state mediation has the effect of placing greater power in the hands of academic institutions such as universities and technical colleges. It has been argued by Dahrendorf that in Germany, for example, the relative power and prestige of academic lawyers has been associated with the degree to which the state has defined and controlled the career structure of law.[1]

One of the major ideological orientations accompanying state mediation is a stress on social service – on the broad social consequences of the provision of services in general rather than upon the personal service orientation of *professionalism*. The 'authoritative' pronouncement common under a system of *professionalism* gives way to the incorporation of practitioners, as advisers and experts, within the context of government decision-making.

It has been argued that where the area of expertise enjoyed by an occupation shrinks as a result of bureaucratisation of tasks, the practitioner will seek to expand the range of his authority by accepting advisory and managerial positions. Where an occupation extends its authority through 'non-professional' means, purely 'professional' sources of authority and the 'community' aspect of the occupation are undermined. Also, where an occupation attempts to maintain inviolate a community of monopolised skills even though the basis of practice is changing, it is likely to lose practice to others. For example, the attempt to maintain the traditional organisation of law in Britain during a period of state expansion has led to the rise of the quasi-judicial administrative tribunals – two thousand of which function in Britain today – as an alternative to the courts.

1. R. Dahrendorf, 'The Education of an Elite: Law Faculties and the German Upper Class', *Transactions of the Fifth World Congress of Sociology*, III (Louvain, 1964), pp. 259–74.

V Legal and Social Change

1. Introduction

The explanation of order may be a central concern of sociology, but for man, the active, meddling, utopian dreamer, the question of change is more exciting. Of course as far as the construction of explanations and theories is concerned they are the opposite sides of the same coin; a totally adequate theory of social order should be an equally adequate theory of social change. One has only to look back at the classical theorists to see this. Durkheim was obsessed with order, and therefore had to have a theory of change. Marx was obsessed with overthowing capitalism, and therefore had to develop a theory of capitalism and social order. The same is true for any sociological theory of law.

In contemporary societies the relationship between law and social change is of more than theoretical interest. In many countries, on matters as diverse as race relations, the position of trades unions, the relative power of suppliers and consumers in a capitalist market, and the protection of the environment, the law has been relied on as an instrument of important change. Yet law and legal institutions are constantly attacked and criticized because, it is said, they are no longer in touch with, or relevant to, a changing social world. Law is certainly believed by governments to be a powerful instrument of change. In Britain successive governments have used law and legal methods to canalize change and to introduce desired reforms, as in attempting to change patterns of employment and sexual inequalities. In the United States law has been seen as the *prime* means for improving the political and social position of blacks. As Massell reports below, law is frequently the chosen mechanism of revolutionary parties to extend the impact of their revolution into the social structure at large.

The problem of the relationship between law and social change is not a simple one. The question is not: Does law change society? or, Does social change alter law? Both statements may be, and more than likely are, correct. Rather we should ask under what specific circumstances can law change society, and to what extent, and vice versa. The writings that follow indicate the variety of strategies and countervailing pressures that emerge as law operates in a changing society. Yet the institutional entrenchment and diffuse effects of legal forms themselves constitute a context for stability that cannot be ignored.

2. Inheritance and Social Change
by H. J. Habukkuk

From 'Family Structure and Economic Change in Nineteenth-Century Europe', The Journal of Economic History (1955) vol. 15, no. 1, pp. 1–12.

The peasant families of Western Europe had two conflicting aims: to keep the family property intact and to provide for the younger children. Families differed very widely, from region to region, both in the relative importance they attached to these two aims, and in the methods they customarily adopted to achieve them. At one extreme the ownership of property descended intact to a succession of elder sons, who had complete discretion in what provision they made for the younger members of the family. At the other extreme the owner-ship was divided between all the children in equal shares. The best example of the former limiting case is provided by England, where the owner had complete freedom to will his property as he pleased, and where, in the absence of a will (or a settlement), the entire property was inherited by the eldest son. Something like the latter limiting case is to be found in France under the Napoleonic Code, which severely restricted the share of his property which an owner could leave by will to a single heir, and in the absence of a will provided for equal division between the children. . . .

There were important differences in inheritance systems from one region to another, and these left permanent marks on the social and economic structure. The influence of an inheritance system was very widely diffused. It affected the distribution of property, and thus the nature of the market. It influenced the type of agriculture and the level of agricultural efficiency. It was not without importance for the supply of capital. In particular, inheritance systems exerted an influence on the structure of the family, that is, on the size of the family, on the relations of parents to children and between the children; and it is with the economic significance of this fact that I am now concerned ...

Almost all writers on this subject agree that rules of inheritance have a profound influence on population growth. But they differ as to the nature of this influence. French demographers have generally been inclined to argue that, in their country, the provision for equal division, in the Napoleonic Code, tended to retard population growth. The peasant who worked to keep his property intact has a powerful incentive to limit the number of children between whom his property would be divided. Friedrich List, on the other hand, in his analysis of the migration from Württemburg in the early nineteenth century, suggested that the application of the Napoleonic Code in the Rhineland had stimulated marriages and hence births. In eighteenth-century Bavaria division of properties was advocated specifically as a means of encouraging population growth, and most German writers lean towards the view that the single-heir system tended to restrain the birth rate. In a peasant society, so the argument runs, children did not marry until they could establish a home; equal division of the family property enabled all the children to acquire an establishment and therefore to marry, whereas inheritance by a single heir made it difficult in a rural society for younger children to set up on their own, and therefore condemned many of them to celibacy.

Clearly it is difficult to bring these views to the bar of empirical verification, and it is therefore difficult in the extreme to disentangle the effects of the rules of succession from the many other circumstances that influence population growth. The general direction of the influence exerted by these rules can, however, be distinguished. In the single-heir areas the owner had relatively slight inducement to limit the number of his children; but his brothers and sisters tended to remain unmarried. In an area of equal division, on the other hand, it was easier for all the heirs to marry, though they may have had some incentive to limit the number of *their* children in order to avoid progressive fragmentation. The typical family in the single-heir region tended therefore to consist of the owner and his wife with a large number of children, surrounded by a penumbra of celibate uncles and aunts, younger brothers and sisters. The typical family in the equal-division regions tended to consist of man and wife with a smaller number of children, but with fewer celibates. My own belief – to state summarily what ought to be argued further – is that, other things being equal, the higher proportion of marriages under the latter system was likely to produce in the aggregate more children than the fewer but more productive marriages of the former. I suggest, that is, that the single-heir system tended to retard population growth and division to promote it.

The writers on inheritance systems also differed when they came to discuss the second question – the effect of different inheritance systems on the mobility of population. To this problem much more direct attention was paid, for it was relevant to one of the most controversial developments in the later nineteenth century, the flight from the land; and consequently a large body of evidence was assembled on the point. Little of this evidence is entirely unambiguous, for it is difficult to isolate the effects on mobility of inheritance systems from the effects, for example, of the distribution of property: all the more difficult because the distribution of property was influenced by inheritance systems.

But this much is clear, that a good deal of the discussion was cast in the wrong terms. The question was not one of mobility versus immobility, but of different types of mobility. Long-distance migration, for seasons or short periods, was common throughout Europe, whatever the prevailing rules of inheritance. This sort of migration was not of primary importance for economic change, for it was essentially temporary. Seasonal migration was not an escape from the peasant family, but a condition of its survival. The peasant went, not to acquire a new occupation in a different society, but to improve his position in the old.

Of much greater importance were the permanent migrations, and where these migrations are concerned there is a reasonably evident distinction between the influence of different systems of inheritance. There are a number of instances of large-scale permanent migration from areas of division. Where division led to a considerable morselization of properties and to a rapid growth of population, a succession of poor harvests might break down the normal resistances and lead to a sudden, explosive, and permanent exodus. South Germany in the early nineteenth century is a case in point. But the inhabitants of division areas were not likely, in the absence of such severe pressure, to respond readily to demands for permanent industrial labor in regions distant from their homes. In the first place, not only was the peasant himself rendered immobile by his property; his sons were deterred from permanent migration by the certainty of succeeding to a share of their family property. Secondly, in these areas, the market in small parcels of land was more active, and the chances of even a landless laborer acquiring some property were brighter than they were in areas where farms descended to a single heir. The retentive effect of property was thus very widely diffused. Finally, though in these areas the peasant often found ways, by agreement, to circumvent the worst excesses of morselization, the division of property did tend to create a class of peasants too poor to find their living outside the village, even had they wished to do so. The poverty of areas of division, as well as the wide diffusion of property rights, might hinder mobility.

By comparison, the inhabitants of single-heir regions responded more easily to a demand for permanent industrial labor. The typical peasant families of these regions tended to contain a higher proportion of celibates, and single men were more likely than families to leave their villages permanently. It was only when there was a breakdown of social morale, such as in Ireland in the 1840s that whole families migrated in large numbers. Moreover, the fact that the share of the younger children was under this system provided in the form of money facilitated their permanent movement away from the family holding. Generally speaking, moreover, the younger children in these areas were not debarred from compounding for their expectations during the lifetime of their parents.

There is thus a broad contrast. The one system provided for the younger children usually on a more generous scale, but in a form that tethered them to peasant society; the other generally provided less generously, but in a form that allowed the younger children to leave that society for good. The division areas may have tended to have the densest populations in relation to their capacity, but they were populations which it was difficult in normal times to induce permanently to leave the area. The population in single-heir areas may have been less dense, but it was more capable of permanent movement.

Now for the effects of these differences in mobility on economic change, on the form and speed of industrial development. In early industrial society, labor was probably a higher proportion of total costs than, in general, it is today, and, in societies that were still predominantly peasant and where transport facilities were few, geographical mobility of labor was certainly lower. The terms on which labor was available to industry were therefore a more decisive influence on the location of industry than it is in modern Europe. Where the peasant population was relatively dense but immobile, industry tended to move to the labor; where the peasant population was more mobile, even if less fertile, the industrialist had much greater freedom to choose his site with reference to other relevant considerations.

But it is a question not only of the location of industry, but of its type. The practice of division of property was favorable to the development of local industry in the home or small workshop, for it tended to create a population with time for by-employments. The relation between division and domestic industry was not indeed a one-way relation. In some areas it was not so much that division facilitated industrial by-employments, as that the independent existence of domestic industry diminished resistance to division; because nonagricultural by-employments were available, properties could be divided and still be capable of maintaining families. In most cases, however, the practice of division appears to have arisen independently of the customs of local domestic industry, and it is a reasonable conjecture in some cases that it directly promoted the development of such industry. It is, for example, perhaps not entirely a coincidence that the medieval woolen textile industry should have flourished in East Anglia, a region of partible inheritance.

Whether or not inheritance customs had much to do with the early distribution of local domestic industry, division did greatly influence the capacity of that type of industry to resist the competition of the factory in the nineteenth century. To attract labor permanently from peasant families in areas of division the factory had to offer a wage sufficiently high to compensate them for renouncing their prospects of rising in peasant society; this fact limited the range of operations over which the factory could successfully compete with domestic industry, decentralized in the small workshop and the home, and drawing its labor from local peasant families of the neighbourhood.

The clearest example of the effect of labor immobilities is Russia in the later nineteenth century where, largely because of the existence of the *mir*, the factory failed to make headway against the village industry. The persistence of old forms of industry in France, and the wide geographical diffusion of French industry are also, in considerable measure, to be ascribed to immobilities arising from the structure of the French family. It is significant that England, the country of the earliest factories and regions of industrial concentration, was the country where, with a few minor exceptions, younger children had no claim at common law to any share of their father's estate, that is, had only such claims as might be specifically granted them by special agreement, for example at the time of their parent's marriage.

The two features I have been discussing – the mobility of a population and its capacity to increase – are closely related. I have argued that a peasant community in which the single-heir system prevails is likely – with the important proviso of other things being equal – to be mobile but unprolific in comparison with one in which division prevails. But because of its capacity to send forth its younger sons to become part of a permanent industrial labor force, the single-heir system made a powerful indirect contribution to population increase. It retarded population increase in the country but accelerated it, and to a greater extent, in the towns and areas of industrial concentration. For in all the Western European countries the industrial wage-earners were the most prolific class. They were not restrained by traditional views, which in peasant societies subordinated marriage to the purposes of maintenance of the family; a higher proportion of them married, and they married younger. And once the initial stages of industrialization had got under way, the natural increase from this source very greatly diminished the extent to which the further expansion of industry needed to depend upon continued migration from the countryside.

In the years before 1914 a large amount of writings was devoted to a discussion of a third consequence of inheritance systems for economic change – their influence on the efficiency of agriculture. It was argued by the opponents of equal division that it starved the land of capital. Regions of division were regions of land hunger; small peasants, anxious to add acre to acre, bid up the price of land to an excessively high level, and often mortgaged in order to buy. As a result, the savings of the peasants were not applied to improving their properties but to extending them; in substance, that is, the savings of the fortunate peasant went in absorbing the fragments thrown on the market by the less fortunate members of their own class. Moreover, the flow of outside capital into agriculture was impeded because the high price of land made capitalists reluctant to buy. On the other hand, it was argued by the defenders of division that the single-heir system often had equally bad effects on agricultural efficiency; where the property descended to a single heir who was charged with an obligation to compensate the younger children with sums of money calculated on the market value of the property, it might become heavily burdened with debt and so starved of capital.

Wherever the truth of this argument about the effect of inheritance systems on productivity may lie, it is probable that any given increase in productivity in the regions of equal division tended to exhaust itself in an increase in population, and to accelerate the process of division; whereas an equivalent increase in the single-heir areas was more likely to increase the surplus available for sale to the nonagricultural population. The agriculture of a single-heir region was therefore more capable of responding to the increased demands for food which arose in the course of industrialization.

3. Law Making: Symbolism and Instrumentality
by W. G. Carson

From 'Symbolic and Instrumental Dimensions of Early Factory Legislation: A Case Study in Social Origins of Legislation' in R. G. Hood (ed.) Crime, Criminology and Public Policy, *London, Heinemann (1974) pp. 107–38.*

In recent years a number of writers have stimulated a renewed interest in the symbolic nature of rules and of the social processes involved in their creation. The major thrust of the argument advanced by Gusfield in *Symbolic Crusade*[1], a term now firmly entrenched in the standard repertory of literature in this field, can be discerned in his own summary of the social forces which under-pinned the emergence of anti-drinking legislation in the United States:

> ... the issue of drinking and abstinence became a politically significant focus for the conflicts between Protestant and Catholic, rural and urban, native and immigrant, middle class and lower class in American society. The political conflict lay in the efforts of an abstinent Protestant middle class to control the public affirmation of morality in drinking. Victory or defeat were consequently symbolic of the status and power of the cultures opposing each other. Legal affirmation of rejection is thus important in what it symbolizes as well or instead of what it controls. Even if the law was broken, it was clear whose law it was.

In arriving at this succinct conclusion, Gusfield had already pro-gressed – somewhat uneasily – through a series of relatively complex steps which can only be summarized. At the heart of the matter lay his dissatisfaction with what he saw as a predominant tendency to interpret American politics in terms of economic and class conflicts. For a society so characterized by 'consensus about fundamentals', the overweening centrality of such interpretations was inappro-priate. Thus, he argued, the vacuum created by such underlying agreement was partially filled by moral issues contested, not along class or economic lines, but along lines drawn by broader social for-mations which were concerned with their status and prestige. Borrowing the distinction between the politics of class and of status, he went on to contend that the two are analytically distinguishable in terms of their orientation and objectives. Class politics involve conflicts over the allocation of material resources; they are oriented towards the 'interests' of particular groups in the economic system; and their goals are 'instrumental' in the sense that they comprise 'alterations in the system of behaviour characterizing the society'. In contrast, status movements involve conflicts over the allocation of prestige, and while they may in that sense be described as 'interest-oriented', they seek their ends in symbolic rather than instrumental goals. Comprising groups which may well transcend economic and class divisions, they vie with one another for the enhanced prestige which stems from public endorsement:

> The fact of political victory against the 'enemy' shows where social and political dominance lie. The legislative victory, whatever its factual conse-

quences, confers respect and approval on its supporters. It is at once an act
of deference to the victors and of degradation to the losers. It is a symbolic
rather than an instrumental act.

In drawing attention to the symbolic significance which projected
legal norms may hold for their instigators, Gusfield has underlined
an important and often neglected aspect of legislative processes. But
this tortuous and indeed, sometimes tortured attempt to rehabilitate
much American political conflict from the baser forms of class
conflict 'so salient in European history' is not without its defects. In
particular, it is important to note that although Gusfield takes care
to enter the heuristic caveat that most movements contain both
symbolic and instrumental elements in varying degrees, the nature
and dynamics of this empirical connection remain largely
unexplored in his analysis. More specifically, while conceding that
the instrumental and the symbolic are frequently yoked, he appears
to neglect the possibility that there is no necessary congruence
between a group's disposition towards the symbolic character of
projected norms, and its stance in relation to their instrumental
potential. Once the possibility of such divergence is admitted, there
then arises the question of whether one element, by becoming the
more salient features of a mooted enactment, may not vitiate a
favourable or unfavourable disposition based upon the other. Instrumentally oriented acquiescence in a measure may be undercut when
the movement for its enactment begins to take on symbolic overtones which are unpalatable to some of the parties involved

Despite his theoretical caution, Gusfield fails to portray symbolic
meaning as an *emergent property* of the interactional sequences
occurring in connection with particular pieces or types of legislation.
Indeed, the whole characterization of crusades as 'symbolic' runs the
risk of confusing ends with processes, and of adopting the stance of a
historian who, in the words of Schutz, 'knows perfectly well what the
actor intended to do because he knows what he did in fact do'.

In 1833 a statute entitled 'An Act to regulate the Labour of
Children and Young Persons in the Mills and Factories of the United
Kingdom' was passed. Applying to a range of textile industries
where steam, water or other mechanical power were used, this
enactment prohibited the employment of children under nine years
of age, limited the labour of those between nine and thirteen to nine
hours per day (up to a limit of forty-eight hours per week), and
restricted the employment of young people between thirteen and

eighteen to twelve hours daily (up to a total of sixty-nine per week). For all under the age of eighteen, a ban was imposed–with some special exceptions–on their employment between 8.30 at night and 5.30 a.m. Children in the younger age group were to receive some elementary education, vouchers to that effect being made a pre-requisite of their employment each week. A complex system of age certificates was also established in order to facilitate enforcement of the various provisions, and in the same context, four full-time Inspectors of Factories were to be appointed.

Although the very necessity for such regulations may seem some-what staggering to the contemporary eye, this enactment was, in some ways, an unremarkable stage in the development of factory legislation. The minimum age for employment in cotton mills and factories had been fixed at nine in 1819, and a start had been made on limiting the hours to be worked by young people of employable age. Subsequent enactments, in 1825 and 1831, had retained the same minimum age and had made further though largely nugatory efforts to deal with problems such as night-working and enforcement. Thus, although the Act of 1833 imposed further restrictions and extended their application beyond cotton, it did not establish the principle of intervention itself. Nor indeed, did its terms represent any particularly dramatic and immediate victory for the burgeoning cause of factory reform. Those who in the preceding months had campaigned vigorously for the hours of all under eighteen to be restricted to ten per day, could derive little comfort from the statute, and would have to wait for more than another decade before achieving their goal.

Yet the Act of 1833 is frequently regarded as an extremely important piece of legislation. In part, this is because it basks in the reflected glory of the Royal Commission which preceded it, one of the famous Blue Books of the early nineteenth century which are so often hailed as testaments to the informed humanitarianism of the age. Apart from the detailed, though not necessarily unimpeachable investigations and arguments upon which the Report of this Commission was based, it is a significant document on account of the proposals that it made with regard to enforcement. The Royal Commission 'made possible a new and effective approach'. This new approach was, of course, the appointment of inspectors, and in taking this step the Act of 1833 fully earned its prominent position in the history of factory legislation. Even if its efficacy sometimes seems no less questionable today than it was at the time of its inception, the Factory Inspectorate still survives as the agency charged with enforcing the now voluminous regulations contained in the Factories Acts.

There is little doubt that the various groups which pressed for further legislation between 1830 and 1833 were indeed interested in possible instrumental effects. In Gusfield's terms, this means that they were oriented towards the actual impact of legislation upon people's actions, towards 'influencing behaviour through enforcement'.

There is no suggestion that the operatives' goals were anything other than instrumental. Their motives may or may not have been 'ulterior', their assumptions may have been mistaken, but their orientation was towards the actual effects that a Ten Hour Act might have. Moreover, whatever the true nature of such desired effects, it is clear that they could not be realized if the law, when passed, were to remain unenforced like so many of its predecessors. A similar instrumental 'integrity' must also be allowed to the men of higher estate who came forward to support the operatives' demands in these years. The possible effects of further legislation were by no means necessarily an anathema to at least some of the manufacturers themselves. A number, for example, could claim that they had already of their own accord introduced considerable improvements in the conditions of employment in their factories. The Act of 1833 was not passed for such people as the Gregs, Ashworths or Ashtons, one of the first inspectors was later to recall; 'had all factories been conducted as theirs are, and as many others I could name are, there would probably have been no legislative interference at any time'. Similarly, the Commission of 1833 alluded, albeit not without qualification, to the improvements which had already taken place in the 'larger branches' of manufacturing, 'not by means of any legislation, but mostly by the voluntary care of more intelligent manufacturers . . .'

Without reducing the factory controversy of these years to a monopolistic conspiracy on the part of some employers–an interpretation which according to one historian appealed only to smaller masters at the time and to uncritical historians since–there is strong evidence to suggest that reconcilement to the instrumental facets of further legislation may have been greatly facilitated by the competitive advantages which might ensue therefrom. In a period when large profits were no longer so easily extracted as they had been in the early days, some larger manufacturers were prone to attribute their slightly straitened circumstances to the chronic malaise of over-production. Coupled with the incentive provided by the prototypical fortunes of the earlier period, they argued, the comparative ease with which production could be started on some small scale had created a situation in which, as John Marshall, the Leeds flax-spinner, put it, 'the trade has been over-done by many new adventurers entering into it'. Thus, a link was perceived between their present troubles and the competition being encountered from the smaller and frequently isolated concerns in which, most observers seem to have been agreed, conditions were worst.

In consequence, throughout the period there runs a thin and sometimes almost indiscernible thread of acquiescence in effective legislation as a means, perhaps the only remaining one, of reducing competition. Thus, in the aftermath of the 1825 Act, a number of leading manufacturers in Manchester attempted to enforce the law themselves, and set up a committee for that purpose. But before such instrumental concerns could be allowed their rein, the manu-facturing class had to fight another and more subtle battle which arose out of the symbolic rather than instrumental connotations which the controversy assumed in the years following 1830.

With the gradual erosion of the social arrangements which had characterized the pre-industrial order, the raw materials out of which the factory controversy might be refashioned as a symbolic issue had been accumulating for many years before 1830. In factory labour, an emerging working class had increasingly encountered a form of discipline which was not only incompatible with a traditional family structure, but also with a traditional style of life. As early as 1818, an astute operative was able to assert that there was now 'a greater distance observed between the master . . . and the spinner, than there is between the first merchant in London and his lowest servant or the lowest artisan'.

On the ideological level, the old order had also been steadily losing ground before 1830. In particular, the ideal of paternalistic responsibility had been outflanked on two fronts: by the admini-stration of theoretical absolution to the ruling establishments, at the hands of men like Burke; and by the deployment of arguments purporting to equate the enlightened self-interest of entrepreneurs with the best interests of their employees–as of the nation as a whole.

Indeed, at a time when it was accepted that 'the best test of social institutions is the condition of the community subjected to their influence', the practice of paternalistic government was not only questioned but often openly indicted. By interfering with the freely competitive operation of capital in the hands of men who were enterprising, industrious and thrifty, it was argued, the ill-conceived restrictions and regulations of paternalism actually militated against the best interests of those whom it sought to protect.

If the ideology of traditionalism was suspect, then if followed that the political and economic hegemony which it had served to legitimate must be equally so. Thus, as the thirties approached, there was not only an increased and surprisingly successful demand for the removal of barriers against freedom of enterprise, but also a more and more vociferous insistence that the political structure itself should be altered in favour of the emergent middle class.

Against this background, it is significant that the men who came to the fore in the public agitation for further legislation in the third decade of the century were unrepentant traditionalists.

Translated into theoretical terms, this historical complexity requires that the symbolic overtones which dominated the factory question by 1833, must be treated as an emergent rather than intrinsic property. The issue did indeed come to be seen as the inseparable counterpart to other social and political divisions; it did indeed become a symbolic focus for a broader contest between competing conceptions of social order; for a time too, the most likely outcome seemed to be a signal legislative victory for the diffuse forces of resistance, and a public affirmation of the cultural and moral inferiority of the manufacturing class. But these additional meanings grew out of the way in which the reformers pursued their instrumental objectives, and, no less important, out of the way in which their activities in this respect were interpreted by others. Moreover, once construed in symbolic terms, their efforts attracted a new order of resistance in which the instrumental acquiescence of some manufacturers became temporarily submerged.

Conditions conducive to reinterpretation of the issue in symbolic terms were fostered, first of all, by the movement's own political strategy and timing, both of which contributed significantly to a process of convergence between the factory controversy and the other questions of the day. An early portent of this approaching fusion was evident in Oastler's decision to couch his initial attack on the worsted mills of Bradford in terms of an analogy with colonial slavery.

The reformers helped to create a situation in which the projected enactment could be interpreted as standing for much more than the straightforward imposition of further restrictions upon the labour of children in factories.

On one level, factory legislation was transformed into a political reciprocal for other issues, a process which was to continue relentlessly through the ensuing decade and the period of what Dicey saw as the 'accidental' coincidence of the movements to abolish the Corn Laws and to secure a Ten Hours Act. On another, we are witnessing a more subtle transformation in which factory legislation is seen as standing for an attempt to reassert a revitalized establishment's entitlement to legitimate political authority, and more particularly, to the allegiance of an emergent working class.

In themselves, such interpretations might have been sufficient both to stiffen resistance on the part of those who were already opposed to further legislation, and to vitiate the acquiescence of some who might otherwise have stood to make substantial gains from a new enactment. As it turned out however, both also discerned an additional meaning in the projected Ten Hours Act, and this supplied an even sharper spur to resistance. To many manufacturers, the passage of such an enactment in the particular circumstances of 1833 would have been a degradation of much more humiliating potential than the public demonstration of someone else's social dominance and political legitimacy. But once again, this additional meaning emerged as much from what transpired in the course of an abortive attempt to make law, as from the unelaborated possibility of legislation itself.

In the first place, the proponents of the measure *were* very determined to make any enactment effective. Inevitably, however, the form taken by this concern was traditional and, in particular, involved stiffer penalties rather than any dramatic alteration in the system of enforcement as such. Moreover, their suggestions in this respect were of such a kind as to foster a public identity of unambiguous criminality for the delinquent mill-owner.

If the thrust of the movement's suggestions for more effective enforcement of the law tended towards the allocation of an unequivocal criminal status to some employers, other aspects of its campaign implied a second and broader moral indictment. At a time when it was commonly held that, 'all legislation upon whatever subject, is an evil only to be tolerated for the purpose of preventing some greater evil', the terms in which the relevant 'evil' was portrayed, and indeed, the evidence which was offered in proof of its very existence, often imputed moral inferiority to the manufacturer, his ideas and his entire factory system. Thus, for example, one propagandist could almost feel compassion for the political economists, even though they might have 'no idea of people save and except as tax-producing and money-gathering animals of the un-plumed biped species'; but what, he asked, could possibly be said of the manufacturer, 'him whose heart is corrupted by the present profit he is making from the suffering and destruction of hundreds of little children; and who is able, with an untroubled face ... to demand these infant hecatombs as a necessary sacrifice to the spirit of manufacturing avarice?'

Statements like these cut deep at the roots of entrepreneurial claims to be both guardians of universalistic interests and practitioners of a benevolence no less real for being self-interested.

Again, then, we can see the meaning of the proposed enactment being transformed in the making. Just as in broader terms the issue became a symbolic focus for emerging ideological and political divergences, so in this narrower context it came to stand–in the minds of manufacturers–for their own moral debasement. For a time indeed, the battle become one, not so much over 'whose law this would be', as over whose 'knowledge' and whose moral inter-pretation of the whole system would be publicly endorsed in the act of legislating. A common attitude was the one expressed by Wilson Patten when he demanded the appointment of a Commission 'for the purpose of clearing the characters of the masters from those im-putations which seemed to be cast upon them by the friends of this measure...' In April 1833, a motion in favour of such a Commission was narrowly carried, and one of the most famous social investigations of the century was duly set in train.

The early Blue Books of which the report from this Commission was one, have sometimes been uncritically accepted as evidence of a profound awakening of social conscience during the first half of the nineteenth century. More sceptically, they have also been characterized as 'a battleground in which reformers and obstructionists fought ... and in which humanitarian causes, as often as not, were buried'. In the present case, the latter inter-pretation seems closer to the truth, though the 'battle' was perhaps

more subtle than the sceptics sometimes appreciate. For the establishment of this enquiry marked a victory for the manufacturers in a
war now being waged on a symbolic level as much as on any other.

If the setting up of the Commission was the first victory for the
manufacturers, its report, when published, proved to be the second.
For although it did come out in favour of some further intervention
and of more adequate provision for enforcement, it also went a long
way towards vindicating the system and the manufacturers as a
body. Endorsing the view that the worst abuses were confined to
small mills. the Commissioners made a point of noting the paternal,
considerate, gentle and beneficent approach adopted by the
proprietors of many large factories. Apart from a tendency to prolong the hours worked by children in order to match those of
adults–a tendency which, anyway, could be obviated by the use of
relays–the system as such was to be exonerated. Not only would 'the
natural course of commercial operations' lead to the smaller mills
giving way before the competitive superiority of the large ones, but
also, with increased size would come a self-interested necessity for
conditions in which injurious 'filth and disorder' could have no
place. Similarly, far from there being any inherent impetus towards
longer and longer hours in the factory system, 'there appears to be a
general tendency in all manufacturers to settle down the extent of the
labour in their operatives to about twelve hours daily'. Indeed, to
exceed the 'ordinary hours of the trade' was likely to be economically
counter-productive. As for the employment of children, while there
was certainly a need for further restriction, factory labour was still
'amongst the least laborious' work performed by them, and of
indoor employments, 'amongst the least unwholesome'. In the
matter of penalties, the Commission was equally at odds with the
proponents of the Ten Hour Bill.

The Report from the 1833 Commission was then, in many
respects, a great triumph for the influential segment of the manufacturing interest. For some of them, as indeed for many historians,
it was to become the embodiment of truth. For some too, it helped to
resolve the dissonance between desirable competitive effects and
unpalatable symbolic connotations, since legislation on the basis of
this information need not carry the same derogatory overtones
which had come to be associated with the Ten Hours proposal.

The statute which resulted was the Factories Regulation Act of
1833. While going further in some respects than the reformers
themselves had envisaged, its passage in no way impeached the

legitimacy of the manufacturing system and its attendant ideology.
Nor, while the Act indeed imposed further restrictions and controls,
did it mark any imminent shift towards a more plainly 'criminal'
status for the offending employer.

   1. J.R. Gusfield, *Symbolic Crusade*, Urbana, University of Illinois Press (1963).

4. Commercial Development and Law
by J. W. Hurst

From The Legitimacy of the Business Corporation, *Charlottesville, Virginia,*
The University Press of Virginia (1969) pp. 155–62.

That business corporations were important in the country's life did
not prove that corporation law was; there might be a great difference
in effect between ongoing organizations and the titles, structures,
and procedures with which law endowed them. In the early twentieth
century Charles W. Eliot and Nicholas Murray Butler reckoned the
corporation, as the law gave it shape, the most important
contrivance of their time for developing the economy. Some fifty
years later Bayless Manning saw corporation law as a rusting framework through which winds of change whistled unhindered; reality
lay wholly in the wills and institutional ways of businessmen.

    The Eliot–Butler–Manning difference points up the marked shift
in public policy toward the business corporation which occurred
between about 1890 and the 1930s. Eliot and Butler put a high rating
on the social impact of corporation law because they spoke in years
of major change in the law as well as of major growth in corporate
business. Manning struck his appraisal in the 1960s, after a
generation's stable acceptance of the enabling-act type of
corporation law, which emerged as a national norm out of developments at the turn of the century. Eliot and Butler rated high the new
style of instrument which the law had just made available; Manning
took it for granted, and in doing so implicitly bore witness to how
integral it had become to the economy.

These commentators were not at such odds as they might appear to be, for they were talking about different things. They all addressed themselves to corporation law, but they focused on different functions of it, and the difference in focus itself reflected changing currents of policy. Butler, Eliot, and Manning all weighed the social legitimacy of corporation law. However, Butler and Eliot measured legitimacy by utility, while Manning measured it by responsibility. The first two found twentieth-century corporation law of large and good effect because it provided a useful tool for expanding economic activity and productive effort. Manning rated the same corporation law of little effect because he found that it provided scant controls over those who wielded practical power within corporate organizations. The three together were faithful to the dominant direction of policy from 1890 into the 1960s, which put the law of corporate structure at the service of top management and for social regulation turned mostly to specialized *ad hoc* standards, rules, and agencies outside the corporation.

The corporate instrument proved useful to economic growth and materially affected its character–by encouraging multiplication of ventures and by assisting the larger scale of enterprise for which technology and expanding markets supplied the prime dynamics. These propositions are plausibly established by the large currents of events. Prime circumstantial evidence is the continued, increasing demands which businessmen made on law to supply them the corporate form of organization; this was a source of pressure too pragmatic to derive from other than experienced conviction of utility. Circumstantial evidence lies also in the law's own institutional responses. Our legal tradition began by regarding corporate status as uniquely created by the sovereign's action and existing strictly on the sovereign's terms. To limits set in legislation, courts added at times their own brand of doctrinal conservatism; legislatures tended to respond to practical demands with more opportunism, while courts developed more tradition of rationalizing policy and more readily fell captive to their rationalizations. Businessmen sometimes found corporation law less than fully responsive to the practical services they wanted from corporate organizations. Yet on the whole, both statute and judge-made law grew in ways calculated to make the corporation a more flexible business tool. Drags derived from the law's own inertias or abstractions did not last much past the point at which businessmen began to make common and large-scale use of the corporate form. Special chartering lingered longer than it should have, but in earlier years it did point up the truly special character of public-utility-type franchises. The general incorporation acts took over the scene rapidly as general industry and commerce claimed the corporation in the last quarter of the nineteenth century; statutory limitations gave way in less than a generation from this turning point to more flexible forms. By the early nineteenth century courts relaxed their insistence on action under the corporate seal; by mid-century decisions were hospitable to finding in charters such implied powers as were necessary or proper to the corporation's business, and this development along with broader statutory grants made obsolete a generation's ponderous learning in *ultra vires*. In mid-twentieth century the most conspicuous remaining institutional drag of law upon the corporate instrument was the uncertainty which could still cloud efforts to adapt the corporation to the close-held firm. The prevailing pattern adapted corporation law to business use; given normal institutional resistance, this adaptation moved fast enough and on a wide enough front to attest that the corporation, as businessmen wanted it, was rated so useful as to generate specially insistent pressure that corporation law should achieve legitimacy by realizing this utility.

If we ask more specifically what prime business utilities corporation law provided, the record of legal development and business practice suggests two outstanding heads. For both small and large enterprises the corporation provided a defined, legally protected, and practically firm position of authority for those in central control. The characteristic internal arrangement of power differed between large and small enterprises. In the small firm the corporate form gave power to the majority investment interest vis-a-vis the minority; in the large firm it gave power to central decision makers (more and more without need of substantial accompanying investment interest) vis-a-vis the bulk of those who had capital at risk in the firm's securities. Mechanisms differed. In the close-held firm, management held power primarily through the combination of a voting majority and the separation-of-powers doctrine, which left directors and officers beyond interference by stockholders, except upon showing of gross negligence or abuse of trust. In the firm with a substantial body of shareholders, these same elements figured, but the more immediate assurance of central control lay in the law's sanctioning of proxy voting, coupled with management's practical control of the proxy machinery for nominating directors and framing issues put to shareholders.

The second prime business utility provided by corporation law was help in mustering capital. Again, the end was served both for big and little enterprises but in different manners. One difference affected the general pattern of firms. The corporation's capital-raising utilities encouraged multiplication of small firms, while they helped a few enterprises achieve larger size. That the corporation allowed limited commitments figured in these outcomes but again in different ways. Limited liability of stockholders could foster investment in small ventures, but the influence of this factor was modified by the tendency of substantial creditors to insist on the personal credit of the principal investors. The corporate form distinctively helped muster capital for small firms by providing a standard format within which to combine investors active in management with investors who desired a more passive role. The corporation helped muster capital for the large firm by legitimating a flexible structure of shares and long-term debt, protecting management's discretion in retaining earnings, and providing assured limited liability for stockholders. In the large enterprise limited liability could provide an effective inducement to limited-commitment investors, because creditors had the assurance of an institutionalized pool of assets, even though they lacked practical means to exact personal responsibility from a diffuse body of capital contributors. However, we must not exaggerate the role of corporation law in mobilizing capital for the large enterprise. Essential to the outcome were the growth of the investment banking industry and the stock exchanges and later the development of institutional investors. The corporation provided the stock in trade of these institutions. But, for their part, these institutions made it possible for corporations to reach large sources of capital. Moreover, the stock market complemented the inducement of limited liability by offering the investor practical options to move in and out of commitments.

To say that corporation law helped multiply enterprises and helped technology and business ambition create a larger scale of firm is not to say that the particular corporation law we had was indispensable to these outcomes. However, it would be equally unreal to conclude that because it was not indispensable the corporation law we had was unimportant to these business outcomes. The functional needs to be served were there–the need of a workable internal division of powers within business organizations, the need to attract capital with appeals varied according to scale and risk and investors' goals. Had we devised some different legal format to serve these needs, the underlying business drives would have required that the other form of organization in working substance must resemble the corporation.

Through most of the nineteenth century corporation law embodied formal efforts to impose social responsibility upon corporate enterprise as well as to provide incorporation as a business utility. One dimension of responsibility was to utility itself. To hold the corporation responsible to fulfil its immediate economic functions, the law gave certain rights to creditors and stockholders and, in effect, trusted their self-interest to attend to the general social interest that the corporate firm behave as a productive entity in market. There are no inventories to measure how much impact creditor and stockholder surveillance had. But the formal record is sparse and episodic enough to suggest that creditor and stockholder safeguards built into corporation law at least lacked steady effect to enforce the immediate utility criterion of legitimacy. After 1890 the main trends of the statutes further reduced the opportunity of creditors to stockholders to police corporate legitimacy through provisions embodied in corporate structure itself. Twentieth-century corporation statutes paid little specialized attention to creditor interests and, in effect, remitted creditors for protection to their own zeal and ingenuity through the law of contract and the machinery of credit ratings and information. The standard twentieth-century corporation statute put such broad discretion in those controlling corporate enterprise–to design articles and bylaws, to shape the financial structure, to control directors' and officers' tenure through the proxy machinery, and to enjoy substantial autonomy in regular operating decisions–as to reduce the general stockholder electorate to a quite residual control function, wielded more through shares trading and take-over threats than through processes set up in the law of corporate organization itself.

To the end of the nineteenth century corporation law often built some regulations into corporate structure to protect general social interests. The statutes did this especially to protect the market as an institution of social control, to this end setting limits on corporate purposes, duration, and size. There is little evidence that these limitations substantially affected business behavior. Special charters often avoided limits put into optional general incorporation acts, and where limits were set, they were not infrequently amended out of existence. By the time the general incorporation act became the exclusive avenue to corporate status, such limits were being relaxed. Insofar as formal restrictions continued, they were rarely enforced. The state might on writ of *quo warranto* seek to withdraw a corporate franchise for abuse of its terms. But this remedy was so drastic that it was not used. Under inherited Equity powers, courts might conceivably entertain suits to enjoin charter violations. But initiative here lay with jacks-of-all-trades public prosecutors, who had little incentive to move in such matters compared with the flow of more ordinary law enforcement business pressing on them. Such public action as was taken through the courts usually focused, not on violations of the terms set for corporate status, but on violations of conditions set for special-action franchises of public utilities. Thus, when it became standard in the early twentieth century to drop from the general corporation statutes regulations primarily directed at general social interest, the change simply made form fit existing substance. In this light Manning's judgement of the lack of general regulatory impact in corporation law of the 1960s is valid, but the fact does not represent a material change from the situation as it had existed, at least since use of the corporate device became widespread in the late nineteenth century.

5. Interpretation for Application
by Sir Rupert Cross

From Statutory Interpretation, *London, Butterworths (1976) pp. 142–50.*

In the law of statutory interpretation there are two kinds of presumption which merge into each other and the sovereignty of Parliament gives the clue to the nature of the first kind. For the purpose of the present discussion let it be assumed that the courts will give effect to any law Parliament sees fit to pass provided it is expressed in clear terms. Allowance must be made for the fact that statutes are not enacted in a vacuum. A great deal inevitably remains unsaid. It is assumed that the courts will continue to act in accordance with well recognised rules:

> The mental element of most crimes is marked by one of the words 'maliciously', 'fraudulently', 'negligently' or 'knowingly', but it is the general–I might, I think, say, the invariable–practice of the legislature to leave unexpressed some of the mental elements of crime. In all cases whatever, competent age, sanity and some degree of freedom from some kinds of coercion are assumed to be essential to criminality, but I do not believe they are ever introduced into any statute by which any particular crime is defined. [Per Stephen, J., in *R. v. Tolson* (1889), 23 Q.B.D. 168, at p. 187]

Long-standing principles of constitutional and administrative law are likewise taken for granted, or assumed by the courts to have been taken for granted, by Parliament. Examples are the principles that discretionary powers conferred in apparently absolute terms will be exercised reasonably, and that the jurisdiction conferred on administrative tribunals will be exercised in accordance with the principles of natural justice. One function of the word 'presumption' in the context of statutory interpretation is to state the result of this legislative reliance (real or assumed) on firmly established legal principles. There is a 'presumption' that *mens rea* is required in the case of statutory crimes, and a 'presumption' that statutory powers must be exercised reasonably. These presumptions apply although there is no question of linguistic ambiguity in the statutory wording under construction, and they may be described as 'presumptions of general application'. At the level of interpretation, their function is the promotion of brevity on the part of the draftsman. Statutes make dreary enough reading as it is, and it would be ridiculous to insist in each instance upon an enumeration of the general principles taken for granted.

But these presumptions also operate at a higher level for they are expressions of fundamental principles governing the relations between Parliament, the executive and the courts. Although the point lacks clear authority, it is probably true to say that some of them can only be rebutted by express words; nothing in the nature of implication, even necessary implication, will suffice. On the other hand, it is tolerably clear that some presumptions of general application are rebuttable by implication which need not always be particularly necessary. The requirement of *mens rea* in the sense of guilty knowledge may be excluded by implication from the purpose and background of criminal statutes; more may well be required to exclude defences such as insanity or duress. The principle that no-one shall be allowed to gain an advantage from his own wrong is of general application for it undoubtedly applies so as to qualify the effects of statutory words which are wholly unambiguous. But it is somewhat easily refuted by the statutory context.

To be contrasted with presumptions of general application are 'presumptions for use in doubtful cases'. The *'prima facie* presumption that Parliament does not intend to act in breach of international law' applies where one of the meanings which can reasonably be attributed to the legislation is consonant with treaty obligations and the other is not.

Presumptions are often said to express 'policies of clear statement'. Whether this is the right way to regard the presumptions, other than the linguistic one concerning words bearing the same meaning throughout a statute, which have been mentioned so far is open to question, but it is certainly an excellent way of describing those to be discussed in the next section. They can all be looked upon as warnings to the draftsman: 'If you do not express yourself clearly, there is a risk that the courts will hold that your words will not have affected the change in the law intended by your instructors.' They are all presumptions for use by the courts in cases in which there is an ambiguity in the draftsman's words.

Presumptions against unclear changes in the law

The main presumption against unclear changes in the law goes back to the days when by far the greater proportion of law was common law and statutes were, for the most part, thought of as minor emendations of that law. In modern times it is possible to make a travesty of the presumption by stating it in some such form as that 'it is to be presumed that a statute alters the common law as little as possible'. So stated the presumption is of course ridiculous when applied to such matters as social welfare legislation concerning subjects on which there is not and never has been any common law. Sensibly stated, the presumption can be of undoubted assistance in resolving ambiguities. To quote Lord Reid in *Black-Clawson International, Ltd. v. Papierwerke Waldhof-Aschaffenburg A.G.:*

> There is a presumption which can be stated in various ways. One is that in the absence of any clear indication to the contrary Parliament can be presumed not to have altered the common law farther than was necessary to remedy the 'mischief'. Of course it may and quite often does go farther. But the principle is that if the enactment is ambiguous, that meaning which relates the scope of the act to the mischief should be taken rather than a different or wider meaning which the contemporary situation did not call for. ([1975] 1 All E.R. 810, at p. 815).

The presumption was one of Lord Reid's grounds for holding, contrary to the view of some other members of the House, in the *Black-Clawson* case that s.1 of the Foreign Judgments (Reciprocal Enforcement) Act 1933 did not apply to judgments given in favour of a defendant simply dismissing a claim made by the plaintiff. In the earlier case of *Maunsell v. Olins* ([1975] A.C. 373), Lord Reid had relied on this presumption in support of his conclusion that the word 'premises' in s. 18(5) of the Rent Act 1968 did not extend to farm land. The provision under construction being, in his opinion, ambiguous, he was entitled to consider how it came to be where it was, and he traced it back to s. 41 of the Housing Rents and Repairs Act 1954 the object of which was to get rid of the decision in *Cow v. Casey* ([1949] 1 K.B. 474) which was not concerned with agricultural leases. The restriction of the scope of a statute to the immediate mischief it was designed to remedy was described by Lord Simon of Glaisdale in his dissenting speech as a misuse of the mischief rule, but Lord Reid was after all only speaking of a presumption to be called in aid in a case of ambiguity. The real difference between the majority and the dissentients in *Maunsell v. Olins* was over the question whether there was an ambiguity.

An earlier instance of the presumption against unclear changes in the law in the form stated by Lord Reid is *Leach v. R.* ([1912] A.C. 305). Section 4(1) of the Criminal Evidence Act 1898 provides that the spouse of a person charged with an offence under any enactment mentioned in the schedule *may* be called as a witness either for the prosecution or for the defence. Subject to irrelevant exceptions, a wife could not be called to give evidence against her husband at common law, and it was held by the House of Lords that s.4(1) had only made her a competent witness for the prosecution in the scheduled cases; she was not compellable: 'the principle that a wife is not to be compelled to give evidence against her husband is deep seated in the common law of this country, and I think if it is to be overturned it must be overturned by a clear, definite and positive enactment, not by an ambiguous one such as the section relied upon in this case.' No useful purpose would be served by multiplying examples, but it should be pointed out that the presumption applies to changes in statute law. Thus, in *Bennett v. Chappell* ([1966] Ch. 391), it was held that a provision in one of the schedules to the Local Government Act 1933 under which a poll might be demanded before the conclusion of a parish meeting 'on any question arising thereat' had not altered the law laid down in a schedule to the Local Government Act 1894 which provided for a poll on any 'resolution'. The 1933 wording was said not to be 'sufficiently plain to indicate an intention to depart entirely from the basic conception of the Act of 1894, that only resolutions were liable to a poll demand'. A change of language on re-enactment will, however, fairly readily be held to indicate a change of law, although this is much less so when the re-enactment is a consolidating statute for there is a well recognized presumption that consolidating statutes do not change the law.

Ex parte Campbell. When a statutory provision is re-enacted in the same words, and those words have been the subject of a judicial decision, it is natural to assume that the draftsman was aware of that decision, and it is not unreasonable to say that there is a presumption that Parliament intended to endorse that decision. This is how the matter was put by Salmon, L. J., in *R. v. Bow Road Justices (Domestic Proceedings Court), ex parte Adedigba* ([1968] 2 Q.B. 572, at p. 583), but James, L. J., used much stronger language in *Re Cathcart, ex parte Campbell*:

> Where once certain words in an Act of Parliament have received a judicial construction in one of the Superior Courts, and the legislature has repeated them without alteration in a subsequent statute, I conceive that the legislature must be taken to have used them according to the meaning which a court of competent jurisdiction has given to them. [(1869), 5 Ch. App. 603, at p. 706]

If this is the statement of an absolute rule the consequences could be somewhat striking. If a high court judge of first instance were to construe a section of a statute in a particular way, and that section were to be re-enacted in the same form, neither the Court of Appeal nor the House of Lords could construe it in a different way. Lord

Buckmaster did not hesitate to draw this conclusion from the rule laid down by James, L. J., which he described as 'a salutary rule and one necessary to confer upon Acts of Parliament that certainty which, though it is often lacking, is always to be desired'. (*Barras v. Aberdeen Fishing and Steam Trawling Co. Ltd.*, [1933] A.C. 402, at p. 412.) More recently, however, Denning, L. J., said he did not believe that whenever Parliament re-enacts a statute, it thereby gives statutory authority to every erroneous interpretation which has been put upon it (*Royal Crown Derby Porcelain Ltd. v. Raymond Russell*, [1949] 2 K.B. 417, at p. 429), and in *R. v. Bow Road Justices*, the Court of Appeal overruled a decision of 1849 on a statutory provision which was re-enacted in 1872 and again in 1957. No doubt the position is simply that the fact that a former decision concerned a statutory provision which has been re-enacted is a reason why courts with power to overrule that decision should be more than ordinarily cautious before doing so.

 Special examples of the presumption against unclear alteration of the law are the presumption against ousting the jurisdiction of the courts, the presumption against interference with vested rights and the presumption in favour of a restricted construction of penal statutes.

Ouster of jurisdiction. It is only necessary to mention *Pyx Granite Co., Ltd. v. Minister of Housing and Local Government* ([1960] A.C. 260) as an illustration of the presumption against ousting the jurisdiction of the courts. Section 17 of the Town and Country Planning Act 1947 provided a special procedure by way of application to the Local Planning Authority to determine the question whether planning permission was necessary for any operations on land. There was a right of appeal to the minister and his decision was to be final. The House of Lords held that the company might nevertheless seek a declaration from the courts that planning permission was unnecessary for the proposed operations. Lord Simonds spoke of what lawyers like to call 'the inalienable remedy of Her Majesty's subjects to seek redress in Her courts'; whatever the true implication of the word 'inalienable' may be, it is obvious that the clearest exclusionary words are required to oust jurisdiction. Quite apart from any question of their constitutional position, the courts take the view that they are the only tribunals really fitted for the task of settling legal disputes, and who is to say them Nay?

Vested rights. 'The well established presumption is that the legislature does not intend to limit vested rights further than clearly appears from the enactment.' One striking modern illustration will suffice. *Allen v. Thorn Electrical Industries, Ltd.* ([1968] 1 Q.B. 487), was concerned with the Prices and Incomes Act 1966 under which the Secretary of State was empowered to make orders imposing a 'wages freeze'. Section 29(4) provided that 'an employer shall not pay remuneration to which this section applies for work for any period while the order is in force at a rate which exceeds the *rate of remuneration paid* by him for the same kind of work before July 20th 1966'. Did 'paid' mean actually paid or contracted to be paid? The Court of Appeal unanimously came to the latter conclusion with the result that, where immediately effective pay increases had been agreed but not paid before July 20th, the increased rate was the rate of remuneration paid before that date. Lord Denning had no doubt but added:

> If I were wrong in this view, I am clear that, at any rate, the requirement in the statute is ambiguous and uncertain, in which case the rights under the contract must prevail. No man's contractual rights are to be taken away on an ambiguity in a statute, nor is an employer to be penalised on an ambiguity.

Winn, L. J., used language which, though less common among modern judges, is surely no less significant:

> I must reject as quite untenable any submission ... that if in any case one finds (a) that a statute is worded ambiguously in any particular respect, and (b) finds also clear indications *aliunde* that Parliament intended that they should have the strictest and most stringent meaning possible, therefore the court is then compelled to construe the section in the sense in which Parliament would have desired it to take effect, by giving the words their most stringent possible meaning. On the contrary, I think the right view is, and as I understand always has been, that in such a case of ambiguity, it is resolved in such a way as to make the statute less onerous for the general public and so as to cause less interference, than the more stringent sense would, with such rights and liabilities as existing contractual obligations.

Strict construction of penal statutes. The phrase 'penal statute' is used to cover both statutes creating a crime and those providing for the recovery of a penalty in civil proceedings. In either case the present position is that if, to use the words of Lord Reid in *Director of Public Prosecutions v. Ottewell*, ([1970] A.C. 642, at p. 649), 'after full inquiry and consideration, one is left in real doubt', the accused or person from whom the penalty is claimed must be given the benefit of that doubt. Lord Reid proceeded to stress the point that it is not enough for the provision under construction to be ambiguous in the sense that it is capable of having two meanings, and the same point is embodied in the following frequently quoted passage from one of Lord Esher's judgements:

> If there is a reasonable interpretation which will avoid the penalty in any particular case, we must adopt that construction. If there are two reasonable constructions we must give the more lenient one. That is the settled rule for construction of penal sections. [*Tuck & Sons v. Priester* (1887), 19 Q.B.D. 629, at p. 638]

So understood, the presumption in favour of a strict construction of penal statutes is simply an example of the presumption against unclear changes in the law.

6. Engineering Change
by G. J. Massell

From 'Law as an Instrument of Revolutionary Change in a Traditional Milieu – The Case of Soviet Central Asia', Law and Society Review *(1968) vol. 2, no. 2, pp. 182–226.*

The modernization process, even when relatively sedate, always contains elements of suspenseful confrontation. In few cases, however, has it been quite so dramatic as in the attempted modernization of Central Asia under Soviet auspices. One reason for this is that the drive toward modernization did not, by and large, come out of Central Asia itself, not primarily from a local elite nor even a local counter-elite commanding the support of an 'expectant people'. The outside powers, moreover, had an exceptionally extravagant vision and explicit ideology, as well as remarkable revolutionary elan and impatience. Per contra, the societies to be transformed were at an especially low level of social and economic development, as different from that postulated by the Marxist theory of revolution as they could possibly have been; they were also, relatively speaking, highly intact and integrated, that is, lacking in relatively large, significant, and politically experienced groups that were both alienated and marginal. The drama of modernization in Soviet Central Asia thus arose from a huge gap between the social structures existing and those envisioned; from the lack of significantly disintegrated structures ready-made for refashioning: and from great verve and urgency on one side and a deep imperviousness to manipulation on the other.

While the overall Soviet assault on Central Asia's Moslem traditional societies proceeded on a number of levels, and with widely varying degrees of success, one essential facet of that assault came to be the deliberate attempt to stimulate and manipulate sexual and generational tensions that would help to induce an upheaval in a traditional system of values, customs, relationships, and roles, beginning with the primary cell of that system: the extended, patriarchal Moslem family.

At least three basic propositions were implicit in the decision to use women to break up Moslem traditional societies. First, that 'class struggle', in some societies, did not need to express itself exclusively through social strata conventionally designated on the basis of property and relation to the means of production. Second, that 'patriarchism' characterized authority relationships not only in large and complex social organizations in Central Asia but also, and perhaps most strikingly, in the primary cell of the native traditional world, i.e. in the extended family. Third, that in such a milieu, social status, and hence potentially social tensions, could be based as much on sexual as on economic or other roles.

The Soviet plan of action may, perhaps, best be visualized in a series of propositions – propositions that constitute a brief and selective projection of the imperatives and premises underlying the Soviet action-scheme, that relate immediate means to ultimate ends, that are interdependent, and that fluctuate in emphasis within a spectrum from moral to instrumental considerations, from revolutionary idealism to cold political pragmatism.

1. *To emancipate women as individuals – and, with women, the young generation –* from 'slavery in the feudal-patriarchical order' of

kinship, custom, and religion, and thereby fulfil the egalitarian strictures of Marxism with respect to the family, as well as engage the humanitarian and reformist impulses of important segments of the emerging male and female elites in Russia and Central Asia.

2. *To undermine the prevailing patterns of traditional authority* – based on lineage, kinship, conquest, custom, religion, and age, as well as on the absolute superiority of men – by endowing women with unprecedented socio-political roles, and backing these roles with an organizational framework, with educational and material opportunities, and with the legal and police-power of the new state. By the same token, to undermine the backbone of a traditional community's political cohesion, and ease and hasten, thereby, the grafting and assimilation of new Soviet authority patterns at the grassroots. As a corollary, *to politicize the latent or actual grievances of the most disadvantaged females.* This would help the regime to gain, in effect, a political fifth column in the Moslem traditional milieu. By being disposed to act in such a role, women could be uniquely suitable elements in depriving native kinship units and village communities of their salient traditional advantages in dealing with outsiders – their secrecy and solidarity.

3. *To undermine the kinship system and the village community* – revolving around clan-loyalties, and ties of family and custom – by endowing women with unprecedented social, cultural, and economic roles, by encouraging and sponsoring divorces initiated by women, and by involving them in massive and dramatic violations of traditional taboos, such as mass-unveiling in public, playing of dramatic female roles on stage, open competition with males in sports events, and assumption of martial roles in paramilitary formations, including the operation of airplanes, the use of parachutes, and the handling of guns. As a corollary, *to compound the power of attraction upon male as well as female youth* – by stressing a new accessibility of the sexes to each other, an accessibility based on free choice and no longer dependent on customary and religious rules, or on tribal, communal, or paternal authority, an accessibility involving unprecedented dimensions of contact, courtship, and romantic love.

4. *To significantly weaken some crucial moorings of Islam in native societies* – especially the codified religious laws of *shariat*, and the main repository of local customary laws, the *adat* – by endowing women with unprecedented civil rights, by backing those rights with

a new and especially tailored judicial system, and by staffing that system, in part, with women. To revolutionize traditional attitudes toward the clergy, by suggesting, among other things, that the latter's presumed spiritual guidance of a man's wives and daughters could easily go hand in hand with sexual exploitation; and by wooing especially women – traditionally the most numerous and submissive clients – away from the influence of Moslem 'teachers', village 'wise men' and 'holy men' and tribal shamans. As a corollary, *to break the monopoly of knowledge, and of political adjudicative, intellectual, educational, spiritual, and consecrative functions*, held by males in general, and by traditional elites – religious, tribal, communal – in particular, thus helping to undermine the status, authority, as well as livelihood of these elites.

5. *To disorient and weaken the prevailing concepts of property* – by bringing into question the woman's role as, in bolshevik interpretation, her father's means of exchange, and her husband's beast of burden, chattel, and property in marriage; by forcefully stressing and challenging the entire range of her legal and customary inferiority, particularly with respect to her control and inheritance of property, including land; and by endowing her with unprecedented roles and capabilities in the sphere of economic activity. As a corollary, *to compound the power of attraction upon poor and socially disadvantaged males* – by stressing a new availability of brides that would no longer be dependent on the social status of a man and his family or clan, or on the requirements of property in the form of the locally traditional bride price (*kalym*) and thus endowing the males' sense of sexual deprivation with overtones of social, economic, and political deprivation, making the conflict over women into a powerful fulcrum for sharpening class conflict.

6. *To gain, in the heretofore secluded female masses, a large and reliable labor pool, and a potentially important reservoir of technical cadres* – so as, in the short run, to maximize the scope and tempo of economic development and, over the longer term, to release the productive and creative potentials of a traditional society. By the same token, by recruiting women en masse into novel forms of economic activity, and by encouraging them to play unprecedented roles in that sphere, to remove the traditional 'middlemen' – fathers, brothers and husbands – standing between women and the economic market place, and thus to create optimum conditions for their economic independence from husbands, families, or clans, and

for their attraction to, and socialization in, the Soviet system. As a corollary, *to compound the emotional pressures upon the whole male population – by exposing it, in every role, in every enterprise and sphere of life, to unprecedented competition from women*, thus, as a minimum, depriving men of the traditional haven of unquestioned acceptance and superiority in the family and in public life.

7. *To recruit, through and among women, political, administrative, medical and educational cadres* – cadres that would reliably staff and expand the network of Soviet influence and control, including the new system of communications, health, education and welfare; cadres that would thus not only dramatize the new relations of the sexes, but would serve directly as sharp political tools, and assist deliberately and actively in the fragmentation of tradition. In this fashion, to gain in women, and especially in young women, unique agents as well as catalysts in the overall revolution of modernization, and in the shaping of new foci of socio-political integration under the auspices of the Soviet regime.

8. *To compound the power of attraction upon other traditional societies – and societies sharing ethnic identity or cultural and historical experiences with Central Asia's peoples – outside Soviet borders*, and hence spur revolutionary ferment in the colonial and semicolonial world, through the buildup of egalitarian and high-achievement imagery in the realms of youth and sex; to open up, thereby, unprecedented potentials for the formation of a revolutionary and modernizing elite and elan.

The use of law as one of the Communist Party's strategic approaches to revolutionary change may be said to have involved the introduction of a *specialized tension-management system into a traditional milieu*, a system combining tension-inducing and tension-controlling purposes. Specifically, the strategic objectives came to be: to induce (positive) tensions that would fundamentally undermine the traditional order (the target system) and, at the same time, to control those (negative) consequences of induced tensions that threaten to affect the stability of the Soviet regime (the sponsor system) and the safety of its developmental objectives. In other words, a new legal system had both to encourage and to maintain a delicate balance between disequilibrium and stabilization, fragmentation and integration, social revolution and orderly development. Moreover, it had to take into account not one homogeneous universe of clients, but, many – and over-lapping – social interests and groups.

The response of indigenous Moslem women to the norms and thrusts of Soviet legal engineering was varied in the extreme. It tended, at least at first, to be dependent on the attitudes and actions of males in general and the tug-of-war between traditionalist and Soviet forces in particular. Broadly speaking, female response may be said to have ranged from what might be called avoidance and selective participation to militant self-assertion and uncontrolled involvement.

The pattern of male response within the traditional milieu may be said to have ranged from evasion and selective accommodation to limited retribution and massive backlash.

The response of native political and administrative personnel may be said to have ranged from circumlocution and selective cooperation to sabotage and uncontrolled self-indulgence.

(1) The realization through Soviet law of new ideal norms in Central Asia tended to be inversely related to the degree of forcible attempts to apply it in reality. (2) Statute law, while evidently a suitable parental surrogate in the Russian milieu, lacked the cultural underpinnings for such a role in Central Asia, and therefore could not be easily transplanted there in its specific Soviet-Russian forms. (3) While law successfully elicited, reinforced, and focused grievances, it tended to be dysfunctional to the extent that it encouraged hopes it could not satisfy. (4) The functioning of law as an instrument of mobilization (as both a repository of ideal norms and a focus of grievances), while powerful in its revolutionizing impact, tended to be directly related to the degree that extra-legal integrative and supportive arrangements were provided for, and coordinated with the mobilization thrust. (5) Given its vivid imagery of justice and of equality of the sexes before the law, the operation of the Soviet legal system as an instrument of recruitment unquestionably made a highly important contribution to Soviet revolutionary objectives, since recruitment through the legal milieu tended to net females cadres that were the toughest, the most disaffected from tradition, the most vengeful, and hence, politically, the most reliable from the Soviet point of view. But the impact of the system, in this case, tended to be diluted to the extent that the manipulations of its native male personnel made female judicial roles purely honorary or menial, and it was relatively narrow in that it tended to appeal

primarily to female personalities with aggressive and authoritarian, but not necessarily imaginative and creative, characteristics. (6) To the extent that Soviet law was intended to be a warning system (a 'tripwire') designed to prevent transgressions and resulting conflicts it tended to be relatively useless (since it was regarded as irrelevant, or disregarded altogether, by traditionalist males) and decidedly dysfunctional (in that, far from preventing conflicts, it helped to trigger and aggravate them). (7) Deliberately fashioned and used as an instrument of class struggle – an instrument dispensing distinctly political justice – Soviet law tended to be eufunctional (from the Soviet point of view) only if class enemies could be readily detected and safely indicted, but tended to be dysfunctional to the extent that the local traditional milieu was alienated in the course of the regime's crude and indiscriminate attempts to identify and apprehend 'class enemies'. (8) Having to function not only as a conveyor of new norms but also as an instrument to extirpate the entire entecedent legal system, Soviet law enjoyed the advantages of (a) a formal monopoly of the legal universe; (b) a formal monopoly and over-whelming superiority of force; (c) a centralized and potentially efficient bureaucratic apparatus; and (d) the backing of an authoritarian party-state committed to an over-arching ideology and uninhibited by moral and democratic constraints. It was at a dis-advantage, however, and hence was congenitally unattractive, or at least not immediately useful, in that (a) it lacked the sacred qualities and personalities of the antecedent system; (b) it tended to be abstract, rigid, and impersonal; (c) it could not easily gain access to traditional communities either because the latter were physically distant, or nomadic-pastoral (hence elusive), or because they were governed by a combination of religious and customary law, and could thus be independent of, and elusive to, formal legal structures. (9) To the extent that it had to function as a protective shield for revo-lutionary agents and converts, Soviet law tended to be not only useless (in that it could do little or nothing to protect defecting Moslem women from violent retribution), but decidedly dys-functional (to the extent that it obliged the Soviet regime to risk the lives of valuable and scarce political activists in the impossible task of protecting the rights and lives of masses of individuals scattered in an extremely hostile milieu). (10) Viewed as an heretical model, the impact of Soviet law on the traditional milieu was exceptionally great. Perhaps no other instrument could hold out to the traditional community, and especially its women, revolutionary standards of human relationships and potentialities as palpably, consistently, and authoritatively as Soviet laws did. Perhaps no other instrument could, in the short run, be as powerful a catalyst of systematic alienation in, and fundamental transformation of, the traditional milieu. But law as a heretical model tended also to be dysfunctional to the extent that (a) it was felt to be forced upon traditional communities by men who were ethnically or ideologically outsiders; (b) it not only posed a threat to the traditional unities and values, but impinged directly upon the most intimate and sacred realms of local life-styles; (c) it stimulated the self-assertion of both Soviet-oriented heresy and traditionalist orthodoxy; (d) it put a discipline-oriented, implicitly authoritarian system in the position of encouraging iconoclastic and libertarian propensities that showed themselves capable of turning just as easily against the Soviet regime as against the traditional order. (11) As a regulative mechanism in a revolutionary situation, Soviet law was at one particularly pronounced disadvantage, apart from all those already mentioned. It had neither the legitimate authority, nor the judicial resources, nor yet the extra-legal supportive structures to be able to control tensions as widespread, pervasive, and corrosive as those induced by the heretical model. A revolutionary instrument that was itself not easily controllable, and was itself seeking legitimation in a traditional world, could not very well control tensions and ensure order in that world while it was enforcing with all the power at its command the very quintessence of illegitimacy: heresy.

(12) Therefore, in its role as a specialized tension-management system designed to induce and control revolutionary change, Soviet law turned out to be an exceedingly volatile, imperfect, inexpedient, and in certain circumstances, dangerous instrument. It tended to be volatile in the sense that it could just as easily go too far as not far enough in inducing and managing change. It was imperfect in the sense that, if devoid of supportive institutions and arrangements that would permit the translation of legal rights into roles and opportunities, it tended to define new goals while failing to supply the means to reach them. It was inexpedient in the sense that it could undermine the traditional status quo, but could not really transform it. It tended also to be dangerous in that, as a heretical model, it maximized undersirable as well as desirable tensions, while, as a regulative mechanism, it could not minimize the impact of those

tensions on the political structures and developmental objectives of the incumbent Soviet regime.

Revolutionary legalism as a strategic approach to social engineering could be self-delusory to its sponsor as well as dangerous. Its perfectionist emphasis on adherence to uncompromising, if seemingly rational, rules, and its heavy stress on the strength and promise of rationally devised legal machinery, served to de-emphasize to the point of neglect or exclusion precisely those initiatives that were needed most for the attainment of revolutionary and developmental objectives, and for the legitimation of the legal system itself – initiatives involving comprehensive, systematic, and coordinated social action whereby human needs, potentialities, and expectations would find a reasonable chance to be fulfilled. Given such omission, revolutionary legalism, intended to induce a strategic conflict in a traditional milieu for the purpose of changing it, tended, instead, to precipitate cataclysmic conflict, verging on civil war.

Faced with the full panoply of implications of massive enforcement and repression, the Soviet regime had the following options: to continue inducing revolutionary tensions as before, to contain them by selective rather than indiscriminate enforcement, to deflect them by retaliating primarily against selected targets, to suppress them at all cost and with all the means at its disposal, or to reduce them at the source. While predispositions to all these choices continued to assert themselves in Soviet ranks, the regime's chief reaction was to attempt mitigating the tensions at their source – through a deliberate reduction of legalistic pressures and a calculated attempt to construct a complex infrastructure of social-service, educational, associational, expressive, and economic facilities.

By early 1929, only two and one half years after the inception of the 'cultural revolution' in Central Asia, the communist party felt obliged to bring the 'storming' activities on behalf of female emancipation and the massive and overt forms of the cultural revolution itself to an abrupt halt.

VI Law, Legality and Legitimacy

1. Introduction

Understanding what constitutes the legality of an act or an institution has long preoccupied writers on jurisprudence. Yet the emphasis in much jurisprudential inquiry has rested on questions about the pedigree and formal validity of legal provisions. Sociology of law is also concerned with notions of legality but its questions are different in form and lend different emphases to subsequent inquiry. For sociologists the interesting question is whether an act or institution making a claim to legality (perhaps via a jurisprudential argument) will in fact be accepted as legitimate by those whose behaviour it seeks to influence. If it is not, then it no longer exercises legal domination – it uses non-legal domination, crude power or else has no effect. For a legal system to maintain legal domination, those subject to its regulation must *believe* that it is acting legally. Any legal system must therefore pay close attention to sustaining a belief in its legality. The legal form is not necessarily enough, as the Nazi regime found in parts of occupied Europe. This same point has been made by Marxists with their claim that law must be analysed as an ideological institution.

The nature of legitimacy is perhaps the most fascinating sociological issue involved in studying law in society. It is the imperative need for legitimacy that constrains the law's use of coercion. Governments are often forced to choose between constraining coercion within an acceptable notion of legality, or risk losing all the authority that is derived from law. It is for this reason that most theorists acknowledge that law possesses an independent authority of its own, a relative autonomy, and cannot be used as a straight-forward instrument of power by any group, no matter how dominant.

A concentration on legitimacy takes us back to the issues raised in our introduction. If law needs legitimacy then it is concerned with social as well as legal order. The existence of law has a necessary connection with the basic structures that order our thinking about and relationship with the world. Different forms of law and approaches to different forms of law reflect the sort of world and the sort of societies men want to live in. The debates that may thus be engendered are indicated in the writings that follow. Ultimately the nature and types of freedoms that men can exercise in all aspects of their life are at stake. That is what makes the sociology of law so interesting and so important.

2. Legal Competence
by Philippe Nonet

From Administrative Justice, *New York, Russell Sage (1969) pp. 78–91.*

Legal Competence and Civic Competence
One of the more fundamental aspirations of the legal order, and indeed a persistent feature of its imagery, is that all men should be able to appeal to the law, irrespective of their power or their social position or the political leverage they command. Obviously this ideal is often frustrated, for the legal system does not work in a social vacuum. It is of course frustrated when a tribunal is corrupt, subject to illegitimate influence, or captive of a political machine; decisions may then have to be bought or won through pressures on those who own the system. Even where, as in the case of the IAC [Industrial Accident Commission] the integrity of legal officials cannot on the whole be seriously questioned, equal access to the law is impaired by the sheer financial burdens involved in initiating legal action, such as

the cost and length of proceedings and the expensiveness of legal services. And of course ignorance acts as a similar obstacle. Such obstacles, however, seem to fade away as the administration of justice assumes greater initiative in meeting needs and processing demands. A lesser burden is put on the means and resourcefulness of the citizen. When the IAC in its early days assumed the responsibility of notifying the injured worker of his rights, of filing his application for him, of guiding him in all procedural steps, when its medical bureau checked the accuracy of his medical record and its referees conducted his case at the hearing, the injured employee was able to obtain his benefits at almost no cost and with minimal demands on his intelligence and capacities.

But participation may be open, and yet remain so impoverished as to be meaningless. An effective use of law requires more than the sheer accessibility of tribunals and legal services. The critical issues appear when we consider the kind and quality of participation the system allows, and the conditions under which they vary. This leads us to a more important aspect of the relations between political resourcefulness and legal competence. Insofar as the IAC aimed merely to open its doors to the poor man, it could very well dispense with the initiative of injured employees and seek and treat their cases on its own. And its doors were wide open indeed. At the same time, however, the only voice the agency heard in the making of its policies was that of organized industry, the only sure pressures on legislative and budgetary determinations came from the employers' lobby, industrial medicine was the captive of private insurance, and the daily administration of the law by carriers practically escaped all controls. Under these conditions, the worker's participation was likely to resemble more a passive submission than an affirmative use of legal opportunities. He could hardly hope to achieve much effectiveness as long as he did not have positive means of influencing the operation of the law and the working of the commission. These means he did not acquire before organized labor gave him an active and articulate representation, with bargaining power and political leverage.

However distinctive it is in other respects, an appeal to law is in the first place an *appeal to authority*. As such, its effectiveness depends to some extent upon much the same conditions as affect political action in general. For law is more than a blind and mechanical application of rules to social life; it is also a means of answering needs and fulfilling aspirations, even though it can do so only through and within the confines of its own authoritative standards. The perfection and growth of law will therefore depend upon *how effectively legal authorities are sensitized and made responsive* to the problems and demands of their constituency. In this the citizen's initiative and his political alertness perform a critical role. As his channels of advocacy and his resources for social action develop, as his ties to the political order become closer and his appeals to authority more potent, the law also can more readily take notice of his condition and give recognition to his claims. Thus a prerequisite of legal competence is the development of citizenship and civic competence. Some may derive this competence from the political and social advantages they enjoy by virtue of their established position in the social structure. Others, however, whose position is precarious, may find it only in the concerted action of organized groups, which articulate interests and provide the power and means of promoting them.

Competence, civic or legal, is of course always relative to the political or legal system appealed to. The more passive the posture of governmental and legal authorities, the more burdens they place on the initiative of the citizenry, the greater the resourcefulness that will be required for achieving civic and legal competence. Conversely, the function of some administrative agencies may be conceived as an attempt to overcome the passivity of ordinary tribunals and the lack of resources of certain classes of citizens. The original mission of the IAC was in part programmatic; it consisted in identifying the problems of the injured and framing policies that would answer their needs. To that extent the commission was, in a sense, compensating for the worker's weakness and making him more competent. An agency may even directly attempt to foster the civic capacities of the governed; through it, the legal order assumes then a positive role in the development of citizenship. Although the IAC never sought to build up this kind of strength among workers, it did have a general idea that part of its role was to stimulate the assertiveness of injured employees. Thus one answer to the problem of competence may be the creation of a dynamic administration, committed to the interests and strength of the citizen. Even so, however, much will continue to hinge upon the latter's own capacities. For commitment and dynamism are not simple products of administrative determinations; they emerge from and find their support in the social organization of the system, that is, the character and perspectives of administrative personnel, the recruitment of leadership, and the structure of groups and interests under which the agency operates. In order to preserve the positive orientations of an agency and to keep it in its active role, a group must be capable of influencing the outlook of administrators, of gaining representation in policy-making boards, of making its pressure felt when decisions are made. And this already presupposes a considerable degree of civic competence.

Legal Competence and Conceptions of Law

However necessary it is, civic competence is not in itself a sufficient condition of legal competence. Social resources and political initiative can be used in a variety of ways, and other conditions must be met before they become focused on exploiting the rights and opportunities provided by the legal order. One such requisite is the development of positive orientations toward law.

To labor, law had first been an endless succession of *obstacles* and restraints on its activities. The first three decades of the century were a period of relentless legal harassment; the labor injunction, anti-trust law, the doctrine of illegal conspiracy, the use of constitutional law to strike welfare legislation, the free employment contract unable to confer any right on the worker, all combined to prevent labor from achieving status and pursuing its aims. Legal action almost never meant more than attempting to overcome a restriction; court appearances were uniformly for the purpose of defending against adverse suits, and to seek legal change consisted in demanding removal of legal obstacles. The only end labor had in law was to free itself from legal tyranny and gain the liberty it needed for its economic struggle. Law was not only a restraint on labor's freedom, it was also its *enemy*. Legal restrictions had become the most powerful weapon in the hands of industry. Even where the laws were good, they only worked as a way of lulling labour into sub-mission. Labor's problems were beyond the capacities of the legal order. Law was not viewed as a means to be used positively for furthering the workers' aims. Labor saw in it an instrument of the state, and thus an interference that could always be weakening or even oppressive and had to be avoided as much as possible. Labor would thus not seek in law the authority or the moral support for its demands; it would rather find this authority in its own private power on the private scene of economic struggles. Although this doctrine undoubtedly drew much of its strength from a generalized perception of law as hostile to labor, it also had clear affinities with widely held cultural notions of the time – the laissez-faire philosophy, its theory of the passive state, its identification of state and law, and its idea of law as protecting freedom through restraint.

With the advent of the New Deal, the legal order suddenly turned from an obstacle and an enemy into a friend and a positive support. The National Labor Relations Act had laid new foundations for labor law and the judiciary had reversed its stand on the constitutionality of government interventions in the economy. All accepted conceptions of the proper roles of law and government had also been shaken up by the social crisis of the depression. The active state was emerging and a new idea of law, already embodied in the flowering legal realism , was not presenting it as an active instrument of political and social change. Organized labor did not immediately respond to these transformations of law and legal conceptions, and throughout the New Deal period it retained much of its apathy towards the legal order. But changes became manifest towards the end of the 1930s. In 1938 the secretary of the California State Federation of Labor concluded his report by strongly stressing the need for workers to learn the laws in their favor and to use and develop them. The 1940s also saw a sudden burgeoning of programs to educate union members, stewards, and business agents in their rights and opportunities under the law. The law was no longer the employer's law, not a hopeless obstacle on labor's road to economic success. Labor law had finally become labor's law. In spite of deficiencies and past failures, the law offered labor a source of rights and strength. Rudimentary as the law was, from labor's point of view, it was now accepted as worthy of sustained attention and positive effort.

Legal Competence and Orientations to Authority
Although an appeal to law is basically an appeal to authority, not all appeals to authority have legal significance. Some may not involve more than a compliant request for a favor; other demands are only part of the process of bargaining and compromise between government and the governed. The distinguishing feature of appeals to law is that they hold authority accountable to rules, and found demands upon reasons derived from rules. Thus an important aspect of legal competence is the capacity for independent criticism of authority on the basis of reason and law.

This capacity is closely related to the character of authority relations and the established conceptions of authority and legitimacy among the governed. When the ruler is accepted as the only competent judge of his acts, when his authority rests upon the personal loyalty of the subject, when it is strongly protected by awe or unconditional respect, legal competence can be severely undermined. Even where such conditions do not result in submissiveness among the governed, even where they allow considerable initiative on the part of the citizen and rich reciprocal exchanges between subject and ruler, they nevertheless remain a serious obstacle to the assertion of rights. For whatever advantages are claimed or gained tend to be perceived as flowing from concession, or good will or favor, rather than as obligations that are due as a matter of right.

An important step in labor's progress toward legal competence has been the shift from welfare capitalism and its paternalistic outlook to bureaucratic management and modern conceptions of the employer's authority under the collective contract.

Paternalism and the merging of rights and charities came to an end when company welfare plans became a subject for collective bargaining, a change fostered by the rise of union power and the restrictions on wage increases under the war administration. As a result, both private and public welfare became governed by definite legal obligations. Whatever advantage the employee was using, he was no longer asking for a privilege in exchange for his cooperation; he was invoking a rule and claiming a right.

Autonomy and Commitment

When we think of a law suit, the image is often suggested of a person freeing himself from and acting against the weight of social pressures, standing alone on his right and invoking the justice of the sovereign on his behalf. The legal man is thus presented as unbound and uncompromising, free to pursue his moral commitment to legal principles. And correspondingly an often celebrated virtue of the legal order is its capacity to lend authority to the individual against the power of groups and society. Although this imagery can hardly be accepted as an accurate description of how the legal process operates, it nevertheless turns our attention to an important condition of the capacity to use law effectively. Legal competence requires a certain degree of autonomy, a detachment of the person from the system of social relations that determines his position and

274 Law and Society

interests. The more dependent a person is on his ties to others, the more he is involved in some going concern he needs to preserve, the less capable he is of assuming the principled posture legal action requires. Dependency makes the person insecure and captive of his social situation; it encourages passive acceptance and accommodating compromises, rather than moral assertion.

One element of autonomy is *security* – being free from the fear or threat of losses and reprisals. Persons depend on others for their economic welfare, their social status, and their sense of worth and dignity. The assertion of a right may upset those social relations in which a man has invested his self and his interests, thus exposing him to risks or threats he cannot bear.

[Now] social insurance, legal protections, and the collective agreement have made the employee much less dependent on his job and his wages and have considerably enhanced his security and his capacity to assert rights against the employer.

There is, however, more to autonomy than sheer security. Submissiveness may reflect normative conceptions of the nature of authority, shared by ruler and ruled, having the effect of perpetuating the dependency of the subject. Similarly, one may be *morally captive* of one's social situation, unable to disassociate oneself from common values and perspectives even when they harm one's interests and aspirations. Moral captivity has been recognized in a variety of settings, perhaps most extremely when the inmate of a concentration camp comes to identify himself with the aims of his guards, when the Negro shares the racial conceptions of his white master, when workers adopt the ideology of industry, or when the recipient of public aid approves the violations of his privacy by welfare agancies. In a more subtle way, the same sort of captivity develops wherever the uncritical acceptance of group perspectives transforms the person into a docile performer of social routines. Whether it is a direct response to oppression, insecurity, or group needs or a more immediate reflection of established value orientations, whether a product of culture or society, this captivity prevents persons from rationally assessing their special interests and developing distinct moral aspirations. Hence it bears critically on the capacity to invoke law. For *the assertion of a right is a form of moral criticism: besides the expression of a demand, it involves an appeal to the authority of principles in support of one's claims.* To assume this posture requires one to take distance from the social world so as to redefine and criticize it in terms of authoritative standards. Legal competence thus rests upon the same moral autonomy in which man finds the ability to set himself apart from the group and to evolve his own moral commitments as a discrete person.

3. Political Justice

by Otto Kirchheimer

From Political Justice, *Princeton, N.J., Princeton University Press (1961)* pp. 3–10.

Every political regime has its foes or in due time creates them. If in its structure and in the ground rules for the circulation of its elites the regime bore the hallmark of Plato's philosopher-king, it might be able to distribute ideological and material goods according to some preconceived pattern. But any regime is more likely to represent the joint product of tradition, the accident of history, plus an accretion of responses to the pressures of its time. Thus the merits of claims presented for validation to the powers-that-be are always bound to provoke controversial reaction. The resulting struggles between the established power holders and their foes, and generally between competitors for political power, assume a great variety of forms. Resort to courts is neither the most incisive not the most frequent form. Dramatic changes in the composition of elites, the rank order of social classes, the authority of political systems, styled revolutions, or equally dramatic reconfirmations of the old order, such as the defeat of a peasant revolt or an attempted establishment of the earthly reign of a spiritual community that is hostile to traditional belief systems – all to a large extent bypass the courts. At best, the courts will be cast into the somewhat placid role of confirming results reached elsewhere. The courts' regular jobs confine them to the middle ranges. They operate in the zone of seemingly endless thrusts and counterthrusts through which power positions are strengthened and the incumbent regime's authority is impressed on friend and waverer; but often, at the same time, new images and myths are pressed forward by foes of the regime who try to expose and erode established authority. Even in these middle ranges, however, the courts function as little as any other official agency, as an exclusive staging area for clashes between conflicting political claims. The battle is likely to be joined simultaneously in the parliament and administrative office, the newspaper and the factory, the school and the church.

The fight for political domination may thus range over wide fields. Yet as long as the territorial state wields final authority, formalized political decisions are bound to be channelled through parliament, executive authority, and the courts. Of the three, the courts' share in the making of decisions is most limited. Parliament creates the law and, at least theoretically, supervises an all-important executive, handling the making of policy decisions as well as being prime mover for administrative chores. The courts' part in the public business consists less in advancing their own substantive solutions of issues of public concern than in holding themselves in readiness for settling a great number of conflict situations. Among these situations, the clash between the authorities of the day and their foes is significant.

Of the manifold devices to rid the regime of political foes, the judicial inquest obtains neither the quickest nor by any means the most certain results. The desired goal – elimination of a political foe from political competition, or seizure of his wordly goods – may be performed by other agencies. Some of them involve informal violence and are highly irregular. Others form the stock-in-trade of politics: the ballot, a recent and partial substitute for the bullet; the pulpit, now partly replaced by its modern equivalent, the media of communications, working the full range of psychological pressures; and last but not least, Philip of Macedonia's ass with sacks of gold, noiseless and leaving behind them few traces. All do similar and, considering the proximate aim, possibly superior service. Do judicial proceedings belong altogether in this same category? Are they nothing but another device in the continuous process of stabilizing or changing power relations? Where rests the qualitatively different element, transcending the level of proximate result?

Judical proceedings serve to authenticate and thus to limit political action. Power holders may have an infinite number of security interests. Some of them, though perhaps far-fetched, are arrived at rationally; others are the products of imagination. By agreeing to a yardstick, however nebulous or refined, to cut down the number of occasions for the elimination of actual or potential foes, those in power stand to gain as much as their subjects. Authentication removes the fear of reprisals or liquidation from multitudes of possible victims, and encourages a friendly and understanding disposition toward the security needs of the power holders on the part of their subjects. The more elaborate the paraphernalia of authentication, the greater the chance of vicarious popular participation in its conundrums. When proceedings remain largely secretive, the character of those sitting in judgment, whether it rests on magic, tradition, or on the much narrower basis of rational professional qualifications, must perforce form the main basis of approval. In proceedings to which the public has some access, authentication, the regularizing of the extraordinary, may under favorable circumstances be transformed into a deeper popular understanding and political participation. Modern means of communication do not restrict participation in or reactions to a trial by those present and, with some delay, by a wider educated public. If the participants wish, proceedings may be thrown open to virtually the whole world. The dynamics of such an undertaking – the vicarious participation of a virtually unlimited public in the unfolding of political reality, re-created and severely compressed for trial purposes into categories within easy reach of the public's understanding – fashions a new political weapon. Such mobilization of opinion may remain a mere by-product of judicial proceedings; but it may and in modern times frequently has superseded the original goal of judicial proceedings, authentication. At the same time it may destroy the proceedings' inherent limitations.

What a state organization does with its statutory arsenal, its security blueprints, and blank checks will depend on the state of mind of its leadership and on the amount of concerted hostility in the body politic. These two influences are not necessarily related. The greater the reservoir of public dissatisfaction, the more the regime's political effectiveness will depend on a planned and discerning use of its legal weapons. If it allowed its administration of justice to run after every incident that could be worked up into a case, it would soon lose breath as well as face. Seeking the spontaneous assent of foes is at best difficult and long-term. To instill in potential foes the habit of prudence and a measure of obedience requires the tracking down of the significant rather than the available foe. Attempts to enforce universal compliance may end up in universal lawlessness, heralding the breakdown rather than the strengthening of the existing order. To develop rational criteria rather than emotional slogans for dealing with political foes, the regime must be able to differentiate between the isolated and occasional foe and the organized group and, within the group, between the leader and his followers. Failing the latter, the regime may incur political risks in inverse proportion to the likelihood of its success. Importuning the isolated foe may be a cautionary device, a seemingly harmless popular pastime – a matter of flexing muscles in self-confirmation. Yet such a move may prove costly if it implants the seed which starts communion with the martyr.

Where the allegiance of masses rather than the action of selected individuals becomes the focal point of contention, formal obeisance rather than retribution seems the more logical goal. The official system has to be kept going and possibly reinforced by its depriving the mass of dissenters of easy incentives to challenge the regime, by allowing the average camp follower to stay on the sideline, by a policy of graduated disqualifications and rewards, and by strategic individual acts of submission. Transferring loyalty conflicts from the ranks of the regime into those of the foe might, other factors being equal, help to hold the outer defense perimeter and obtain outward conformity rather than multiplying the opportunities for martyrdom; the more spectacular task of reclaiming lost souls would be left as the penultimate hope and aim. The reservoir of potential followers of the foe of the regime fills and empties in accordance with the tidings of the battle. If the right kind of key is used, these followers are rarely locked completely from either side.

The differentiation between followers and leaders, facilities for which are found in criminal codes, enforces a certain amount of passive obedience and keeps the machinery of enforcement from breaking down or becoming a mere apparatus of registration. If it does not help a regime on the downgrade to survive catastrophes due to deeper and more encompassing causes, it saves it from wasted motion and embarrassment. If this differentiation, which permits followers to move to the sidelines, is dismissed without simultaneous resort to crude, sweeping, and often bestial forms of 'disqualification', such as deportation or execution, according to 'objective' criteria of race, social status, religion or nationality, the regime is confronted by a dilemma. Mass prosecutions follow unavoidably from the failure to differentiate between leaders and followers in a politically hostile organization.

These cursory remarks on the differences between prosecuting deviant leadership and containing their followers point up two major problem areas. The first concerns the institutional patterns of relations between a regime and its political foes, viewing the foes as a movement rather than as obstreperous and dangerous individuals. In our period hostility to an existing regime is rarely any longer the isolated expression of loosely joined individuals or an inchoate sentiment among the upper echelon of society. Nor, if hostility is organized, is it restricted to upholding a particular segment (religion, property) against the encroachment of today's rulers who would be willing to compromise on almost anything else. Since the nineteenth century, the days of Irish Nationalists, English Chartists, and the German Social Democrats, the fine art of loyalty-absorbing counter-organizations has been developed parallel to the growth of state power. Whenever such full-fledged counterorganizations fuse the ideological and material interests of larger groups, any state organization which does not want to turn to the Fascist or Communist pattern of total repression of political deviation may face major problems of political mass control.

Another problem put into bold relief by the accelerated rate of political change in our time concerns the feasibility of trial by fiat of a successor regime. Keeping a present political foe at bay is one thing, prosecuting him once he has been vanquished another. Considerations governing both situations are not all necessarily identical. Reversals of political fortunes have not been uncommon and many a Hydra supposedly slain by its foes has raised a head again. The very possibility and danger of a reversal points up many a successor regime's preoccupation with delving into its predecessor's record, holding it up to contempt, and instilling into the public feelings of loyalty and gratitude towards those who have delivered them from the evil. In doing so, however, the regime faces the ticklish problem of casting its pedagogical goal into a suitable legal form. It must attempt to minimize the partisan element which inevitably mars such proceedings and to differentiate between accountability for mere political misjudgment and responsibility for criminal and inhuman behavior committed during such political action.

4. Revolution and Legitimacy

by Michael Barkun

From 'Law and Social Revolution: Millenarianism and the Legal System', Law and Society Review *(1971) vol. 6, pp. 118–35.*

It is important to indicate as precisely as possible what I mean by revolution and, more specifically, to underscore its intermittently millenarian character. The distinction between 'revolution' and 'rebellion' is apposite here. Rebellion, though it involves collective violence, leaves the constitutional framework unaltered. New incumbents occupy old office. Indeed, the rebel frequently see himself as acting in defense of the established order, whether defending the institution of kingship against a usurper or parliamentary prerogative against executive power.

Rebellions of all kinds share similarly limited aims; they leave the social and political frameworks very much as they found them. This paradox of violent change amid institutional continuity ties together African tribal rebellions, medieval peasant revolts, and military coups. The seizure of power, unaccompanied by a coherent political or social program, necessarily leaves most relationships and the rules regulating them intact. Then, too, there is a whole category of rebellious or quasi-rebellious outbursts which are not even focused on the seizure of power, but are merely the expression of discontent, the desire to alleviate very specific economic and social conditions, or some free-floating sense of hostility.

Since rebellions leave alone more than they change, the bulk of the legal system continues on its conventionally incremental course. There does in fact seem to be some kind of natural affinity between the operation of a legal system and incremental change.

A system of legal rules and institutions is expected to enhance social stability. However, the reciprocal character of the relationship means that legal rules cannot stabilize interactions if interactions do not already possess some modicum of predictability. Lest this sound entirely circular, it comes down simply to this: Rules and institutions conventionally called 'legal' have their own prerequisites. They cannot be expected to perform as some kind of social gyroscope if there is not already a relatively high level of consensus and manageable rate of social change. The latter point means that the rate of social change may not be faster than the rate of legal adaptation and administration.

Revolution intentionally destabilizes a social system, building upon pre-revolutionary sources of instability. In so doing, the polity enters a period characterized both by lack of consensus and by an unmanageable rate of social change.

Movement along the rebellion–revolution continuum necessarily constitutes movement away from accepted bases of legitimacy and away from rule-governed behaviour; in short, away from law. Revolution seeks at the very least to produce structural alterations in the political system, as for example by altering the character of political offices in addition to removing their incumbents. But of course the categories of 'rebellion' and 'revolution' are not properly regarded as dichotomous at all. An indefinite number of hybrids separate the two extremes, each incorporating value dissensus and consensus in varying proportions. It goes without saying that all revolutions leave some facets of the old regime and society untouched, while virtually all rebellions have some effects, however unintended, upon structure.

As one moves along the continuum in the direction of an extreme form of revolution, the commitment to structural change necessarily broadens. The movement is in the direction of 'millenarian revolutions'. Millenarian movements may be most succinctly defined as social movements which anticipate immediate, collective, total, this-worldly salvation. To the extent that they rely for the ultimate consummation wholly upon external, supernatural forces, they lie beyond our present concern. They do, however, frequently manifest a pronounced activism, either through a desire to help the inevitable along or as a result of escalating disagreements with the regime in power. At any rate, it is part of the ideological baggage of such movements to regard the present society, whatever it happens to be, as irremediably evil and to desire to displace it with a new and totally just social order. A large number of movements approximate this holistic approach to social change.

Millenarian revolutions, with their commitment to the construction of Utopia, logically entail the total destruction of existing society and its supersession by a totally new and different one. Now in point of fact the break is nowhere so clear cut. Indeed in many cases the drive for political and social redemption is linked to the restoration of a legendary golden age, 'paradise lost'. While *total*

change is an ideal which is inherently unrealizable, the very statement of it is an act of primary political and legal significance. First,
millenarianism mandates change in precisely those expressive and
evaluative activities where 'normal law' appears least competent to
act, e.g. status, sexual morality, and religion. Second, revolutions
are preceded by, and themselves produce, substantial instability. As
I have already indicated, in the very strictest sense no revolution can
really be millenarian; all face unsuperable obstacles in the resilience
of institutions, the habit-following propensities of persons, and the
limits of technology. But in a slightly less strict sense, certain
revolutions (many obscure by usual historical canons) can be classified as millenarian. Concerning the rest: those that normally come to
mind when the word 'revolution' is mentioned contain millenarian
elements and, more importantly, *may well have been millenarian* at
certain points in their life histories.

Insofar as a revolutionary movement is millenarian in any of the
senses discussed, it poses special difficulties for the continuation or
establishment of a system of legal rules. In the early stages of
millenarian revolutionary upheavals, members of dissident movements often attempt radically and consciously to withdraw themselves from the evil society they perceive about them. This withdrawal may take the form of actual physical movement to a remote
area or through a process of 'inner emigration'.

Separateness creates substantial problems for the existing legal
system. Where separation takes the form of an internal psychological process of dissociation, there is a corresponding process of
legal de-socialization. In addition, where the separation is physical,
groups can build up elaborate systems of counter-rules. And in both
cases, there may be recourse to ritualistic violation of traditional
norms.

As social movements approach the ideal type of total millenarian
commitment, they demand more and more of their members.
Adherents must cut themselves off completely from prior allegiances
and attach themselves to a very different and comprehensive set of
loyalties. The political prophet or putative messiah comes less as the
bearer of a specific doctrine than as the catalyst of his followers'
political conversions. Again, the more sweeping the changes in
process, the more a political movement comes to resemble a religion.
The new states of Africa and Asia, in the throes of modernization,
are predictably rich in charismatically based political religions.

Unfortunately, so far as the legal system is concerned, charismatic authority is incompatible with law. In Max Weber's formulation, traditional authority, based upon immemorial usage, was roughly comparable to customary law; rational–legal authority draws upon conventionally understood concepts of a legal system. Only charismatic authority, based upon the leader's possession of extraordinary gifts, lies outside legal categories. Genuine charisma is not rule-governed.

Millenarian revolutions almost always focus upon a supernatural or extraordinarily gifted leader, at some times the messiah whose very presence seals the doom of the existing order, at other merely the uniquely perceptive spokesman for higher forces. In either case, the leader possesses a form of authority peculiarly his own, neither shared nor subordinated. The crisis of legitimacy, caused when individuals withdraw from the commitments to which they were once socialized, can now be dealt with; for there is in charisma an alternative basis for commitment, a focus around which individuals may be, as it were, 'resocialized'. It is important to recognize, therefore, the dual role of the charismatic leader *vis-a-vis* socialization: He is the catalyst of 'political conversions' which draw persons away from past allegiances and at the same time offers an alternative source of legitimacy for those who have been withdrawn from conventional commitments.

... I take it as axiomatic that charismatic authority flourishes when large numbers of people perceive the social system as inadequate to their needs. Times of perceived stress and deprivation constitute a necessary if not a sufficient condition. Hence traditional and rational–legal bases of authority give way to charisma in times of depression, war, epidemic, modernization and culture-conflict. Millenarian revolutions, as political instability in general, similarly occur in periods characterized by abnormally severe deprivations, dislocations, and changes. These circumstances, with which both charismatic authority and millenarian revolution are associated, constitute 'disasters', in the special sense in which social scientists have used the term:

> ... a severe, relatively sudden, and frequently unexpected disruption of normal structural arrangements within a social system, or subsystem, resulting from a force 'natural' or 'social', 'internal' to a system or 'external' to it, over which the system has no firm 'control'.[1]

'Normal' forms of authority are seen to have failed, although of course this says nothing about their 'objective' levels of performance.

There is a significant legal dimension to disaster situations. Law, for the complying majority, constitutes a set of internalized concepts fitted into rules. This map or model of society allows people to orient themselves to others, as well as to make fairly accurate predictions of their behavior. Such legal functions as the de-escalation and resolution of conflict, the control of deviation, and the implementation of policy all grow out of and depend upon the primary function of the attainment of social predictability. A society that experiences rapid social change and increasing conflict – the kind of society we associate with such phenomena as revolution, mass movements, and charismatic authority – is a society in which *law no longer provides an adequate means for the attainment of predictable expectations in social interaction.* There are limits to how fast law can adapt to changed circumstances. Stress-producing change, so rapid that law cannot adapt or which occurs in areas that law cannot effectively restructure, produces a crisis in social predictability. The environment simply becomes unmanageable and, increasingly, incomprehensible. In this connection, we ought not to lose sight of the fact that law is in a very real sense a kind of explanation of why people behave as they do. In a period of pronounced change and upheaval, legal categories and rules tell people about a world which no longer exists, imparting less and less information about situations in which they presently find themselves.

When law is thus undermined by events, the most immediate solution lies in an alternative base of authority. The imputed gifts of the charismatic leader are of course vulnerable to death, to the stubborn character of reality, and to inevitable routinization. However, in the short term situation where law – any law at all – appears inoperative, such considerations are bound to seem irrelevant. Even the quixotic nature of personalized authority seems somehow fitting. Rapid social change and revolutionary movements are neither wholly the products of uncontrolled circumstances nor solely the outcome of deliberate planning. Nor, to carry the process one step further, are they independent of each other. The inner integrity of the legal system, as it has been adumbrated in Fuller's legal morality, cannot withstand the increasing levels of demands and the shifting environment.

The final paradox of revolutionary messianism lies in its inability both to tolerate law and to exist without it. The systematic breakdown of former patterns of socialization, the reliance on charismatic authority, and the frequent commitment to antinomian ideas all bespeak a desire for a world without norms. At the same time, resocialization demands an elaborate alternative rule system, charismatic authority cannot be indefinitely sustained, and large-scale administration demands continuity. Millenarian revolutions, in their periods of greatest activism, consequently maintain the form of rules while infusing them with precisely the kinds of contents and functions that violate their 'morality'. They thus come to resemble the legal systems of Lewis Carroll and Franz Kafka, which is to say that the terms 'law' and 'rule' can be attached to them in only the loosest way.

1. Gideon Sjoberg, 'Disasters and social change' in G. W. Baker and D. W. Chapman, *Man and Society in Disaster*, New York, Basic Books (1962) p. 357.

5. The Unfinished
by Thomas Mathiesen

From The Politics of Abolition, *London, Martin Robertson (1974) pp. 13–25.*

I have gradually acquired the belief that the alternative lies in the unfinished, in the sketch, in what is not yet fully existing. The 'finished alternative' is 'finished' in a double sense of the word. If it is correct, this view has considerable consequences for political life. It means that any attempt to change the existing order into something completely finished, a fully formed entity, is destined to fail: in the process of finishing lies a return to the by-gone. Note that I am here thinking of change and reversion in terms of structure. The existing order changes in structure *while* it enters its new form. This was the meaning of the oracles: they provided sketches, not answers, as entrances to the new. This is the meaning of psychotherapy. In the sketches of the oracles and of the therapist to him who asks and to the patient – in the very fact that only sketches are given – lie their alternatives.

Existing order changes in structure *while* it enters the new. The first political question, then, becomes that of how this 'while' should be started, how the sketch should be begun, how it should be mobilized. The second question, which is politically almost as central, is that of how the sketch may be maintained as a sketch, or at least prolonged in life as a sketch. An enormous political pressure exists in the direction of completing the sketch into a finished drawing, and thereby ending the growth of the product. How can this be avoided, or at least postponed? The answer to this question requires a new understanding of the social forces that work for the process of finishing. Through both of these questions, *abolition* runs like a red thread. Abolition is the point of departure.

I shall first explain in more detail why the alternative lies in the unfinished. Next, I shall approach the two questions mentioned: the inception and the maintenance of the unfinished. I will hardly give complete answers to these questions, but I hope to be able to give some suggestions.

The alternative is 'alternative' in so far as it is not based on the premises of the old system, but its own premises, which at one or more points *contradict* those of the old system. In other words, contradiction is a necessary element in the alternative. It is a matter of contradiction in terms of goals, or in terms of means together with goals. The alternative is 'alternative' in so far as it *competes* with the old system. An arrangement which does not compete with the old system, an arrangement which is not relevant for the members of the old system as a replacement of the old system, is no alternative. I emphasize that the concept of competition takes, as its point of departure, the subjective standpoint of the satisfied system-member being confronted with an opposition. The political task is that of exposing to such a member the insufficiency of being satisfied with the system. When this is exposed, the opposition competes. This is the case whether the system-members in question are on top or at the bottom of the system. Often those we try to talk to will be at the bottom, because these are considered more mobile for actual political action.

The main problem, then, is that of obtaining the combination of *the contradicting and the competing*; the main problem is that of avoiding that your contradiction becomes non-competing and that your competition becomes agreement. The main aim is that of attaining *the competing contradiction*.

An opposition may seek to bring a message which is (1) foreign and (2) fully formed. The fact that a message is 'foreign' will mean that the message in fact does not belong to, is not integrated or woven into, the old system. The opposite of being foreign will subsequently be that of being 'integrated': the message one seeks to bring has in fact already got its defined place, integrated into the old thinking. The fact that a message is 'fully formed' will subsequently mean that the consequences of the actual carrying-out of the message are clarified, or approximately clarified. The opposite of being fully formed will in the following be 'suggested': the consequences of the actual carrying out of the message are not yet clarified.

The opposition that speaks (1) in a foreign way and (2) in a way that indicates a fully formed message, thus brings a message (a) which does not belong to, is not integrated in, the old system, and (b) which at the same time is clarified in so far as the consequences of its actual practical carrying-out are concerned. The contradiction of this opposition stands in danger of becoming non-competing. Since it is clear–beyond doubt, definite–that the message, when carried out, does not belong to the old system, the satisfied member of the old system may disregard the message as of no importance to himself and his system, as irrelevant, as of no concern to the system. The contradiction of the opposition may be disregarded as permanently 'outside', and thereby be set aside, because it is beyond doubt that the message does not belong to the established system. The message which is foreign and full formed thus contains a contradiction, but the contradiction easily becomes non-competing. This analysis, of course, is couched in ideal-typical terms.

Let us for a moment take a look at the opposite extreme: the message with a content (1) which in fact is woven into, or integrated in, the old system, but (2) where the content is only suggested, so that the consequences of the actual carrying-out of the message remain unclarified. This message will not so easily be written off as non-competing. Since the question of what the message will lead to is not clarified, the message cannot simply be set aside. But at the same time the message does not contradict the establishment. In fact, it is integrated into, and therefore in accordance with, the premises of the old system. In sum, the message constitutes what may be called a 'competing agreement', a fictitious competition. The pipe-smoking, casually philosophizing district attorney in an exclusive interview with the Sunday newspaper may be a case in point. Nothing new is being said, but the old is stated in such a way that the reader is given the impression of interesting depth. Competition takes place–about nothing.

The important thing at this point is that neither of the two cases discussed above provides an understanding of the alternative. Logically there are two other main possibilities.

The first is that of (1) the integrated and (2) fully formed message. The main thing to say about the integrated and fully formed message is that this is a message which brings nothing new. The integrated and fully formed message constitutes what we may call a non-competing agreement. The 'able' student reproducing textbook material from rote learning is probably the core example. This student does not give any hint of an alternative. His examination paper contains no contradiction, and no message experienced as competing. It contains only memorization. The sociologically significant point is that considerable parts of life in our society consist of such reproduction or non-competing agreement, interspread by a few meditating district attorneys.

The remaining possibility is that of (1) the foreign and (2) suggested message. Here we are faced with a contradiction, and finally at the same time competition. The unclarified nature of the further consequences of the contradiction makes it impossible for the (satisfied) system member to maintain that the contradiction is certainly outside his realm of interest. Contradiction and competition are united–in the alternative.

This is at the same time the definition of 'the unfinished'. To be sure, the foreign and fully formed message is unfinished in the sense that it is outside the established–empirically tested and tried–system, but it is at the same time finished in the sense that its final consequences are clarified. The integrated and suggested message is in fact fully tried out, and thereby finished, even if its consequences are unfinished in the sense of not being set down on paper. The integrated and fully formed message is finished in a double sense of the word: it is in fact fully tried out, and its consequences are even clarified, on paper. The foreign and suggested message, however, is unfinished in the sense that it is not yet tried out *as well as* in the sense that its consequences are not yet clarified. Thus, the alternative constitutes the double negation of the fully formed or finally framed world.

The forces which pull away from the unfinished–away from the competing contradiction–are many and strong. Figure 1 schematically presents the material we have covered so far.

The forces that pull away from the unfinished–away from the competing contradiction–move in two directions, as the arrows show. In the first place, there are forces which finish in such a way that the contradiction becomes non-competing; in such a way that competition is abolished. The vertical arrow shows this movement. Language provides a road to it. The pressure in the direction of finalizing language, the pressure in the direction of clarifying what we mean, may lead to a contradiction in this direction. When language is finalized, the answer is given, and the contradiction–though stubbornly maintained as a contradiction–is finished in the sense of becoming fully formed. When fully formed, the foreign language may be rejected, and is rejected, as clearly and definitely of no concern.

Far stronger are the forces that *abolish* the contradiction, the forces that change the contradiction to an agreement rather than making it non-competing. The horizontal arrow shows this finishing movement. Language is important also with regard to the doing away with the contradiction and its change into agreement (rather than the maintenance of the contradiction and its becoming non-competing). To amplify, in a specific and important way, language is related to power. Those in power decide (by and large) what language is to be spoken. The opposition is not in power, and in order for the opposition to ensure that it is defined as a competing

The message is	Foreign	Integrated
Suggested	Competing contradiction (alternative) ——	Competing agreement
Full formed	Non-competing contradiction	Non-competing agreement

FIGURE 1

party, it must begin to speak the language of those in power. But language not only provides a possibility for transmitting information. It is also active in structuring and defining the problem at hand. The more we use the language of the powerful, the more attuned we become to defining the problems at hand *as the powerful usually do;* in other words, the more integrated we become into the old system. We define the problems at hand in this way in order to persuade the powerful that our contradiction is sensible. But competition is then maintained at the cost of the contradiction itself; the contradiction is abolished and turned into fundamental agreement; the forms which compete are both integrated into the old system, tested out, and finished.

I will give an example. In penal policy there is, from the side of one opposing group, a stress on the use of 'treatment'. To the opposition, the concept of 'treatment' has a professional and specific meaning, and treatment is in itself a goal, though a part of a means–end chain. To make the concept understood and competing, the opposition characteristically translates it into the language of the ruler. For example, the opposition tries to talk of 'influencing', or 'persuading', the 'deviant'. In doing so, however, the opposition has straight away defined the issue as the other party–those in power–usually does. To the other party, the goal is that of creating better 'morals', and the concept of treatment has now been defined in these terms. When the lawyers in the Prison Department have finally understood, those who are out of power–those in opposition–have finally managed to express themselves perfectly in the language of those in power. And at the same time, the contradiction is gone; the problem at hand is defined according to the usual standards of the powerful.

I am basing my argument on an interpretation which is in dispute. Any society has certain general needs which must be satisfied. Furthermore, a society has limited ways in which to satisfy these needs, if it is at the same time to exist as a society. The very existence of 'society' is, in other words, in itself structure-forming in a limiting way; it is in itself anti-alternative. The limitations are partly embedded in the society's relations to other societies; other societies which are not changed. But the limitations are also built into the very phenomenon of 'structure'. The new society is therefore–when it is finished as an established order–in fundamental ways like the old society. This is like the new prison which is–when it is finally established–in fundamental ways like the old prison.

What are the general features of structure which are so recurrent? In particular, I have in mind the two dimensions of 'differentiation' and 'integration'. These are quite general processes, and the point is that they appear in combination: a differentiation becomes established, or is ossified, through an integration of the differentiated parts.

But imagine that we have aroused an interest in the unfinished among those who have so far been satisfied with their system. How is the unfinished to be started in more practical terms? The question is complex.

The most general answer is that the inception of the unfinished takes place through *abolishing* the established order. Only the abolishing of what is finished gives the unfinished a chance to appear.

But at this point we may easily fool ourselves. A change through which we leave one order in favour of another *which is waiting,* is no abolishment. It is only a substitution, which certainly may involve differences in detail, and 'improvements' in detail, but which does not involve a change of structure. Structurally, a finalized fully formed new order perpetuates old solutions; our relationship to what is waiting is structurally like our relationship to the old order. Abolition in other words takes place when we break the established order and at *the same time* face unbuilt ground. This is to say that the abolition and the very first phase of the unfinished are one and the same. The moment of freedom is that of entering unbuilt ground. Freedom is the anxiety and pleasure involved in entering a field which is unsettled or empty.

The abolition, and thereby the transition to the unfinished, is triggered through making those who are implicated conscious of the fact that one is necessarily faced with a *dilemma;* through the conscious experience of in fact having to *choose* between a continuation of the prevailing order (possibly with minor changes) and a transition to something which is unknown. Such a conscious experience is no sufficient condition for the inception of the abolition and the unfinished, but it is certainly a necessary one. It implies that veiled, unprincipled reliance on combinations, which deceives you into continuing the old structure, must be unveiled, and the choice between the horns of the dilemma must be clearly presented.

6. State Control
by Nicos Poulantzas

From Facism and Dictatorship, *London, New Left Books (1974) pp. 301–8.*

Ideological Apparatuses as State Apparatuses

Ideology does not only belong to the realm of ideas: it is not a 'conceptual system' in the strict sense of the term. As Gramsci firmly stated, it extends to the mores, customs, and 'way of life' of the agents in a social formation. It is concretized in the *practices* of a social formation (bourgeois, proletarian, and petty-bourgeois practices). Ideology, the dominant ideology, is furthermore an essential *power* of the classes in a social formation. As such, the dominant ideology is embodied in a series of institutions and apparatuses within a formation: the Churches (religious apparatus), parties (political apparatus), unions (union apparatus), schools (educational apparatus), the means of 'communication', i.e. papers, radio, television, cinema (communications apparatus), the 'cultural' domain (publishing etc.), the family in a certain sense, etc. These are the ideological State apparatuses.

Such apparatuses are relatively distinct from the 'repressive' State apparatus, i.e. from that apparatus which fulfils its role under the *principal aspect* of organized physical repression, which the State legally monopolizes (though ideology plays a part here too): this is the State apparatus in the strict sense. The ideological apparatuses have as their *principal aspect* the elaboration and indoctrination of ideology (though various forms of repression are at work here too). Why should they be described as ideological *State* apparatuses?

1. Ideology is not something 'neutral' in society: *the only ideologies are class ideologies*. The dominant ideology consists of power relations which are absolutely essential to a social formation, and sometimes even assume the dominant role in it. But this is not enough to make the ideological apparatuses State apparatuses. Political domination cannot in fact be maintained through the use of physical repression alone, but demands the direct and decisive intervention of ideology. It is in this sense that the dominant ideology,

in the form of its ideological apparatuses, is directly involved in the State apparatus, which concentrates, guarantees and gives expression to political power.

2. This brings us to the Marxist definition of the State. In the Marxist classics, the State, as a class State, is not defined solely by its control of repressive physical 'force', but mainly by its social and political role. The class State is the central instance with the role of preserving the unity and cohesion of a social formation, of preserving the conditions of production and therefore the reproduction of the social conditions of production. In a system of class struggle, it guarantees political class domination. This is precisely the role of the ideological apparatuses; in particular, the dominant ideology is the 'cement' of the social formation.

3. The State apparatus in the strict sense is the condition for the existence and functioning of the ideological apparatuses in a social formation. Although the repressive apparatus does not generally intervene directly in their functioning, it is still continually there behind them.

Branches of the Repressive State Apparatus: Characteristics of the Ideological State Apparatuses

1. I have just said that the State apparatuses fulfil their role either under the *principal aspect* of repression or under the *principal aspect* of ideology. But I should specify that *this does not mean that the only 'functions' of the State are repressive and ideological.* Depending on the modes of production and their stages, and depending on the phases and periods of a social formation, the State can even have what could be called a 'direct economic function'. This function is direct in that the State is not limited to reproducing the social conditions of production, but intervenes decisively in the reproduction of the production cycle itself–notably in certain cases of the interventionist form of capitalist State, where the State, as Lenin showed, intervenes 'even in the detailed workings of the economy' (i.e. in the very cycle of capital reproduction). This economic function of the State can be carried out both by the repressive apparatus (government and administration), and by the ideological apparatuses (the trade unions). The important point, however, is that the economic function of the State is always articulated to its overall political role. In other words, this economic function, which may be dominant over the other functions, is in fact

carried out under the principal aspect of either repression or ideology.

2. As a corollary, the concept of 'apparatus' cannot be restricted to the State apparatuses alone. In other words, the *concepts of 'apparatus' and 'State' do not cover exactly the same ground.* The firm, for example, is not merely a 'unit of production'. It also plays a part in reproducing the social conditions of production, and ideology and relations of political domination are involved in it. As an effect of the relations of production, the 'firm' gives concrete form to the relationship between social relations of production and political and ideological social relations. Revolutionary practice experienced this with the 'workers' councils' and 'soviets'. However, the 'economic apparatus' cannot be described as an economic State apparatus, although the State intervenes to guarantee 'order'. On the one hand, the Marxist definition of the *State* is that its apparatuses are basically designed to preserve the cohesion and unity of a formation divided into classes. This definition emphasizes political class domination and does not therefore apply directly to the economic apparatus. On the other hand, as 'production units' in a system of class exploitation, the main role of the economic apparatus in relation to the masses is to *exploit* them. The 'authority' or 'despotism' of the exploiting class is directly determined by exploitation, while the State apparatuses do not exploit in the full sense of *directly extracting* surplus value (this at least is not their main role).

There are some important consequences for the problem of the socialist revolution. The Marxist classics *explicitly* indicated that a socialist revolution means not only a change in *State power,* but must also *'smash'* the repressive State apparatus. It can be argued that this thesis does not apply only to the *State,* i.e. to the repressive *and* ideological State apparatuses, nor is it enough just to extend it to the ideological State apparatuses. *This thesis in fact involves the whole 'apparatus', including the economic apparatus;* Lenin always maintained just this position. None the less, the distinction between State apparatuses and economic apparatus is *still basic.* In particular, it is clear that the *State* apparatuses and the economic apparatus cannot be smashed *at the same time or in the same way.* The same is of course true for the distinction between the repressive and ideological State apparatuses, which can also not be 'smashed' at the same time or in the same way. But the difference between the

State apparatuses (repressive and ideological) and the economic apparatus is of quite a different kind. The economic apparatus in particular contains, in its 'production units', the hard kernel which Marx called the 'technical basis of production'. This is not to be met with in the State apparatuses, and it poses quite specific 'problems'.

3. The fact that the ideological State apparatuses are often of a 'private' character, and are not officially recognized as *State* apparatuses, should not be surprising. The distinction between 'private' and 'public' is purely juridical. Contrary to a certain conception that there is a 'pre-juridical', almost ontological distinction between private and public, a demarcation line between 'civil society' and the 'State' (i.e. the place at which the State is constituted), it has to be understood that the distinction is established by *law*–in effect, by the State itself–and its *only* meaning is therefore a juridical one. The distinction between 'private' and 'public' does not basically affect the question of the ideological State apparatuses. Gramsci understood this perfectly when he described 'bodies normally referred to as private' as belonging to the State. This in no way means that the 'private' or 'public' character of the ideological State apparatuses is of no importance, or that it comes about merely by chance. On the contrary, this signifies different forms of functioning, according to the different types and forms of State. The normally 'private' nature of these apparatuses, moreover, often relates to their *relative autonomy* both from each other and from the State apparatus.

4. We are close to the heart of the matter. It is possible to refer to *the* State apparatus, narrowly defined, *in the singular,* whereas one speaks of *several* ideological State apparatuses. It would be wrong to think that the State apparatus in the narrow sense was some kind of indivisible monolith. The repressive State apparatus is itself composed of specialized *branches;* the army, the police, the administration etc. But in their relations with each other and with the repressive State apparatus, the ideological State apparatuses display *a degree and form of relative autonomy* which the branches of the repressive State apparatus do not posses. The repressive State apparatus, the *central nucleus* of the State system and State power, has a much stronger and more vigorous internal unity than the ideological apparatuses. The internal unity of the branches of this apparatus makes it possible to speak of them as a *virtual sub-system* within the system of State apparatuses.

One of the main consequences is that the 'destruction' of the State cannot be identical for the State apparatus and for the ideological State apparatuses: the ideological apparatuses cannot be 'smashed' at the same time nor in the same way as the State apparatus, or as each other.

Why do the ideological State apparatuses have this relative autonomy, expressed in their own multiplicity?

(a) The relative distinctness of class ideologies from the State apparatuses is not jeopardized by the institutionalization of the dominant ideology in State apparatuses. These apparatuses do not 'create' ideology, and their main function is to develop and instil it. This relative distinctness of ideology stems from the fact that the apparatuses themselves are no more than the effects of the class struggle. I cannot go into this here, but its implications were understood by the Marxist classics. They saw the remarkable ability of the dominant ideology to *outlive* the transformation of the apparatuses (including the ideological apparatuses) and of State power.

(b) It is based on fundamental features of the class struggle, firstly in the realm of ideology. The dominant ideology is not the only ideology in a social formation: *there are several contradictory ideologies or ideological sub-systems,* related to the various classes in struggle. The dominant ideology itself is only formed by its successful domination of these other ideologies and ideological sub-systems: it does so through the ideological State apparatuses. This in turn implies that the apparatuses condense the intense ideological contradiction expressed in splits among the 'ideological spokesmen' who are a part of them. The result is the relative autonomy of the ideological apparatuses.

(c) The relative autonomy of the ideological State apparatuses therefore finally relates to the relations of political power in the strict sense, and is expressed in major dislocations of *State power.* Firstly, State power is generally formed by an alliance of the dominant classes or class fractions, the power bloc in a capitalist socialist formation. So despite the fact that one class or fraction normally has hegemony, the political power of the other classes or fractions 'in power' involves dislocations among the State apparatuses. It is not possible to discuss State power, political class power, without locating its concrete expression in the State apparatuses. In particular, it is possible for one class or fraction to have power in all or some of the ideological apparatuses of the State, while another controls the State apparatus proper. One characteristic example is that of the transition from feudalism to capitalism, where there is an alliance between the bourgeoisie and the landed nobility. In such cases the Church often acts for a long time as the nobility's seat of power, while the bourgeoisie entrenches itself in the State apparatus.

The important point to stress is that these dislocations in State power appear mainly between the ideological State apparatuses themselves, or between them and the repressive State apparatus. Despite the internal unity of this sub-system, it is even possible for similar divisions to appear within the State apparatus proper. The army, the administration or the judiciary can at times be the privileged seats of power of different classes or fractions within the power bloc. But as the repressive State apparatus is the central nucleus of the State, the hegemonic class or fraction generally controls this apparatus. Its internal unity ('centralization') means that while non-hegemonic classes or fractions may control certain of its branches, its internal organization is, according to the form of State, generally under the direct domination of the branch controlled by the hegemonic class or fraction. This is precisely why it is possible to speak of a concrete unity (not a 'sharing') of State power within the State apparatus, when several classes and fractions are in power.

With the ideological apparatuses things are different. These are in fact the apparatuses best able to concentrate in themselves the power of non-hegemonic classes and fractions. They are therefore both the favoured 'refuge' of such classes and fractions, and their favoured spoils. The classes and fractions in these apparatuses may not even be allies of the hegemonic class, but in bitter struggle against it. These apparatuses are therefore often the *last ramparts* of a waning class power, as the Church was for the landed nobility, or the *first strongholds* of a new class power, as publishing and the schools were for the bourgeoisie before the French Revolution. Lastly and most importantly, the struggle of the masses is not only reflected in the ideological apparatuses, but often has a particularly marked influence on certain of them, in particular those aimed at the masses, such as trade unions and parties of the social-democratic kind.

The 'game' of class power played out between the repressive State apparatus and the ideological apparatuses, which is due to the *class struggle,* appears to be the basic cause, and one of the effects, of the relative autonomy of the ideological State apparatuses.

5. One last point, which I can only touch on here. Only revolutionary organizations and organizations of class struggle can in the end 'escape' the system of ideological State apparatuses.

7. Norms and Inequality
by Ralf Dahrendorf

From 'The Origin of Inequality' in Essays in the Theory of Society, *London, Routledge and Kegan Paul (1968) pp. 167–74.*

Human society always means that people's behavior is being removed from the randomness of chance and regulated by established and inescapable expectations. The compulsory character of these expectations or norms is based on the operation of sanctions, i.e. of rewards or punishments for conformist or deviant behavior. If every society is in this sense a moral community, it follows that there must always be at least that inequality of rank which results from the necessity of sanctioning behaviour according to whether it does or does not conform to established norms. Under whatever aspect given historical societies may introduce additional distinctions between their members, whatever symbols they may declare to be outward signs of inequality, and whatever may be the precise content of their social norms, the hard core of social inequailty can always be found in the fact that men as the incumbents of social roles are subject, according to how their roles relate to the dominant expectational principles of society, to sanctions designed to enforce these principles.

Let me try to illustrate what I mean by some examples which, however difficult they may seem, are equally relevant. If the ladies of a neighborhood are expected to exchange secrets and scandals with their neighbors, this norm will lead at the very least to a distinction between those held in high regard (who really enjoy gossip, and offer tea and cakes as well), those with average prestige, and the outsiders (who, for whatever reasons, take no part in the gossiping). If, in a factory, high individual output is expected from the workers and rewarded by piecework rates, there will be some who take home a relatively high paycheck and others who take home a relatively low one. If the citizens (or better, perhaps, subjects) of a state are expected to defend its official ideology as frequently and convincingly as possible, this will lead to a distinction between those who get ahead (becoming, say, civil servants or party secretaries); the mere followers, who lead a quiet but somewhat anxious existence; and those who pay with their liberty or even their lives for their deviant behavior.

One might think that individual, not social, inequalities are in fact established by the distinction between those who for essentially personal reasons (as we must initially assume, and have assumed in the examples) are either unprepared for or incapable of conformism and those who punctiliously fulfil every norm. For example, social stratification is always a rank order in terms of prestige and not esteem, i.e., a rank order of positions (worker, woman, resident of a certain area, etc.), which can be thought of independently of their individual incumbents. By contrast, attitudes toward norms as governed by sanctions seem to be attitudes of individuals. There might therefore seem to be a link missing between the sanctioning of individual behavior and the inequality of social positions. This missing link is, however, contained in the notion of social norm as we have used it so far.

It appears plausible to assume that the number of values capable of regulating human behavior is unlimited. Our imagination permits the construction of an infinite number of customs and laws. Norms, i.e. socially established values, are therefore always a selection from the universe of possible established values. At this point, however, we should remember that the selection of norms always involves discrimination, not only against persons holding sociologically random moral convictions, but also against social positions that may debar their incumbents from conformity with established values.

Thus if gossip among neighbors becomes a norm, the professional woman necessarily becomes an outsider who cannot compete in prestige with ordinary housewives. If piecework rates are in force in a factory, the older worker is at a disadvantage by comparison with the younger ones, the women by comparison with men. If it becomes the duty of the citizen to defend the ideology of the state, those who went to school before the establishment of this state cannot compete with those born into it. Professional woman, old man, young man, and child of a given state are all social positions, which may be thought of independently of their individual human incumbents. Since every society discriminates in this sense against certain positions (and thereby all their incumbents, actual and potential), and since, moreover, every society uses sanctions to make such discrimination effective, social norms and sanctions are the basis not only of ephemeral individual rankings but also of lasting structures of social positions.

The origin of inequality is thus to be found in the existence in all human societies of norms of behavior to which sanctions are attached. What we normally call the law, i.e., the system of laws and penalties, does not in ordinary usage comprise the whole range of the sociological notions of norm and sanction. If, however, we take the law in its broadest sense as the epitome of all norms and sanctions, including those not codified, we may say that the law is both a necessary and a sufficient condition of social inequality. There is inequality because there is law; if there is law, there must also be inequality among men.

This is, of course, equally true in societies where equity before the law is recognized as a constitutional principle. If I may be allowed a somewhat flippant formulation, which is nevertheless seriously meant, my proposed explanation of inequality means in the case of our own society that all men are equal *before* the law but they are no longer equal *after* it: i.e. after they have, as we put it, 'come in contact with' the law. So long as norms do not exist, and insofar as they do not effectively act on people ('before the law'), there is no social stratification; once there are norms that impose inescapable requirements on people's behavior and once their actual behavior is measured in terms of these norms ('after the law'), a rank order of social status is bound to emerge.

Important though it is to emphasize that by norms and sanctions we also mean laws and penalties in the sense of positive law, the introduction of the legal system as an illustrative *pars pro toto* can itself be very misleading. Ordinarily, it is only the idea of punishment that we associate with legal norms as the guarantee of their compulsory character. The force of legal sanctions produces the distribution between the lawbreaker and those who succeed in never coming into conflict with any legal rule. Conformism in this sense is at best rewarded with the absence of penalties. Certainly, this crude division between 'conformists' and 'deviants' constitutes an element of social inequality, and it should be possible in principle to use legal norms to demonstrate the relation between legal sanctions and social stratification. But an argument along these lines would limit both concepts–sanction and stratification–to a rather feeble residual meaning.

It is by no means necessary (although customary in ordinary language) to conceive of sanctions solely as penalties. For the present argument, at least, it is important to recognize positive sanctions (rewards) both as equal in kind and similar in function to negative sanctions (punishments). Only if we regard reward and punishment, incentive and threat, as related instruments for maintaining social norms do we begin to see that applying social norms to human behavior in the form of sanctions necessarily creates a system of inequality of rank, and that social stratification is therefore an immediate result of the control of social behavior by positive and negative sanctions. Apart from their immediate task of enforcing the normative patterns of social behavior, sanctions always create, almost as a by-product, a rank order of distributive status, whether this is measured in terms of prestige, or wealth, or both.

The presuppositions of this explanation are obvious. Using eighteenth-century concepts, one might describe them in terms of the social contract *(pacte d'association)* and the contract of government *(pacte de gouvernement)*. The explanation sketched here presupposes (1) that every society is a moral community, and therefore recognizes norms that regulate the conduct of its members; (2) that these norms require sanctions to enforce them by rewarding conformity and penalizing deviance.

It may perhaps be argued that by relating social stratification to these presuppositions we have not solved our problem but relegated its solution to a different level. Indeed, it might seem necessary from both a philosophical and a sociological point of view to ask some further questions. Where do the norms that regulate social behavior come from? Under what conditions do these norms change in historical societies? Why must their compulsory character be enforced by sanctions? Is this in fact the case in all historical societies? I think, however, that whatever the answers to these questions may be, it has been helpful to reduce social stratification to the existence of social norms backed by sanctions, since this explanation shows the derivative nature of the problem of inequality. In addition, the derivation suggested here has the advantage of leading back to presuppositions (the existence of norms and the necessity of sanctions) that may be regarded as axiomatic, at least in the context of sociological theory, and therefore do not require further analysis for the time being.

It is hard to imagine a society whose system of norms and sanctions functions without an authority structure to sustain it. Time and again, anthropologists have told us of 'tribes without rulers', and sociologists of societies that regulate themselves without power or authority. But in opposition to such fantasies, I incline with Weber to describe 'every order that is not based on the personal, free agreement of all involved' (i.e., every order that does not rest on the voluntary consensus of all its members) as 'imposed', i.e. based on authority and subordination. Since a *volonté de tous* seems possible only in flights of fancy, we have to assume that a third fundamental category of sociological analysis belongs alongside the two concepts of norm and sanction: that of institutionalized power. Society *means* that norms regulate human conduct; this regulation is guaranteed by the incentive or threat of sanctions; the possibility of imposing sanctions is the abstract core of all power.

I am inclined to believe that all other categories of sociological analysis may be derived from the unequal but closely related trinity of norms, sanction, and power. At any rate, this is true of social stratification, which therefore belongs on a lower level of generality than power. To reveal the explosiveness of this analysis we need only turn it into an empirical proposition: the system of inequality that we call social stratification is only a secondary consequence of the social structure of power.

The establishment of norms in a society means that conformity is rewarded and deviance punished. The sanctioning of conformity and deviance in this sense means that the ruling groups of society have thrown their power behind the maintenance of norms. In the last analysis, established norms are nothing but ruling norms, i.e. norms defended by the sanctioning agencies of society and those who control them. This means that the person who will be most favorably placed in society is the person who best succeeds in adapting himself to the ruling norms; conversely, it means that the established or ruling values of a society may be studied in their purest

form by looking at its upper class. Anyone whose place in the co-
ordinate system of social positions and roles makes him unable to
conform punctiliously to his society's expectations must not be
surprised if the higher grades of prestige and income remain closed
to him and go to others who find it easier to conform. In this sense,
every society honors the conformity that sustains it, i.e., sustains its
ruling groups; but by the same token every society also produces
within itself the resistance that brings it down.

8. Law and Forms of Freedom
by Harold E. Pepinsky

From Crime and Conflict, *London, Martin Robertson (1976) pp. 91–9.*

On the surface, application of the Chinese form of legal system may
appear clearly and simply to be repressive. Not surprisingly, in the
United States the practical absence of utilised formal written law is
generally viewed as a fearsome prospect. The threat of repression is
commonly held to be foreboding enough, even if, as is apparently the
case in the People's Republic of China (PRC) today, it is rare to find
someone actually 'punished according to law'. The threat of political
repression is not all that is aversive about the thought of a curtailing
of reliance on formal written law. The prospect of a breakdown of
social order, of rampant social conflict, of anarchy is also foreseen
(although a simultaneous state of anarchy and state repression is
evidently paradoxical). Conversely, reliance on a formal written law
is seen to restrict both each citizen's freedom to act uncontrolled by
the demands of others and others' freedom to control each citizen's
freedom of action. This view is also paradoxical. Each notion
implies that citizens' freedom from control by agents of the state co-
varies directly with state agents' control of citizens' freedom of
action. The paradoxes are eliminated only by making logically
tenable the possibility of a simultaneous increase and decrease in
citizens' freedom from control by state agents, accompanied by a

simultaneous decrease and increase in state agents' control of citizens' freedom of action.

It is therefore possible that Americans' typical visions of the consequences of lesser reliance on formal written law might be qualifiedly valid. In one sense, freedom of citizens' actions from control by state agents might be increased, while in another sense it would be decreased. The way in which persons' freedom would be increased and that in which it would be restricted remain to be projected.

Indications are that commitment to maintaining particular relationships is lower in the United States than in the People's Republic of China. Commitment as here used is the probability that social relationships with the same persons will be maintained over time.

Social statistics are easier to obtain in the USA than in the PRC, though ordinal comparisons between the two polities remain possible. To begin with, geographical mobility is higher in the USA than in the PRC. One fifth of all Americans move from one residence to another each year. In China, one lives where assigned. Unauthorised and authorised movement from countryside to cities are both apparently kept infrequent in a predominantly rural country. Most of those who are sent to the countryside are sent only temporarily to learn the meaning of working with the masses, though some stay in the countryside for long periods of time. Community members sent to cities are generally sent temporarily for education and training to use back home. To be sure, a number of Chinese are permanently assigned to work far away from their homes. However, the rate of geographical mobility, especially from one neighbourhood to the next in the same metropolitian area, appears to be far higher in the USA than in the PRC.

Occupational mobility is rather high in the USA if one includes horizontal mobility as well as the less frequent vertical mobility. The latest American data on frequency of job change are unfortunately rather old (from 1949), but there is no reason to believe that frequency of job change has decreased since that time. The findings, by Lipset and Bendix in Oakland, showed unskilled workers having held an average of more than ten jobs. Business managers and executives, at the other extreme, had averaged over three jobs apiece. The overall average number of jobs held by all those sampled was 6.3.[1]

The rate of change of occupation would have to be lower than the rate of change of jobs, but even in this category only 29.3 per cent of American males between the ages of 25 and 64 were found not to have changed occupations as of 1962.[2]

Apparently, in the PRC occupational mobility is minimal. Once trained, urbans workers are reported to change jobs either only as a job is eliminated in favour of another or temporarily from managerial status to work among the masses. Rural workers may perform different jobs as local needs change, such as from cultivating to harvesting of crops or to construction of irrigation facilities. Very much like the small American farmer, the rural Chinese is apt to be more a generalist than a specialist. However, the work setting is not apt to change for the rural resident. Hence, at home and at work, Chinese tend to stay with the same people far longer than their American counterparts.

While divorce is rather commonplace and ever easier to obtain in the USA, divorce is seemingly rather difficult to obtain in the PRC since the Cultural Revolution (in the late sixties). Lubman describes a divorce trial he attended in Peking. The district judge went to the tractor factory where the estranged husband and wife worked. He 'had already interviewed husband and wife singly and together as well as their neighbours, fellow workers and supervisors. All past attempts to keep them together had failed, however, and the wife had persisted in her demand for a divorce.'[3]

The judge interviewed the couple singly and together once again. With him were a group of the couples' neighbours and fellow workers, or 'masses' representatives'. Duties under two of the few laws in the PRC, the Constitution of 1954 and the Marriage Law of 1950, were vaguely described to 'mutually love and respect each other' and to 'participate in Socialist construction'. The husband had committed adultery and had struck his wife in a quarrel, but these were considered past problems to be overcome in a reconciliation, not grounds for a separation. Following the counsel of the 'masses' representatives', the judge ordered the husband to sign a 'statement of guarantee' that he would not again strike his wife. Failure to keep the guarantee would ostensibly be grounds for a divorce and injury to the wife would result in 'punishment according to law' (threatening, but remote). The representatives would continue to 're-educate' the husband and 'assist' in the reconciliation process. Lubman concludes, 'The trial expressed the ideal of Chinese justice–to avoid formal adjudication of disputes between citizens and to strengthen the social solidarity of the working class'.

Professor Victor Li of Stanford University Law School had a similar reconciliation attempt described to him during a visit to the PRC. Apparently, a husband had constantly been late to work and was making mistakes on the job. His work group had asked him for an explanation. He replied that he and his wife were fighting because they saw so little of each other that he was losing sleep and could not focus on his work. The wife worked another shift at the same plant. The group sent the husband's supervisor to the wife's supervisor to arrange for the husband and wife to work on the same shift. The husband was exhorted to study his mistakes and improve his work.

Two contrasts in domestic relations with the USA are noteworthy. First, much greater emphasis in the PRC than in the USA (with parades of faceless people moving through routine and often uncontested divorce hearings) is put on keeping spouses together in the same relationship. For a spouse simply to abandon a family would be inconceivable in the PRC. Second, one's co-workers and supervisors get much more thoroughly involved in the intimate details of a person's home life than would characteristically be the case in the USA.

As Cohen describes, groups and mediation mechanisms exist for residents of urban areas similar to those for workers.[4] 'Mediation' is something of a misnomer, for it is practically unheard of for disputants not to defer to the counsel of their 'mediators', though the process lacks the formal written guarantees of authority of what we know as arbitration. The point is that reconciliation and persuasion will be tried repeatedly and with involvement of many familiar faces at work and in the neighbourhood before the disputants may be released from the burden of trying to resolve their differences within ongoing relationships.

Extended observations of the police, corroborated by police officers from various parts of the country, have suggested that the situation in US urban neighbourhoods is different. A large portion of citizen complaints to patrolmen call for the patrolmen to act as the citizens' agents in resolving petty problems with relatives and neighbours. One common complaint, especially in apartment buildings, is that neighbours are playing music too loudly. Usually, in these cases, the complainant has not approached his neighbour directly and stays away while the police convey his demand. The complainant is apt not even to know the neighbour. Other common complaints would be of neighbours parking in front of the complainant's home, of neighbours' children or pets causing minor damage or simply a disturbance on the complainant's property, of landlords locking tenants out of apartments or rooms, of alcoholic or infirm elderly neighbours or a family needing removal (somewhat like garbage), or of petty but voluble family arguments. The police may not enjoy being called upon to handle such problems, but in practice generally concur in the wisdom of their separating the disputants. The police also generally consider it good practice to end their own involvement as rapidly as possible, believing that the most they can do is to cool down the conflict of the moment.

Citizen complaints to police exemplify the source of a second type of mobility far more commonly found in the USA than in the PRC. Not only are American citizens more apt to move from one place of residence or work to the next and to do so at will, but Americans in a number of cases use third persons to take care of (removing, if necessary) people with whom Americans get into conflict in residence situations. According to Rothman, both forms of mobility became salient simultaneously in the Jacksonian era in the USA. The American does not rely solely on removing himself from others; he can have the others removed or restrained while he remains aloof from them, and, literally, relatively unmoved himself. Characteristically, a Chinese would not be permitted to absolve himself or herself of responsibility for carrying on relationships with family and neighbours throughout periods of conflict and need. The Chinese can remove himself or herself, or others, from troublesome situations only rarely, and then in the guise and with the consensus of comrades that in the overall task of Socialist construction the person is more valuable elsewhere.

This set of examples indicates consistently a greater tendency in the USA for citizens to move among relationships than is the case in the PRC. Presumably, too, there is more occasion for citizens to express themselves in private, as by painting, alone, than would be the case in the PRC, where all action is to be public. The right to privacy has in fact been held to be implicit in law as law is known in the USA. On the other hand, PRC citizens seem more consistently to stay involved in ongoing relationships through problem situations than do their US counterparts. As a result, the scope of the relationships in the PRC appears characteristically to extend beyond that of corresponding relationships in the USA. Hence, the state which restricts less – and even encourages – social mobility is also the one that relies more heavily on formal written law.

The freedom more typical for Chinese than for Americans is

difficult to describe. It is a kind of freedom with which Americans are largely unfamiliar. For Americans this freedom has a subtlety corresponding to its salience for the Chinese. The freedom is that of developing access to new economic and social resources within the context of existing relationships.

The improvement in the economic lot of the average Chinese over the last twenty-five years is dramatic and well know. Where famines periodically took millions of lives, all people have enough to eat. All in the cities have shelter, where many once had only the streets on which to live. Middle-school education has become universal where illiteracy was the norm. Myrdal and Kessle found that through collective effort the 'five guarantees' of enough food, enough fuel, health care, an honourable funeral and education for the children had become a reality for everyone even in a relatively poor village in Yenan in 1969.[5] Myrdal and Kessle provide perhaps the most detailed, vivid and credible description of the form of the collective effort in the PRC. However, for those accustomed to relative affluence, as in the USA, any description of collective accomplishment in the PRC is apt to seem trivial. The general strength of inter-personal competition has become an American assumption. The following scenario has been developed to translate the recent Chinese experience into an American context.

The US President has just made a nationwide television address telling Americans of a fuel crisis and asking them to curtail petrol consumption as much as possible. No formal action is contemplated, full faith is being placed in the voluntary cooperation of the citizenry, in accord with the political ideology that has become nationally dominant in recent years.

Outside the city of Gotham, at the 2100 block of Rich Street in the suburb of Pleasantview, darkness has fallen. It is 8.00–time for the nightly block meeting. Jack and Doris Stormann generally host the meeting in their spacious home. Tonight is no exception.

Almost everyone has arrived. The children are being watched tonight by Dan and Barbara Spinoza, who are taking their turn in the babysitting rotation. In the living room, about thirty people are sitting in a circle–each already engaged with his neighbours in discussion of the President's speech. Conservation among them is relaxed, for most of them have known each other, in and out of meetings, for years. Then block chairperson Mary Geller, bearing in mind that her responsibility is to elicit a cooperative response to the fuel crisis, calls the meeting to order.

'Obviously, the President's speech is in all our minds', she begins. 'Anyone who wants to comment on it may speak.'

'Apparently, the fuel crisis is real. We simply have to use our cars a lot less than we've been doing.' Heads nod in agreement. Bill Samuels has expressed a preliminary consensus of the meeting.

Discussion moves quickly to the ways in which members of the group can help one another to meet the agreed objective. Use of the bus service is suggested, but a number of disparaging remarks about the service lead to abandonment of this idea.

Then a member of the group raises the notion of a car pool. A car pool is acceptable to everyone but George Jones, who likes to be alone on the way to work. 'How can you be so selfish in a matter of such importance?' he is asked. George argues a while for his conception of his rights, but eventually his resistance gives way to assent. Even if he had left the meeting to escape the group pressure, he soon would have been visited by a delegation seeking to 'help' him with 'his problem'. It has come to be taken for granted by all participants that no one can expect to get away with pursuit of private interests in matters of public concern. And so it is agreed that eight car pools will be established to take the neighbours to and from places of work in various areas of the community. The membership of each pool is established, and each pool is asked to work out its own schedule, rotation of driving and plan for sharing expenses.

Then it is noted that a substantial number of housewives in the neighbourhood have shopping to do and other errands to run. With little deliberation, the notion of car pools is extended to meet these needs. On a rotating schedule, individual housewives accept the responsibility for taking calls from those who plan to go out during the day. The first to call who has use of a car and who cannot make use of transport in a car already scheduled to go on a trip is to be a driver, and the coordinator of the day refers subsequent callers to her as passengers. Also on a rotating basis, two housewives a day are enlisted for child care while both parents are away. Thus, mothers and fathers are freed from having to take small children with them on their various trips. Such a child care programme has already been tried and proven for evening babysitting. Children have learned to look forward to staying even overnight with neighbours as a kind of adventure. From previous experience, any inequities in allocation of responsibilities versus utilisation of services are left to be adjusted as they arise in future meetings.

The meeting has been going on for nearly an hour. By convention, it is about time to adjourn. Alice Ladinsky mentions that she and her husband have been having marital difficulties, and asks leave to discuss them in the next meeting. Her husband, Mark, concurs. Without objection, the chairperson approves the request. The meeting is over.

Over the years, the need for social services in the block has declined markedly. The police have not been called for the past two years. A few would-be burglars have been scared off by watchful neighbours. Loans have been arranged by the group for families in a financial crisis. Members of the group have effectively acted as informal therapists for one another. The rate of movement in and out of the neighbourhood has declined to insignificance, for the social support provided there has been proved generally more valuable to the residents than occupational mobility.

The scenario is designed to highlight the kind of freedom offered by a social system geared to collective accomplishment rather than to social mobility. It is closely modelled on accounts of group activity in the PRC, such as those by Myrdal and Kessle.[6] The co-operative effort of a stable group (or groups) provides opportunities and services closely tuned to the needs of the members. Each member has a freedom to choose among services that would otherwise be unavailable or not so well suited to his or her requirements. In the process of restricting social mobility by organising people into groups, and, initially at least, of trying to enforce members' participation in them, the role of the state in providing rules and institutions especially for conflict resolution and provision of services tends to become superfluous. The kind of individual freedom from control by state agents changes as one moves from a social system relying heavily on formal written law to one resisting such reliance. However, the overall quantum of freedom cannot be shown to differ between the two systems.

1. Seymour M. Lipset and Reinhard Bendix, *Social Mobility in Industrial Society*, Berkeley, University of California Press (1959).
2. United States Bureau of the Census, 'Lifetime occupational mobility of adult males, March, 1962', *Current Population Reports* (1964) series P-23, no. 11, May.
3. Stanley Lubman, 'A divorce trial Peking style', *Wall Street Journal* (5 June 1973).
4. Jerome A. Cohen, *The Criminal Process in the People's Republic of China: 1949–1963*, Cambridge, Mass., Harvard University Press (1968).
5. Jan Myrdal and Gun Kessle (Paul B. Austin, trans.) *China: The Revolution Continued*, New York, Pantheon Books (1970).
6. *Ibid.*